STUDIES IN BRITISH ART

THE DIARY OF
FORD MADOX BROWN

EDITED BY

VIRGINIA SURTEES

PUBLISHED FOR THE PAUL MELLON CENTRE
FOR STUDIES IN BRITISH ART BY
YALE UNIVERSITY PRESS
NEW HAVEN AND LONDON
1981

Set in Compugraphic Baskerville
by Red Lion Setters, Holborn, London.
Printed in Great Britain by
Biddles of Guildford.

Published in Great Britain, Europe, Africa, and Asia
(except Japan) by Yale University Press, Ltd,
London. Distributed in Australia and
New Zealand by Book and Film Services, Artarmon,
N.S.W., Australia; and in Japan by Harper & Row,
Publishers, Tokyo Office.

Library of Congress Cataloging in Publication Data

Brown, Ford Madox, 1821–1893
The diary of Ford Madox Brown

(Studies in British art)
Includes Index
1. Brown, Ford Madox, 1821–1893. 2. Painters—
England—Biography. I. Surtees, Virginia.
II. Title. III. Series.
ND497.B73A2 1981 759.2 (B) 81-51344
ISBN 0-300-02743-5   AACR2

CONTENTS

List of Plates   vi

Acknowledgements   vii

Abbreviations   ix

Introduction   xi

THE DIARY   1

Appendix I   225

Appendix II   226

Index   228

LIST OF PLATES

1	A Page from the Diary, Ashmolean Museum, Oxford	xii
2	*Chaucer at the Court of Edward III*, Art Gallery of New South Wales, Sydney	3
3	*Hampstead From My Window*, Samuel and Mary R. Bancroft Collection, Delaware Art Museum, Wilmington	19
4	*Wycliffe Reading his Translation of the Bible to John of Gaunt in the Presence of Chaucer and Gower*, City Art Gallery and Museums, Bradford	19
5	*The Young Mother*, Wightwick Manor, Wolverhampton (National Trust)	47
6	*Windermere*, Lady Lever Art Gallery, Port Sunlight	51
7	*Lear and Cordelia*, Tate Gallery, London	51
8	D.G. Rossetti, *Ford Madox Brown*, National Portrait Gallery, London	73
9	*Emma Brown*, City Art Gallery, Birmingham	75
10	*Christ Washing Peter's Feet*, Tate Gallery, London	77
11	*Work*, City Art Gallery, Manchester	79
12	*An English Autumn Afternoon*, City Art Gallery, Birmingham	79
13	*The Last of England*, City Art Gallery, Birmingham	81
14	*Two Studies of Girl's Head*, City Art Gallery, Manchester	89
15	*The Brent at Hendon*, Tate Gallery, London	89
16	*Carrying Corn*, Tate Gallery, London	147
17	*The Hayfield*, Tate Gallery, London	147
18	*Stages of Cruelty*, City Art Gallery, Manchester	179
19	*The Coat of Many Colours*, Walker Art Gallery, Liverpool	203
20	*The Nosegay*, Ashmolean Museum, Oxford	205

ACKNOWLEDGEMENTS

For permission to quote those passages from Ford Madox Brown's diary still in copyright, I wish to thank most sincerely Mrs Imogen Dennis, Mr John Lamb, Mr Harold Rossetti, and the Lady Stow Hill for giving me this authority, as well as the Directors of the Ashmolean Museum, Oxford, and the Pierpont Morgan Library, New York, owners of the diaries, for making them available to me.

Once again, as in the past, my debt to Mr John Gere is great. As mentor and critic he has catechized, advised, and helped me immeasurably and I welcome this opportunity of renewing my thanks.

To Miss Mary Bennett I owe much for having willingly shared with me her knowledge of the diarist while completing her own *catalogue raisonné* of his works, and I should like to record how invaluable her catalogue to the *Ford Madox Brown* exhibition at Liverpool, 1964 has been to me.

In addition I wish to thank most particularly Mr Herbert Cahoon, of the Pierpont Morgan Library, for his sympathetic consideration of my enquiries; and in the same context Mr David Brown, Miss Eileen Gainfort, Mr Jeremy Maas, Lady Mander, Miss E. Mitchell, Mr and Mrs Harold Rossetti, Mr Christopher Tower and Mr Clive Wainwright. I have been fortunate in the help of Mrs Elizabeth Bonython, Mr John Christian, Mr John Constable, Mr Fred Davis, Professor W.E. Fredeman, Mrs J. Hancock, Miss Diana Holman-Hunt, the Rev. W.G. Knapper, Mr Lionel Lambourne, Mr Michael Lang, Miss Elizabeth de Leeuw, Miss Valerie Lloyd, the Rev. Prebendary Harold Loasby, Miss Glenise Matheson, Mr David Muspratt, the late Professor W.D. Paden, Colonel R.N. Seddon, Mr Peyton Skipwith, Mr M.G. Smith, Mr A.J. Tibbles, Mr Julian Treuherz, Miss K.J. Wallace, Mr Stephen Wildman, Major-General C.G. Woolner. Also the staffs of Bruce Castle Library, Haringey, the Local History Museums of Blackheath, Finsbury, Hendon (where Mrs J. Corden gave me great assistance), Holborn, and Swiss Cottage, and the Public Libraries of St Pancras, Huntingdon, and Rothesay, Isle of Bute.

The following have kindly granted me permission to quote from unpublished material in their possession: the Huntington Library, San

Marino, California, the Pierpont Morgan Library, New York, and the University of British Columbia, Vancouver. I have been allowed to quote from the first two volumes of the *Letters of Dante Gabriel Rossetti*, ed. O. Doughty and J.R. Wahl, Oxford at the Clarendon Press, 1965; Angus Davidson *Edward Lear*, John Murray Ltd, London, 1968; *Munby, Man of Two Worlds*, ed. Derek Hudson, 1972, John Murray Ltd, London; *Sublime & Instructive*; ed. V. Surtees, 1972, Michael Joseph Ltd, London. I wish to thank the publishers for their courtesy.

ABBREVIATIONS

Ashmolean	Ashmolean Museum, Oxford
Birmingham	City Museum and Art Gallery, Birmingham
Graves	A. Graves, *Royal Academy of Arts Exhibitors*, 1904
Hueffer	F.M. Hueffer, *Ford Madox Brown*, 1896
Huntington	The Huntington Library, San Marino, California
Letters	*Letters of D.G. Rossetti*, ed. O. Doughty and J.R. Wahl, i and ii, 1965.
Liverpool	Walker Art Gallery, Liverpool
Manchester	City Art Gallery, Manchester
Morgan Library	The Pierpont Morgan Library, New York
Port Sunlight	Lady Lever Art Gallery, Port Sunlight
P.R.B.	Pre-Raphaelite Brotherhood
R.A.	Royal Academy, London
Ruskin	*Works of John Ruskin*, ed. E.T. Cook and A. Wedderburn, i-xxxix, 1903-12
Wilmington	Delaware Art Museum, Wilmington, Delaware

INTRODUCTION

This journal is the working diary of a painter. At its start in 1847 Ford Madox Brown was twenty-six years old, a widower with a young child, scarcely any money and with no acknowledged reputation. It was a cheerless life, aggravated by a tendency to imagine a slight where none was intended; this, and an outspoken contempt for authority, were ingredients unlikely to make for an easy relationship. His crusty exterior, his deeprooted taciturnity and markedly suspicious nature led to harsh and often mistaken judgments. His work absorbed him totally; in the early years of the diary each rearrangement of drapery, each outline of a sketch, every reduction of head and limb were carefully chronicled. The hours given daily to his work were noted, apparently not always with great accuracy. To his close friends and to his family, he was warm-hearted, loving and generous, and to those he considered ill-used by worldly circumstances he showed the keenest sympathy. To one friendship in particular, which probably became the strongest influence in his life, the diary testifies.

In 1848 D.G. Rossetti wrote as a stranger to Brown in terms of appreciation such as he had done the previous year to Robert Browning and to W.B. Scott; but on this occasion he asked the older painter for tuition. Brown's acceptance proved to be the foundation of a deep and constant friendship despite the disagreements recorded in these pages.

Ford Madox Brown was born in Calais on 16 April 1821. His father had served during the Napoleonic wars as ship's purser and had then retired and married. The family led a nomadic life, chiefly abroad where Brown spent the first twenty years of his life. This may account in some degree for his unusual, and frequently mystifying form of expression and for his unconscious phonetic spelling, seemingly often derived from the French. But if his spelling was idiosyncratic and his occasional use of Latin startling, he owed these defects to a lack of formal education, whereas his lifelong use of malapropisms was derived from his inability to remember names and was of a very individual order. His art studies, from which he received a thorough grounding, were pursued at Bruges, Ghent, Antwerp and Paris. His marriage took place in 1841 and after the death of his wife

2 bob – Emma's tender state made it a matter of prudence more than economy not to go a well we did not pay the other shilling for! mark the sequel, we two nothing buckram about us as yet went & found ourselves opposed by one abbey door which would not open – then one rectors maid servant came towards us two & said that it did not open till 10. & moreover that service began at half past & that if we wished to see the place she had better go for the verger. Well we two being there quite in the dark as to what all this meant naturally concluded that the rector, his maid, the verger & the whole conclave were of a plot to rob us, so we declined the offer saying it was scandalous conduct & that we would go to the vergers – So having got there a stout woman told us plainly no verger should open the door before ten o'clock. So seeing there was no remedy we wandered forth to spend the time somehow and at 10 we got in baiting the verger who confessed they had been shown up but a short while before in the papers. I of course promise a most renomer letter to the "times" but somehow looking over the there workings up & scrapings down of so many centuries, our little tiff about half an hour

1. A Page from the Diary, Ashmolean Museum, Oxford

he returned to England and the diary was begun, though from 1850 Brown's life for the next four years is not easy to follow as the diary was allowed to lapse.

A child had been born to Emma Matilda Hill, his model, at the end of 1850. This was an additional worry for he was responsible for their support as well as for Lucy's, the child of his early marriage, and his pictures were not selling. While retaining his studio in Newman Street, Brown, by his own account, rented a cottage at Stockwell from the spring of 1851 and lived there with Emma and their baby. He mentions June 1852 as the time of their leaving Stockwell but it seems likely that their departure was a few months earlier since the baby was baptized at Old St Pancras Church on 18 April 1852, the parents giving their address as Weedington Street, Kentish Town, their Christian names as Ford and Matilda, and Hill as their surname. Since they were not yet married a degree of secrecy and mystification were essential. The child was baptized Catherine Emily Brown and the date of birth noted in the register as "11 November 1851" in place of "1850". Twenty-five other baptisms were held in the church at the same time and a glance at the register shows that the child baptized immediately before the "Hill" baby was Emily Gandy, whose mother was Emma's elder sister. It was perhaps the Gandys who had urged the baptism that day, when in the confusion of some fifty parents and twenty-five infants, the dimensions of the "Hill" daughter in contrast to her recorded age might hope to pass unnoticed.

By September 1852 Brown had taken a lodging in Hampstead High Street. His landlady was a Mrs Coates, and it is possible that the house was used partly as a china warehouse. Privation and lack of artistic success dogged him mercilessly, he became solitary and appears to have suffered from melancholia. Emma's precise whereabouts and occupation are uncertain though at about this time she was living in the house of John Hardiman, a young farmer at Hendon, either earning a wage as a servant, or working in return for her and the baby's keep. Hardiman's father farmed two hundred acres and the thirty-three year-old son had charge of the land at the northern end of Parson Street, Hendon, where he had his house. Writing to Holman Hunt, Brown begged him to join him one evening at his painting room in Hampstead and then go with him by omnibus to Hendon where, "entre nous", he said, he spent a great part of his time (undated letter at Huntington).

By the spring of 1853 Emma was at North Hill, Highgate, living at North Wood Cottage. No such cottage exists in the directories of the period or in the 1851 Public Census but an envelope (University of British Columbia) so addressed from Rossetti to Emma reached its recipient and it is probable that Brown, renowned for his confusion of names, had misinformed Rossetti of the address. Several small cottages still stretch along the leafy rise of North Hill which at that time housed several "Ladies Seminaries". That Brown felt it necessary for Emma to acquire the rudiments of education is based on family legend and is not unlikely at a time when this was no uncommon occurence among artists aware of the inequality of background and upbringing of the women they hoped to marry. Perhaps Emma went through some kind of schooling at one of these places while lodging at a nearby cottage. When signing her name in the marriage register at St Dunstan-in-the-West in 1853 her writing is wholly unformed though "Emma", the first of her Christian names, is written with a firmer hand, perhaps indicating that the formation of this word alone had been learned at an earlier age.

After their marriage, according to the diary, the family lived at Hendon, Brown retaining his painting room at Hampstead where he continued to work until about February 1854, though the previous September he had bought a cottage, 1 Grove Villas, Church End, Finchley. The house has gone but its site is recognizable. When Brown went to live there the cottage had been recently rebuilt on land within a triangle formed by Hendon Lane, Gravel Hill, and (now) Regent's Park Road. In the apex of this triangle were fair-sized grounds (where now stands a Roman Catholic Church). Closer to Brown, and his immediate neighbours, were Albion Villas and Grove Cottages. His own villa came next, fronting Regent's Park Road, with a yard at the back where he set up his easel, and a narrow stretch of garden. Beyond that a field (where Salvin built Christ's College in 1857) with a quick approach across Hendon Lane to St Mary's Church. Beside him were Nos. 2 and 3 Grove Villas. After Brown's departure a further four villas were built, two still remaining (now Nos. 289 and 291). Grove Lodge, the next in the row still fronts the road, neat, square and early Victorian; two further Grove Villas complete the frontage onto Regent's Park Road. According to W.M. Rossetti, who had known it well, Brown's cottage consisted of a parlour, a kitchen and a bedroom, a tight fit on the occasions when it lodged five Browns and the servant. On 24 October 1854 Brown refers to a "morning lost with workmen for house", which seems to indicate some building. This is borne out by references at a slightly later date to "Lucy's room" and to Miss Siddal "having my room". Besides, Christina Rossetti would scarcely have emulated her brother Gabriel and slept on the parlour floor. The installation of a shower bath was a feature which was daily referred to. This was probably a portable contraption which released water from a cistern overhead after a brief period of pumping. By 1855 the Browns had outgrown Grove Villas and in October moved into 13 (now 56) Fortess Terrace, Kentish Town, set well back from the street, for which they paid half yearly rates of £2.16s, and where now a blue plaque commemorates Brown's sojourn. In the front a strip of garden already planted with trees ran down to the road. Prominent in the foreground of Brown's *Hampstead from my Window* one of these trees is recognizable by its three stout branches, upright and distinctive, though now reaching well up to the height of the first floor, from which the water-colour was made in 1857 (Plate 3). At the back of the house a garden stretched for some distance, and, still identifiable, are the steps which led down to it with its railing and the adjacent wall familiar from *Stages of Cruelty*, though the lilac bush has vanished.

Later still the Browns moved to nearby Grove Terrace, but the diary with its many omissions is silent about this, as it is on the founding of the Hogarth Club and the Morris Firm, and on Brown's drawing class at the Working Men's College and his one-man exhibition in 1865. Towards the end the entries lose their vividness and become uneven; only Brown's lessons to Marie Spartali are regularly chronicled. These were more prosperous days than Brown had yet enjoyed. He had work and he was respected and acknowledged. He died in October 1893 at 1 St Edmund's Terrace, Regent's Park, Emma having predeceased him.

Ford Madox Brown's Diary is made up of six exercise books, ruled and unruled and varying slightly in size. Those extending (with lengthy omissions) from 1847 to 1855 were published in *Pre-Raphaelite Diaries and Letters*, 1900, by W.M. Rossetti who omitted passages, remedied the punctuation and spelling and occasionally rearranged the phraseing. These five books belonged to Mrs Helen Rossetti Angeli and were later acquired by Mr John Bryson who bequeathed them to the Ashmolean Museum, Oxford, in 1977. They have their binding threads broken and the pages are loose. Of the remaining diary, covering intermittently the years 1856 to 1868, Ford Madox Hueffer to whom it belonged, published a brief selection in his *Life* of his grandfather in 1896. Miss Violet Hunt sold the diary in 1913 to the Pierpont Morgan Library, New York, for £100. Rebacked and given new corners, the volume still retains the Kentish Town bookseller's small label on the inside marble cover.

The books are now reassembled, the corrupt text rectified, the punctuation (sufficient to make the text intelligible) has been silently inserted but Brown's distinctive spelling has been allowed to stand.

Diary of my Painting 4th September 1847

As the work I am at present engaged upon is the most extensive as well as the most interesting to myself of any that I have yet undertaken I shall begin in this book by a short retrospectary glance at the events which have led to my undertaking it. In the summer of [18]45 I went to the British Museum to read Sir James Mackintosh's history of England,[1] having heard that it was of a phylosophical nature, with a view to select some subject connected with the history of this Country of a general and comprehensive nature. I was already wavering in my mind between two that struck me, one was "The first naval victory", and the other the Origin of our native tongue. The former subject had first engaged my attention but the sight of M'Clise's [Maclise] cartoon of "Chivalry"[2] and the wish to handle more luxurient & attractive materials afterwards changed the current of my thoughts.

In this mood, glancing over the pages of the above named history I fell upon a passage to this effect as near as I can remember "And it is scarcely to be wondered at, that English about this period should have become the judicial language of the country, ennobled as it had recently been by the genius of Geoffrey Chaucer." This at once fixed me, I immediately saw

[1] Sir James Mackintosh (1765-1832), philosopher and barrister, wrote the earlier part (55 B.C. – A.D. 1572) of the history of England for Lardner's *Cyclopedia*, 1830.
[2] Following the overall design of Sir Charles Barry, the Palace of Westminster was rebuilt after the fire of 1834 in the Gothic style and it was decided that the interior should be decorated with frescoes illustrating incidents in British history, or else from the works of Shakespeare, Milton or Spenser. Artists were invited to submit full-size cartoons and, to demonstrate their familiarity with the technique, samples of painting in fresco. In 1844 Brown submitted a cartoon and a fresco sample of *Adam and Eve* and a sketch of *The Body of King Harold Brought to William the Conqueror after the Battle of Hastings*; and in 1845 a cartoon, a water-colour, and a fresco sample of *The Spirit of Justice*. This last gained him some recognition. The artist Benjamin Robert Haydon (1786-1846), who had first proposed as the initial step towards an extensive scheme of state patronage of the arts that the new palace should be decorated, wrote in his journal: "The only bit of fresco fit to look at is by Ford Brown. It is a figure of Justice, and is exquisite so far as that figure goes" (*Autobiography and Memoirs*, ed. Tom Taylor, 1853, ii, p.790). None of Brown's entries were successful: *The Spirit of Justice*, like *The Spirit of Chivalry*, was carried out by Daniel Maclise (1806-70) in the Chamber of the House of Lords, where they both still are.

visions of Chaucer reading his poems to knights & Ladyes fair, to the king & court amid air & sun shine.

When I arrived at Rome, from the library of the English Academy I procured the works and life of our first poet and fortunately I found that the facts known respecting him perfectly admitted of the idea I had already conceived of the subject to wit, Chaucer reading his poëms to Edward the 3rd & his court bringing in other noted characters such as the black Prince etc, I immediately set to work & after many alterations & great labour I brought the Composition to its Present state.[3]

At first I had intended calling it the "seeds of the English language", and putting Wickliff [Wycliffe] on one side as a wing and some one else on the other but I could find no one to suit, Gower was too poor a Caracter & John of Gaunt for the harmony of ideas would not suit, it being inappropriate to put the patron on one wing & his protegées one in the center & the other on the other side compartment.[4] I then changed my idea to that of The seeds & fruits of the English Language but I soon found that in doing so after having given a place to our greatest poëts there would be none left for the prose writers and little liking the trouble of cutting & contriving for *them*, I determined on leaving them out & calling the work the "*Seeds & fruits of English poetry*". Such is the exposal of the train of Ideas which led to the composition of the work in its present state, whether it may ever diserve the pains I am now taking about it remains to be seen, very likely it may only add one more to the many kicks I have already received from fortune, if so I am quite able to bear it & dispise her — of one thing she cannot rob me — the pleasure I have already extracted, distilled I may say from the very work itself; warned by bitter experience I have learned not to trust only to hope for my reward, nor consider my toil as a sacrifice, but to value the *present*, the pleasure that I have received & daily yet receive from the marking out of a subject after mine own heart, a love offering to my favorite poëts, to my never-faithless Burns, Byron, Spencer & Shakespear. Never can I forget the pleasure with which I could muse over my work in Rome, at a time when visited by the most bitter afflictions & apprehensions for the future, at a time when all other satisfaction was impossible; never can I forget that *she* gave it her disqualified

---

[3] Originally designed as a triptych with Geoffrey Chaucer as the central figure, the work was intended to incorporate all the great English poets. Conceived in Rome, with the help of books from the Academy founded by British artists and where life classes were held, it was begun there in 1845 and redesigned in London in 1847. The side wings were soon abandoned. The painting, now known as *Chaucer at the Court of Edward III* (Sydney Art Gallery), was completed in 1851, by which time the figures were again substantially altered (Plate 2).

[4] Both Chaucer and the fourteenth-century religious reformer John Wycliffe had been befriended by John of Gaunt, fourth son of Edward III. John Gower was a contemporary poet who wrote in French and Latin, but whose best known English poem was the *Confessio Amatis*, published by Caxton in 1483.

2. *Chaucer at the Court of Edward III*, Art Gallery of New South Wales, Sydney

approbation, prophecied that it would ensure me ultimate success, regretted that she would never live to see it, and *ardered* me to complete it after her death; in fulfilling her behest I am breaking one of her strongest recommendations, I have parted from Lucy[5] O! God! ought not that thought to make me strive & struggle agains indolence. O! the hell of poverty!!!

Today I have done little or nothing but sketch in the figure of Chaucer in white chalk, & have been to the Strand about some costumes after writing a list of them. I must not omit to say that In Rome I painted a sketch of it in oil, afterwards made a drawing of it in chalk & then an outline of the whole as it now is since which I began first to fill it up in colour at Southend, afterwards went on a little with it at Hampstead & since touched it & marred it at Tudor's Lodge.[6] I have long intended beginning this journal, praise be God it is begun at last.

5th Got up late, got to work late, did little, scratched in three figures in white chalk, left off at ½ past 2 dressed & went out to dinner, then went to the Cemetary[7] found it full of cockneys walked over to Hampstead, saw a glorious sunset, got back to My studio by 8 – going to finish my letter to Casey.[8]

6th Have not worked to day – tried to do so but could not having been out all the morning to the costume shop & other places, came home quite tired, rested & went out again. Got a lay figure from Barbe's at last, bought 10 yards of flannel for draperies, engaged a model for tomorrow, lost myself in Somerstown got into a place where there was no gas thought I should get my throat cut, persevered and after almost breaking my neck got into the Kings Rd at last, have just been looking at Mogg's Map find I had crossed the kings Road without knowing it – good thing I found my

[5] His wife having died abroad and there being no established home for his four-year-old daughter Lucy, Brown felt obliged to place her in the care of Helen Bromley, the child's maternal aunt. Mrs Bromley had recently started a school for young children at Milton Lodge, Gravesend, Kent.
[6] After his return from France, Brown stayed with relations in Kent, moving from there successively to Southend, Cheapside, and Hampstead. A temporary studio had been made available to him by the painter Charles Lucy (1814-73) at Tudor Lodge, Camden Town. This house contained numerous studios and here Lucy (not to be confused with Lucy Brown) held classes for life-study in his own "Atelier". Brown was now settled at 20½ Clipstone Street (running east from Great Portland Street) where a studio had been converted from a carpenter's workshop, and (according to Holman Hunt) he had a lodging close by. Other tenants in the same house numbered a sofa manufacturer, a furniture japanner, a pianoforte maker, and carvers and gilders.
[7] At Highgate, where his wife lay beneath a gravestone of his own design. She had died on 5 June 1846, and in the early years Brown tried to visit the grave on the 5th of every month.
[8] Daniel Casey (fl. 1842-1880), Irish painter of genre and biblical scenes, lived in Paris. He was first known to Brown in 1837 when they studied under Baron Wappers at Antwerp Academy. Their friendship continued until Casey's death in 1885.

4

way back to it again, reached it just by St Pancras' Workhouse.[9] Went to Cooper's & ordered a movouble seat for my painting steps; have sent my stove to be mended for winter use the weather is getting cold.

7th Got up at seven, model came, worked well all day – drew some legs – had the stove put up – worked hard all the evening at pasting up the fire-place – bought materials to make a blind.

8th Got up at Seven, worked hard at fitting my blind up till four – wouldn't do after all, dinned & afterwards fell asleep till John Marshall came in, went out with him & then called to see my aunt Brown.[10] Lost a day like Titus but dined like Lord Byron on his birth day on eggs & bacon & ale[11] – am very sulky with myself – !!!!!

9th Got up at seven, breakfasted & then went to Greenwich, came back saw my uncle & Tom ye lauyer,[12] bought some plaid draperies dined & set about aranging the draperies for Robert Burns[13] in the Lay figure – sweated over it till dark but got it to do at last – Went out till bed time.

10th Got up at Seven. Worked on the blind again till ten o'clock, got it to do beautifully, breakfasted & set my pallet. A horrid tooth ake came on & I

[9] Having obtained his requirements at Lechertier Barbe, artists' colourman in the Quadrant, Regent Street, Brown lost his way in the poor and overpopulated district of Somerstown. At the junction of King's Road and old St Pancras Road stood the workhouse, greatly enlarged since its opening in 1809. Edward Moggs, mapseller and publisher of Great Russell Street, supplied handbooks with stage fares. The volume in Brown's hands was probably the *New Picture of London, or Stranger's Guide to the British Metropolis*, which in 1845 had reached its seventh edition. (*Mogg's Cab Fares* was immortalized by R.S. Surtees, as the favourite reading of Mr Soapy Sponge.)

[10] John Marshall (1818-91), an early and loyal friend, had started practice at Mornington Crescent, close to Tudor Lodge, which was no doubt where Brown made his acquaintance. In 1847 he was appointed assistant surgeon at University College Hospital, London, and later promoted Professor of Clinical Surgery. His appointment as Professor of Anatomy at the Royal Academy ("so dignified and authentic in the position above named", Brown to F.G. Stephens; Bodleian) brought him great renown. Aunt Bessy Brown, a governess in earlier days, was the author of tales of fiction. She was living in Great Coram Street, perhaps, in view of the family connexion between the Brown and the Bromley families, at No. 29, recorded as the address of "Joseph Bromley, solicitor".

[11] The Emperor Titus (A.D. 7-79) made famous his saying: "Amici, diem perditi" ("Friends I have lost a day"), if he had not done some good deed or benefited someone in the course of it. "... the day I came of age I dined on eggs and bacon and a bottle of ale' (*Life, Letters and Journals of Lord Byron*, ed. Thomas Moore, 1830, i, p.122).

[12] James Fuller Madox, solicitor, Brown's maternal uncle, lived at Foot's Cray, Kent, had an office off Lombard Street, and owned property at Greenwich derived from his family. From the same source, through his mother, Brown had inherited some property, consisting of shares in various small-holdings in Kent and in Ravensbourne Wharf at Deptford Creek on the River Ravensbourne, slightly to the west of the junction of the Greenwich and Blackheath Roads. In his diary the neighbouring district of Blackheath, where Brown had relations, figures prominently. It is possible that he collected rents in both. Tom, the lawyer, is unidentified.

[13] Whole-length figures of Robert Burns, Milton, Spenser, Shakespeare, Byron, and Pope were represented in the wings of the triptych.

hardly did any thing inconsequence, tried all sorts of remedies, went to sleep, & afterwards walked all round Regents park came home & went to bed –

11th Laid awake more than half the night in great pain, went to sleep at last & woke up at seven with a swelled face, got up, breakfasted got to painting about 10½, painted in part of a study for R Burn's Tartan with Copal varnish, worked till ¼ to 6. Dined & walked out to Regents park. Tomorrow being Sunday I must try & get to sleep early.

12th Got up at ½ past 6 – got to work by half past seven. Worked from then till 9 – from ½ past 10 till 20 minutes to 3 & from 20 minutes past till 6. Dined & went out a little way – rained. Tomorrow I shall have a days rest & see Lucy bless her. Worked at the plaid again.

13th Went to Gravesend to see Lucy dear.

14th Got up later. At eight Finished the plaid & began a drawing for the robe of R.B. Mr. & Mrs Lucy came in afterwards. Thomas[14] interrupted & did not do much. Have bought a rat trap. Studio swarms with them.

15th Got up at Seven. Worked well the first part of the day finished the robe for R.B. afterwards got disgusted at arranging the Mantle for Milton & did nothing more but read, diner & walk out called on the Lucys – came back & wrote to Dr Deakins[15] & Helen.

16th Got up at ½ 7. Cut out a fresh Mantle for Milton. Set it & began drawing it, went out, in the evening set about preparing a togum – bought more flannel for it.

17th Got up at ¼ to Eight. Worked all day at the cloak for Milton, & all the evening till twelve at the togam went out about the middle of the day to the city about Casey.

18th Got up very late finish Miltons cloak – cut out the togam & arranged it on the lay figure for Lord Byron, did nothing else before 6 o'clock diner. This evening casting up accounts. Got to call on my aunt Brown.

19th Got up very late – My aunt Brown made me drink too much Wiskey – very sulky with myself – did not do much but worked all day till 6 – afterward called on the Lucys.

[14] William Cave Thomas (1820-1906), the eldest of a large family, genre and biblical painter, and later drawing master to the Princess of Wales, had twice won a competition prize at the Westminster Hall cartoon exhibition. Working under Hess at Munich he had been influenced by the German Nazarenes, as had Brown in Rome in 1845. In 1849 he devised *The Germ* as the title for the new Pre-Raphaelite magazine. He is also known as an ineffective writer of theories on Fine Art.
[15] Dr Richard Deakin practised in Rome. He had probably attended Brown's first wife there in the last months of her life.

20th Got up very early for a wonder, got to work at ¼ past seven, worked very hard all day finished the drapery for Lord Byron dined & walked round the Regents park with Thomas, left him about to go and tell them at a Shakespear meeting of the Church Mason Society, that he thought it all humbug & that the old House had better be pulled down & monument put in its place[16] – afterwards I came home & had the energy to arrange the lay figure for Shakespear before going to bed, *I* am honoring him in the right way.

21st Got up at seven worked pretty well all day. The Lucys came in, and in the night the rats run away with a mutton chop – could fine no trace of it not even the satisfaction of seeing the bone.

22nd Got up rather late finished the drapery for Shakespear and although Late in the day & Lazy Laid in the shirt for Lord Byron in coulor, with linsead oil & copal varnish in eaqual parts as a vehicle.

23rd Got up late. Painted till five at the study of the shirt, find that when I have painted some hours I get tired & cannot see the colour, but can see the shape. Memo ought not to paint to long if I want to do good.

24th Got up at past nine, sick of myself went to the city on business – came back & set to work about 3 painted till ½ past 5 finished the study – find the second painting sinks in unlike painting with M'Guilph.[17] Walked up Hampstead Hill with Thomas & over Primrose Hill. Going to bed.

25th Got up Early – & got to work late, fumbled till 12 o'clock over the Hood of the left hand corner figure of the "knight" made a lirlipipe[18] for it about twelve set to work at a small drawing of – – had not finished it by dusk – am a very swine – shall never get the painting done in time – am a beast & a sleepy brute.

26th Finished the drawing of the Hood & a drawing of the cloak for one of the Men next him, "the chamberlain".

27th drew in the other cloack next it & the cloak of the back figure conversing with the knight & began placing the cardinals head was dissatisfied with it & left off early – went in the morning to see my aunt & in the evening went to oxford st to get my hair cut, then to the city, then bought a

[16] On 16 Sep. 1847 Shakespeare's birthplace in Henley Street, Stratford-on-Avon (of which Thomas seems to have doubted the authenticity), was bought for the public for £3000. Thomas was a member of the Freemasons of the Church, a society founded for the development of architecture in conjunction with kindred arts.

[17] Megilp, a mixture of linseed oil and turpentine much used in the nineteenth century, eventually caused cracking and discolouration of the paint.

[18] Many studies for *Chaucer* exist (Birmingham) including the head of the figure for which Brown made the liripipe (long tail of a hood).

7

Shakespear & Milton of an italian in the Tottenham court Rd for 1/& 10 the two. Came home & dressed & went for my aunt to grt Coram st came home very late.

28th tuesday got up at 8. Arranged the cardinals cape again began a drawing of it. Lucy came in about 1. Made me go out with him – did nothing more but went to Richmond, back with him to tea – came home by eleven read Shelley & got to sleep about 12.

29th Got up *past nine* worse & worse it is horrible to reflect – finished the cape about 1 went out to see Thomas & my aunt, came back & began arranging the hood for "Alice Perrers" old Edwards Misstress – found the hair of the lay figure wanted curling – put it in paper & made a fire to heat the tongues & curled it then oiled it. Alas did nothing afterwards, went for a walk with Thomas.

30th Painted at the capuchon.

1st Octr Ibid finished it.

2nd Went to Hampton court to see the cartoons[19] with Thomas & Lucy.

3rd Went to Richmond with Thomas to see Lucy. Had a row on the Thames up as far as Popes villa & the Eal Pie House.[20]

4th Got up late; felt Low & dejected, never feel Happy – got to work about 12. Arranged the white capuchon for the lady with her back to you, nearly finished it.

5th Set my pallet intending to work, found the capuchon quite wet, could do nothing; went out to look for damasks etc found none, went to Thomas to make a sketch of some vine leaves – found him at work on his designe of the Penseroso for the Art Union[21] – but out of sorts & dejected – about 3 left off & went to the cemetary at Highgate.

6th got up at 8 finished the capuchon, then dined & went out to see after

---

[19] Mantegna's cartoons for the *Triumph of Caesar* were, as they still are, at Hampton Court, but by 'the cartoons' Brown probably means the more famous series by Raphael for the Vatican tapestries which also hung there from about 1819 to 1865, and are now in the Victoria and Albert Museum.

[20] The inn on Eel Pie Island at Twickenham provided its own popular refreshment and was a favourite resort of picnickers. Pope's villa was destroyed in 1809 and another house erected in its place.

[21] Founded in 1836, the Art Union of London organized a lottery for subscribers, the winners of which were entitled to the choice of a work of art from approved exhibitions in London. The vine leaves appear as decoration in the upper parts of the original *Chaucer (The Seeds and Fruits of English Poetry*; Ashmolean).

stufs & a pourtrait of Chaucer published by C. Knight,[22] could get nothing tired & dejected – went to Lucys stopt by the rain till eleven.

7th Got up at 8, went out after draperies & Lay figures bought some blue satin & a peice of damask came back & dined too late to begin anything, went to sleep. Thomas came in & we had a walk. He thinks of going to Cambridge to become wise & learned in all matters – I am a brute & a sleepy beast.

8th Got up at 8 – arranged the drapery & head dress for the figure of a female in blue satin cloak – began and painted the white silk head cushion with copal varnish & drying oil in equal parts. Find dries quick & does not sink in on retouching, went & drank tea with Lucy, engaged Miss Chamberlain [Chamberlayne][23] for Tuesday – began making a green velvet hat of the time of Edward III.

9th Got up at nine – Painted in the blue satin cloak (the study for) & part of the veil went out to see Mr Bamford – found him out walked back & went to the Princess's Theatre, came in late with wet feet & a cold. Have been suffering 8 or 10 days from indigestion, live upon mutton chops & tea & coffee, quite a teatotaler.[24]

10th Sunday got up at 8 – & to work by ten, worked 6 hours finished the study of the feamale & began painting the furred cap of one of John of Gaunt's two pages, walked out, came in & had tea & bacon, read, smoked, and now writing my diary.

12th (11th) Finished the furred cap went & bought stuff for a blind to have two lights if necessary, to give the appearance to those figures which are not in the sunlight, of being in the open air, Lawrence[25] did not come to put it up so I began the green velvet Hat of the old lord who is conversing with the knight.

12th Had Miss Chamberlayne all day, a very devil, a very devil, made outlines of the nudes of several female figures.

13th Finished the green Hat – Wrote 4 letters & called on Thomass to see

[22] Probably the title page engraving in *Cabinet Pictures of English Life: Chaucer*, by J. Saunders, published by Charles Knight, 1845, which is a head and shoulders portrait of him, wearing a hood. The book gives a description of life and manners in Chaucer's day.
[23] A professional model, evidently of uneven temperament.
[24] References to members of the Bamford family occur frequently in the early years. There appears to have been some family connection through the Bromleys. Mr Bamford is probably James Bamford, silk manufacturer of Milk Street, Cheapside, whose portrait Brown had painted the previous year in the style of Holbein. Finding Bamford out, Brown, who loved the theatre, went to the Princess's in Oxford Street. The bill consisted of Goldsmith's *She Stoops to Conquer*, *A Romance of the Rhine*, *Ladies Beware*, and ended with *Love, Law and Physic*.
[25] A Lawrence Castlemain, cowkeeper, lived at 42½ Clipstone Street. He may also have worked as an odd-job man.

some sketches of his, some fine ideas, one in particular a scramble for lawrels – grandly satyrical. Came back to the studio & put up the blind with Lawrence. Afterwards waked half over london in quest of draperies bought some crimson cotton velvet.

14th got up at 7½. Miss Chamberlayne come. Worked well till 4 in spite of her talking propensities. Made outlines of the nude of the two figures of "Muses of impassioned & satyrical poëtry",[26] & several other center figures – dined & called on my aunt Brown. Walked down Holborn in quest of stuffs & found some germon velvet, a bargain at 10¾ a yard, took six yards of it for the gown of Chaucer. Came back & am now writing this.

15th Got up at ¼ past 7. Did nothing all day but arrange the cloack for the female figure, foreground figure to the left of the spectator. Dined & went to Lucy's.

16th Went to Greenwich – to see young Elliots painting at Westminster Rd and to the abby to see some of the old effegies. Lawrence did not fetch my lamp. I went to Reeves's to get some millboards & canvas for Studies – & then with Thomas to the Princess's Theatre to see Miss Cushman & Cooper in the Stranger, both nature to the life, & "She stoops to conquer" a fine *fine* play, went & supped with Thomas & stopped till ½ 1!!!![27]

17th Got up at 11 worked at the cloak from 1 till half past 4, dined, washed & dressed, am writing this & going to Lucy's.

18th Got up at ¼ to 9 began work late, did little, worked at the cloak, went out to buy things for my sweet dawter. Had Thomas's lamp brought me, sent it to be cleaned & went with Thomas to the Lucy's.

19th Got up at ½ past five, went to Gravesend[28] to see my sweet child found her quite well came back & went to bed.

20th got up at 8 set to work by ten finished the cloak. Arranged the lay figure for the old king & began a drawing of his gown. Went out to dun a fellow for Helen Bromley – & called on my aunt Brown. Dined and arranged the lamp, began drawing in the draperies of Lord Byron by nine & worked till ¼ past 10, smoked & am going to bed.

[26] Presumably Byron and Pope, for the right wing.
[27] Brown's day had started at Greenwich, perhaps in the collecting of rents, and included the viewing of a painting, *Negro Emancipation: An Allegory*, by Robinson Elliott (1814-94), which had received lukewarm notice. At Westminster Abbey discussion had arisen concerning alterations in the north transept which was encumbered with monuments. Reeves, the colourman's shop at Cheapside, was his next call, and the day ended at the theatre where John Cooper and the notable American actress Charlotte Cushman were playing leads in *The Stranger*, a translation from a German tragedy.
[28] In October of this year there were special rates for trains from Bishops Gate Station, and steam packets which made the journey to Gravesend every hour.

21st Got up at 9 finished the kings gown – painted a study of a knee of the dress of Alice Perrers – drew in the draperies of Lord Byron at night, went to bed at 11.

22nd Got up at ½ past 5 got to work by 7 painted in the kings cloak (study), workwoman came set her to make the gown for Chaucer myself made ears for the jester's hood & began a drawing of it – in the evening began drawing in the draperies of milton on the canvas. Thomas came in he is going to paint Christ & the decilists [disciples].

23rd Got up at ¼ past five, arranged the figure of Chaucer till 10, began a study of it & then drew at the jester's hood. At 2 dressed to go to Greenwich got wet. Till ¼ past 6 on cursed collecting work – came home dined & writing this & going to cast up my accounts.

24th Sunday got up at ½ past 6 & to work by 9 painted at the study for Chaucer & drew a little at the Jester's hood. In the evening began drawing the draperies of Shakr. on the Canvas.

25th Got up at ½ past 6 worked at the figure of Chaucer (study). In the evening drew at Shakspear.

26th Got up at 7 painted a little at the study of Chaucer then went out to the city, come back by 12 paid the Carpenter for my stretcher £6.5s. (the canvas cost £5.12s.), finished the study for Chaucer. Went out a long goose chase after some velvet could get none to match came back very tired & did nothing more that evening. Was foolish enough to drink a glass of ale which gave me the head ake.

27th Got up at ½ past 7. Went out to seek for velvet & brocades, got some velvet to suit & an old yellow satin dress. Saw some fine old brocade told the Jew to bring it me to my study to bargain some old cloath against it. Came back very tired drew a little at the Jester & in the evening at the draperies of R. burns.

28th Got up at ¼ to 7, work-woman came at nine. Worked at the Jester's head. At 10 Master Lawrence came in & the poor brute became insolent & wanted to fight me because I wanted him to be off again, had to kick him out at last, & then he came to the window & abused me – threatened him with the police. Richard Bromley came to see me on his return from Ireland for a few days.[29] The Jew came & went off sulkey because I would not give him his price & the old cloaths in to the bargain – did little all day

[29] Richard Madox Bromley (1813-65), later Sir Richard, was Brown's first cousin. A civil servant, he had been employed in Ireland during the famine. His mother and Brown's were sisters, while his sister, Elizabeth Bromley, had been Brown's first wife. He had inherited property in the same manner as Brown though on a larger scale. He lived with his wife's family in Tavistock Street (see p.24, n.4).

but superintended the workwoman. Went to see the Lucy's, came back & worked at R Burns on the Canvas.

29th Got up at ¼ past 6. At 8 began arranging the lay figure for the forground female back figure with a nosegay. New boy came. Interruption. Arranged the figure by ½ past 10 & began the study. Went out on business, saw my aunt Brown, wrote a note to Helen Bromley, began painting the satin *sideless* dress,[30] laid it in almost pure white with a little yellow chrome to finish it by glazing tomorrow. Painted till 20 minutes to five, dined & set work about ½ past 6 drew chaucer & the old king in on the canvas. Am writing this & going to bed 20 minutes past 10.

30th Painted at the sideless gown al day – in the evening did little, Lucy came to see me.

31st Sunday Got up very late, painted at the sideless gown – & then at the Hair & cap of the troubadour in the center of the picture. Laid in the study for it, dined, walked a long way to find my washerwoman – called on Mark Anthony stopped there till 12. He told me that Hurlstone had wished to get me to join the suffolk street set which has been trying to regenerate.[31]

1st November Got up at 7 felt very tired walked half over London, bought a portrait of Lord Byron & some yellow brocade & hired some ermine. Come in about 3 finished the hair of the troubadour – dined, felt very tired. John Marshall came in stopped till 10 (1 hour work).

2nd Got up at 7 & to work by 9, painted the study of the ermine cloake of ye ladië with ye sideless gown. Workwoman all day, cut out the yellow brocade Hood & cape & muddled away the rest of the evening (6 hours work).

3rd Got up at ¼ to 7 & to work by ½ past 8, finished yesterdays work & painted at a study of the ermine cloak of ye black Prince & at 2 had to leave off in consequence of ye fog – which like Foggo was nogo.[32] Wrote a letter

---

[30] As illustrated in *Knight's Pictorial History of England*, 1837, i, p.870. The "sideless dress" was very full and the bodice trimmed with fur, giving the impression of a jacket. In the completed canvas the same figure is wearing her hair enclosed in a caul of net-work, copied from p.867. Brown took many ideas from this volume. The Chaucer reading desk is an exact copy of that on p.864 and the headdress and sleeve of the seated woman beside the Cardinal are taken from p.751.

[31] Mark Anthony (1817-86), landscape painter, lived in Percy Street. The Society of British Artists of which F.Y. Hurlstone (1801-69), portrait and historical painter, was President had their premises in Suffolk Street, Pall Mall.

[32] The brothers James (1790-1860) and George (1793-1869) Foggo were lithographers and also produced immense and unsuccessful canvases of historical and biblical scenes. Brown used their name as a punning jest.

& am writing this (¼ to 4). Work woman here making ye yellow brokade hood (7 hours work).

4th Got up at 7 – & to work by ½ past 8. Worked at the study of the ermine cloak till 1. The fog was so bad that I was forced to have the lamp to finish it by – finished the study by 6. Howlet[33] came in then Thomas – I then went to see the Lucy's & got to bed by 12 (8½ hours work).

5th Got up at 7. Dressed, Breakfasted & went out by 9 to the Highgate cemetary, came back & called on Thomas. Set to work about 2 at the hair of the black prince (a study from the lay figure), at 6 set to work at drawing in Chowcer. Again worked at it till 10, have not yet succeeded (5 hours work).

6th got up at 7 have not slept last night, what is the reason of it? Drank some tea just before going to bed. Hope I shall sleep to night. Got to work before 9 finished the hair. Arranged the lay figure for the figure in the yellow brocade hood – began painting it did little before 4 – at 7 went with Lucy to a meeting of the Shareholders of the free Exn. We both refused to be on the comittee, Martin in consequence is afraid they will turn him off, – poor Martin hon sec! we have written to him to say that if they do we will have nothing more to do with them. Marshall Claxton & his party want to make Dibdin Secretary,[34] what a set of Muffs! what will be the upshot of it I dont know & dont care – went to bed at 12 (6 hours work).

7th Got up at 9 – breakfasted & at eleven ment to go to work – felt so miserable and dejected that I could not. Went to find Thomas & walked with him over Regent's Park, up the Finchley Road, by the Swiss cottage, through the lanes up to the top of Haverstock Hill, fine weather but muddy. Enjoyed much. Afterwars went & dined with the Lucy's & spent the day there, come back by ½ past eleven (000 [sic] work).

8th Got up at 7, felt indolent, wrote a note & began work by ½ past 10. Painted at the study of the yellow satin hood till ½ past 3 – am now writing this & going to dine – 4 o'clock. After Diner worked at a drawing of the Head of Byron in charcoal till eleven (9 hours work).

9th Got up at 7 went for a walk with Thomas till 10, worked at the yellow

---

[33] Probably D. Hewlett, sculptor, exhibiting at the R.A. in 1847.
[34] The Free Exhibition of Modern Art (later National Institution of Fine Arts) was in its second year at the Chinese Gallery, Hyde Park. Brown paid a fee per foot of wall space used, which entitled him to be a shareholder. Martin, probably J.F., genre painter. Marshall Claxton (1812-81), painter of historical and biblical subjects, failed to make a reputation and subsequently lived in Australia, India, and the Holy Land. In 1860 his daughter, Florence Claxton, exhibited her parody of Pre-Raphaelite painting, *The Choice of Paris: An Idyll*, at the Portland Gallery (see W.E. Fredeman, *Burlington*, Dec. 1960, pp.523-9). T.C. Dibdin (1810-93) water-colourist, was nominated Secretary.

brocade hood. My aunt Brown came in, did little, left off at half past 3, dined & set to work again at the drawing of Byron and that of Burn's till 12 (8 hours work).

10th Got up at 7 got to work by 9, painted at the study of the green gown with the yellow hood till ½ past 3, went out for a walk till ¼ to 5 – set to work again at 7 & worked till 12 at a drawing of Burns (10 hours work).

11th Got up at 7 & to work by 9. Workwoman came & made sleeves for the robes of the muses etc. I worked at the study of the Green robe as before till 3 – did nothing – & nothing *at all* all the evening (5 hours work).

12th Got up at 7 & to work by 9 – painted at the green gown till ¼ past 3, walked out, went to see my aunt Brown, dined, went to see Mark Anthony about a Daguerotipe, think of having some struck off for the figures in the picture to save time – came back & set to work at a drawing of the head of Spencer. Work from 9 till 12 (8½ hours work).

13th Got up at 7 & to work by ½ past 8, painted at the study of the yelloy hood and Green dress till ¼ past 10 – dressed & went out about this Daguerotipe to Isecole[35] & another man – came back & worked two hours at arranging the lay figure for the skirt of R. Burn to draw that over again, then went out again to the Photographic place, came back & dined & set to work on Spencer again till Lucy came in at 10 o'clock. Stopped till eleven & walked home with him – came to bed at past twelve (6 hours work).

14th Got up at 10! drank beer the night before & eat Bread & cheese! set to work by eleven at the drapery of R Burns, arranged it by 12, drew at it till ¼ past 4, walked out. Dined, wrote to Bamford & am writing this ½ past 7. At 8 set to work drawing a study for the head of Spencer, draw at it till 12 satisfied with it (9 hours work).

15th Got up 7 & to work by ½ past 8. Drew at the robe of R. Burns till ½ past 12 then arranged the sleeve of the female with the white cowl & began a study of it at ½ past one till ½ past 3. Went out for a walk came back & am going for diner. Drew at the figure of Byron on the canvas from 7 till 9 & from ½ past till ½ past 11 (10 hours work).

16th Got up at ¼ to seven & to work by ½ past 8. Worked at the study of yellow sleeve till ½ past ten, then cleaned my pallet & set the lay figure for the cloak of The fair Maid of Kent,[36] painted at it from 12 till 3. Dressed & walked round the park, called on Thomas came back to dine by 5 – he is

[35] Probably Professor Highschool, of Philadelphia, who ran the Daguerreotype Institution in the Strand (open 9a.m. to dusk) where he took portraits "in a most exquisite manner".
[36] The wife of the Black Prince for whom Emma Hill, Brown's second wife, was the eventual model.

hard at work knocking metaphysical art on ye head & bringing each thing sentimental to a positive state. Lucy called on me. Did not get to work again till 9, worked at the head of Byron 2½ hours (7½ hours work).

17th Got up at ½ past seven & to work by 9, cogitated on what I was to do till ½ past 10. Drew at the Cardinal & the 2 Ladies till 2 then painted at yesterday's work & finished the study by 3. Dressed & went out to Roney's[37] & the hairdressers. Come back by 5, am going to dine. Set to work at 7 painted the first bit on the canvas worked till 1 laid in the head & neck of Lord Byron (10 hours work).

18th Got up at ¼ past seven to work by 9, worked slowly at Drawing in the center fourground figures in white chalk till 3. Dressed & walked out till I went to the Lucy's, found a roast hare for dinner, was made to stop, stopped till ½ past 7. Came back & lighted the lamp & set to work. Worked about ½ an hour & then fell asleep, got down off the steps sat down by the fire & smoked & fell asleep & then went to bed (5 hours work).

19th Got up at ¼ past 7 & to work by 10. Drew in several figures in white chalk. The knight the chamberlain etc. Worked till 3. Lucy came in & I walked home with him to hear their decision about whether or not he should take Dickinson's offer to superintend his accademy,[38] he half decided that if Dickingson would give £150 per annum, he would. Roast beef for dinner, obliged to stop. After dinner Mark Anthony & his wife come in we talked a very great deal about the Suffolk Street, the free Exhibition. Stayed till past 12 (5 hours work).

20th Got up at ½ past 7 & to work by 10. Worked till ½ past 12 by lamp light at Laying in the shirt of Lord Byron in white & black with M'Guilph then drew 2 hours at the Lady with the little boy beside her − Left off by ½ past 3 & went out for a walk & to dun Mr Simpson for Helen. Came back & dined. Thomas came in & stopped talking till 9, I then set to work & painted in a part of Lord Byrons togam, the lights in grey & the shaddows & reflections in reddish colour. Worked till 12 (7 hours work).

21st Got up at ¼ past 11, sunday, had nothing to wake me. Am writing

---

[37] Rowney, artist's colourman of Rathbone Place.
[38] The Dickinson Brothers were a firm who dealt in print and lithograph publishing and selling and acted as photographic agents. Their premises were at 114 New Bond Street where they held their exhibitions. Robert Dickinson was head of the firm. His brother, Lowes Cato Dickinson (1819-1908), a popular portrait painter, was an original founder of the Working Men's College where he taught drawing with Rossetti and Ruskin, and coming under F.D. Maurice's spell was converted to Christian Socialism. At about this time the brothers had started a Drawing Academy at 18½ Maddox Street for life study, four evenings a week from 7 to 10 p.m. at a fee of half a guinea a month. Their prospectus made a distinction for "ladies classes in the day. Artists in the evening." Charles Lucy was engaged as a drawing master.

this at 10 minutes past 1 & going to set to work at the Togam of Lord Byron. Have got the Ague. Worked at Chalking in the center figure of the troubadour for one hour & a half, retired from 3 to 4, very ill. Painted at the Togam of Byron from 4 till ¼ to 6, dined and painted from half past 6 till 1 in the morning. Finished laying in the Togam with grey for the lights & reddish colour for the shaddows – have spoilt the drawing of it (8¾ hours work).

22nd Got up at ½ past 7, felt ill, went out on business, wasted my time & took a walk till 12, came back & worked a very little, about 1½ hours – wasted my time & dined. Martin has just dropped a note in my letter box which seems to say that they have ejected him from the place of Secretary to the free Exhibition, if so we have done with it & there is no necessity for me to get this work finished. It has rather cooled my working ardour – worked a little in the evening about 2 hours (3½ hours work).

23rd Got up at 8, still got the ague. Set the study in order had it swept out & hung some of the painting in fresh places. About 1 I began work, about 2 hours. John Bromley & Collingwood Smith[39] & father called to see my studio stoped till ½ past 5. I then went & dined & called on the Lucy's & stayed till eleven. Took wine & brandy & water yesterday for the ague (2 hours work).

24th Got up at 8 rather agueish still, went for a walk with Thomas, bought some cloathes, boots, come back to work about 12, worked from 1 till 4 & going to dine. Hewlett came in & stopped till 6 afterwards Mark Anthony & stoped ½ an hour. Afterwards Thomas & stopped an hour & a half – did not do much before 9 worked from then till ½ past eleven at the figure in the yellow hood chalking it in on the canvas (6 hours work).

25th Got up at 8, walked out, wasted my time. Got to work by ¼ to 11, worked till ½ past 3, about 3½ hours – went out, am writing this expecting my uncle Madox. Old gentleman came. Made himself quite Jolly went away by Six. Mrs Murcott[40] came. Worked from ¼ to 7 till ¼ past 11 (7½ hours work). Lucy came in on his way to a meeting about the free Exhtn & Martin hon Sec.

26th got up at 8 began work at ½ past 9, worked till 12½ at a head of Shakspear did nothing fit to be seen, went out wretched weather, Lucy came back & dined with me, about half past six I set to work at drawing hands but could not work. Drew one, worked little better, then 2 hours. I

---

[39] W. Collingwood Smith (1818-87), landscape painter. For John Bromley, see below (n.41).
[40] Probably Mrs Anne Murcott of Russell Court, Drury Lane, who undertook "dress-making" and was probably the workwoman first mentioned on 22 Oct.

have been reflecting seriously about my large composition that I had better paint the middle compartment small for next years exhibition & recompense it for the large one on a grander principle. I have been reflecting on the subject & have almost made up my mind to do so. I have sat up thinking of the new composition to see if I could make a better one so as not to risk sacrificing the present one to no purpose & I believe I have succeeded to my satisfaction (2 hours work, 2 do. thought, 3 wasted).

27th Got up I know not at what hour. Have been thinking about my change & have decided to go & order the small canvass – am going to Blackheath[41] to sleep & to Foot's Cray tomorrow to return Monday to work. Have called on Thomas he has dissuaded me from changing the large work. Called on Lucy & went to the Royal Exchange & down to Blackheath to sleep.

28th Left Blackheath for foots Cray by 2 oclock Eltham bus. Walked from thence, got to Uncle's by ¼ to 4 Slept there came up next Morning.

29th came up from Foots Cray – payed the carriage of a picture to Rome for Dr Deakin, called on Bamford. Thought of what I should do. Thought of a subject as I went along. Wycliff reading his translation of the bible to John of Gaunt, Chaucer & Gower Present – arranged it in my mind, called on Lucy, saw Martin, in a precious stew about the free Exhibition. Dined, came home Made a slight scetch of it (3 hours work).

30th got at it ¼ to 8. Went out to see about the Museum for consulting authorities, called on Mark Anthony, went to the reading room of Museum, saw Levis's life of Wycliff, Southeys book of the church. Met Lucy there in search of documents for his landing of Puritans in New Plymouth.[42] Came home. Dined & scetched a little at the subject (3 hours work).

1st Decr got up at 8 went out to the print shops and to the national gallery. Then to the Museum, read Godwin's life of Chaucer,[43] came back at 4 to dine am writing this & going to cast up my accounts. Worked a little at my scetch, John Marshall came in & I did nothing more.

2nd got up at ½ past 7 went out to the British Museum got there by ten.

---

[41] To John Bromley, a cousin who lived at Blackheath Hill.
[42] The books of interest to Brown were John Lewis's *An Account of Dr Wiclif*, 1728, and Robert Southey's *Book of the Church* in two volumes, 1824. At the R.A. exhibition of 1848 Lucy exhibited *The Landing of the Primitive Puritans . . . on the Coast of America* A.D. *1620*.
[43] William Godwin, *Life of Geoffrey Chaucer including memories of John of Gaunt*, 1803, 2 vols.

Made a drawing of an gothic alphabet read Knights chaucer,[44] dine, called on my aunt Brown. Set to work by 8 worked the scetch till 12 (4 hrs & museum).

3rd got up at 8 went to the Museum by ½ past 9. Finish the alphabet & consulted Pugin on furniture.[45] In the evening worked at the composition till ½ past 12 (5 hours) (6 hours Museum).

4th went to Highgate & to Gravesend to see my sweet child.

5th Slept at Gravesend, drew a little head of my beautiful babe.[46] It is to day 18 months since the death of my poor dear wife. These are thoughts that I must banish it unnerves me. I have dedicated the day to my child & the memory of her mother. Yesterday I brought her fushia down from her grave & have given it to Mrs Lucy to take care of for the winter. I left Gravesend by the five oclock boat & have come back intending perhaps to do some work (2 hours).

6th Got up at ½ past 8, boy did not come, had to light my fire myself – got to work about eleven at arranging the designe of Wiclif.[47] Worked till ½ past 3, went out for a walk, am writing this & going to dine. Thomas came in, I began to work again at ½ past 7 & slowly worked on till 12 (9 hours work).

7th Got up at half past 8, got to work before ten, drew at the scetch till ½ past 2, went out & called on Thomas to see a designe he is making – & on Lucy. He & his wife & child have been all ill with this influenza. Came back & dined & set to work – about 8 till 12 (8 hours work).

8th no entry, worked nevertheless all day.

9th Got up at 8. The night before I had finished the drawing of the scetch about 10. I began to draw a tracing of the scetch to make it in oil, muddled & worked & muddled till ½ past 3 – went out half inclined to work no more – came back, dined, Mr & Mrs Lucy came in to see me – good excuse I went home with them & stopped till 1!!

10th got up at 8 went out by 9 to take a walk – could not. Wretched weather. Got Thomas to come & see my scetch – went with him to his studio saw some german prints – come back to work about 11. Drew at the outline for my oil scetch till ½ past 2 felt Lazy began writing this in consequence – dined & began work again about 6. Worked till ½ past 8 went out for a walk (6 hours).

---

[44] See p.9, n.22.
[45] A.W.N. Pugin *Gothic Furniture in the Style of the 15th Century*, 1835.
[46] Private Collection. Signed with monogram and inscribed: "Dec 5/47 Lucy To Cathy". The last two words were added at a later date.
[47] The *Chaucer* was now laid aside and *Wycliffe Reading his Translation of the Bible* begun (Bradford City Art Gallery, Plate 4).

3. *Hampstead From My Window*, Delaware Art Museum, Wilmington

4. *Wycliffe Reading his Translation of the Bible to John of Gaunt in the Presence of Chaucer and Gower*, City Art Gallery and Museums, Bradford

11th Saturday got up about 8 set to painting by 10, painted till ½ past 3 at the figures of Wickliff Chaucer & Gower & that side of it. Went out & called on Lucy, come back & dined – & am writing this. Set to work by ¼ past 7 muddled till 10 did little good (8 hours work).

12th Sunday got up at 8 set to work before 10 painted till 3 at the figure of John of Gaunt etc. Went out & dined & spent the evening with Lucy (5 hours work).

13th Monday got up at 8 – went out for a walk by 9 walked all over primrose hill & haverstock hill come back & call on Lucy. *Buss*[48] has been bothering him about the free Exhibition. Went with him to Roney's came back dined & set to work about 6, waisted 1½ cleaning a damned pipe, worked till 11 (5 hours work).

14th Got up at ½ past 8 ready to go & take a walk by ½ past 9. Look for a prescription till 10. Found, and suffering at my chest from indigestion going to take more exercise & doctor myself. Walked till ¼ to 11 – came back settled the size of my canvas went out to order the stretcher could not find cooper saw Lucy – Thomas got the influenza again – going after model & found none, did nothing, went to Lucy's & spent the evening till 12 (no work).

15th Got up at 10 read in bed, went out by 11. Called on Thomas at home, ill with influenza, stopped till near one – took a walk all over hyde Park, dined & came back to studio. Stretcher came home spent the evening straining canvas for my Wicliff. Read Anthony & Cleopatra again. Went to bed at 12.

16th got up at ½ past 8 went for a walk by ½ past 9 – came back by ½ past 10 set to work about 12 worked till 3 chalking in the figures on the canvas – went out for a model unsuccessful. Got Smith[49] coming tomorrow. Set to work about ½ past 6, left off for want of chalk, am writing this & going to write damned letter for money etc. Can do no more work for want of chalk have been as far as Oxford St but can get none – drew a little at the ornamental part of the designe (4 hours).

17th Got up at ½ past 7 took a walk & to work by 10. Model came made scetches of the figure of Chaucer & Gower worked till 3 went out saw Lucy & Thomas. Set to work again by ½ past 6 – did about an hours work. Smith came at ½ past 8, I worked till ½ past 10 at scetches of John of Gaunt (8 hours).

18th Set to work about ½ past 10. Painted at the scetch till 3 – afterwards went to the city & spent the evening at Bamfords (4 hours work).

[48] R.W. Buss (1804-74), book illustrator and genre painter.
[49] A model.

19th Sunday got up at ½ past 9 – went out by 11 to see Lucy & then to Mr Bamfords to go & dine with John Bromley at Blackheath.

20th Got up at about ½ past 8. Mrs Yates & child from 10½ till 12½, scetched a little at the outline head. Garret[50] in the evening for scetches of Wicliff (6 hours work).

21st breakfasted in bed got up about 10 worked all day at the outline on the canvas, about ½ past 3 went out for a walk & to dun this raskel for Helen, he won't pay, came back, went to diner, drew at the outline again. Hewlet came in & brought a Chrismas *box* for my sweet Lucy – after he went I worked again as before till ½ past 11 (8 hours work).

22nd breakfasted in bed got up at ½ past 9 & to work by 10. Drew at the outline till 3 went out for a walk till 4 – Came back in the evening worked about 4 hours at the outline (9 hours).

23rd Got up at 9 after Breakfasting in bed, Fog came, & Thomas also – went out with him & made Purchases for Chrismas boxes – did nothing but Run about all day – in the eveg went to the Lucys.

24th went to Gravesend my sweet child quite well.

25th Christmas. Got up at 8. Dined with my sweet child at Aunt Helen's – in the evening we went to the Lightfoots'.[51]

26th Sunday Stayed at Gravesend.

27th Came up to London did nothing all day called on the Lucy's in the evening. On coming home to my studio at Past 12 found a drunken Man groaning in one of the work shops with a Candle amid the shavings. Fetched a policeman & the Master, got him safe out.

28th Tried to work did nothing all day but arrange the lay figure for Wiclif & superintend the making of a gown for Chaucer, I am sadly Idle!!

29th Got up at ½ past 8 & to work by ½ past 9, worked till 11 at arranging the dress of Wicliff. The Lucy's came in I muddled at a drawing of it till ½ past 2. Then went out for a walk & to have my hair cut. Dined. Afterwards Thomas & Mark Anthony came in till 9. I did nothing but write a note to Martin about the free exhibition (4 hours).

30th Went to Foot's Cray.

---

[50] Garret was a model as was Mrs Yates, presumably for Constance (Gaunt's second wife) with the child in her lap. Later her husband stood for a figure in the same picture (see 28 Jan. 1848).
[51] Probably friends of Helen Bromley. Robert Lightfoot, gent., was listed in Parrock Street, Gravesend.

31st Foots Cray. Music & young ladies. Afterwards Tristram the saylor[52] sat up with him till 3 in the morning after seeing the old year out Drinking rum & water & smoking.

[52] Tristram Maries Madox, only child of Brown's Uncle Madox and thus his first cousin. A rather disreputable figure, he was sent to Australia in the next few years; he died at Ramsgate where he worked in a steam-laundry. In 1847 he appears to have been a seaman.

1848

1st Janry 48 Came back to London & dined at Lucys, in the evening Thomas came in & we settled to illustrate Pope's essay on Man between us, I proposed the subject.[1] Came to bed by 1.

2nd Got up at ¼ past 9 Sunday. Got to work by ½ past eleven drawing at the draperies for Wickliff till ½ past 3 – went for a walk over Regent's Park – dined & read the papers till ½ past 6. Set to work by half past 7 drew at the outline of the picture in white chalk till 11. Am going to bed 12 o'clock (6½ hours work).

3rd Got up at 8 & to work by ½ past 9, drew at the draperies of Wicliff till ½ past 3, finished the study, went out for a walk, dined & called on my aunt Brown, came back & set to work at 8 worked till 11 at the outline of the painting – afterwards fiddled at a peice of poetry till ¼ to 1 (8 hours work).

4th Got up at 8, went for a walk from 9 till 10, set to work at half past 10 at placing the lay figure for Chaucer, began drawing it at 1 till ¼ to 4. Walked out, came back (Got a bad cold) dined, wrote to Helen, Lucy called on me. Set to work at 9 till 11 at the outline on the Canvas (6½ hours work).

5th Got up at 8 went out by 9 to Highgate cemetary had some standard roses planted on my poor Wife's grave, too high, ordered lower ones to be put, came back by 11, worked at the drapery of chaucer till 1. Maitland[2] came, drew his head a study for Gower till 3, worked at the drapery till 4, walked out till ½ past 5, called on Lucy came back, dined, wrote a note. Seddon[3] called on me did nothing more (5 hours work).

---

[1] *Essay on Man*, published 1733. Nothing came of this proposal.
[2] A professional model whom Rossetti employed the following year to pose for the archangel in his *Ecce Ancilla Domine!* (Tate).
[3] Thomas Seddon (1821-56), landscape painter, though as yet still employed at his father's furniture works, for which purpose he had studied decorative art in Paris.

6th worked from ¼ past 9 till 11 at the study for Chaucer's drapery, finished it, had Lucy's lay figure taken back – beautiful day walked up to Hampstead with Mrs Lucy, came back, dressed & called on Mrs Mosa,[4] & on John Marshall. Spent the remainder of the evening with the Lucys.

7th breakfasted in bed set to work by ½ past 9, drew at the outline till ½ past 12. Maitland came drew a study of his legs for John of Gaunt till ½ past 3, dined, called on my aunt. Maitland came at 6 drew at his feet for Wicliff till ½ past 8, had tea, cleaned my pipe, smoked & cast up my accounts etc till now ¼ past 10. Worked at the outline from then till 12 (9 hours work).

8th Breakfasted in bed set to work by 10 at the outline worked at it till 3. Hughes came made a drawing of his head till 4. Dined & went out for Miss Wild,[5] saw Lucy. Came back & set to work by 7 till 10 on the head of the female, made a wretched drawing of it, Thomas here all the time, reading passages of a work on Sylogisms[6] (8 hours work).

9th Got up at ½ past 9 to work by ½ past 11 worked at the outline till 2, began drawing one of my hands in the glass for John of Gaunt – dined, walked round Regents park, first day of frost, set to work again at ½ past seven, drew my other hand for John of Gt finished it by ½ past 9, had tea and set to work at ½ past 10 at the one I had began by daylight. Finished it by ¼ to 12, a good drawing for a wonder. Now 12 going to smoke a pipe & go to bed (7 hours work).

10th Got up at ½ past 8 and to work by ½ past 9. Drew my two hands in the Glass for Gower's. Mrs Lucy called to ask me something – I afterwards drew a little at one of my hands for Wicliff when that devil Miss Chamberlain called. Walked round regents park, dined. Thomas came in & with Lucy we went to Dickinson's accademy, Madox Street. Saw Foley there & Paris & Saulter[7] (5 hours work).

11th Got up at 8 to work by half past 9 drew my two hands for Wicliff & drew at the canvas, figure of John of Gaunt. At 2½ dressed to go & dine with Lucy on his wedding day. Thomas there and Marshall who walked all the way to my study with me at 2 in the morning (4½ hours work).

---

[4] Mrs Robert Moser, of 30 Tavistock Street. Robert Moser was a partner in Crawshay & Co., a firm of iron masters in South Wales. Their daughter Clara had married Richard Bromley in 1843 and this was also his London address.

[5] Julia Wild, "celebrated as model & prostitute also for black eyes". Hughes was also a model.

[6] An anonymous publication had recently appeared under the title *The Syllogism considered as an Analysis of the Reasoning Process and an Inquiry into the Nature of the Induction*, and was dismissed rather peremptorily by the *Athenaeum* (28 Feb. 1848).

[7] Distinguished as a sculptor, J.H. Foley (1818-74) taught modelling at the Academy. E.T. Parris (1793-1873), portrait painter, had invented Parris's Medium which presented a dull fresco-like surface when mixed with oil. W. Saulter (1804-75), historical painter.

12th Breakfasted in bed, drew all day at the canvas. Lucy came in to go to Dickinson's with me, found I was making my figures of Chaucer & Gower to short, quite took me aback. Went & began a pencil drawing at Dickinsons walked home with Lucy, came back bought a bottle of Wiskey to drown care with (8 hours work).

13th White the model[8] came for an hour & a half about 2. I drew at the canvas the rest of the day. Went to dickinsons drew about 1 hour there. Lucy came home with me & drank some wiskey & water (7 hours work).

14th Old Coulton came for 5 hours. Thomas brought me an outline of the proportions according to Vitruvius.[9] I went to the Maddox Street accy. as usual & came back & worked a little, finished little study (9 hours work).

15th I went to Greenwich to collect Rents & to Gravesend.

16th Gravesend still. Made a little study of Lucy in sunshine[10] (1½ hours work).

17th Came back by the 8½ boat. Went to see John Bromley & to make a scetch of the hand of his little girl for the female in the painting. Dined & went to see Thomas' scetch Faith hope & Chary to the Chapel of the Mercer's company.[11] Come back & set to work drawing at the figure of Wicliff, went to Maddox St came back again at 10 & worked till ½ past 11 (5½ hours work).

18th Got up at ½ past 8, set to work by 10 at drawing in a hand & the sleeves of Wicliff. *Began painting.* Laid in the head & feet of Wicliff. Turned my canvasses of the Poëts round to the wall so as to be able to admit persons if necessary. Painted till ¼ to 4 dined & walked out, come back, work an hour at lessening Chaucer's legs, had tea & went to Dickingsons accademy. Came back worked from ¼ past 10 till ½ past 11 at lessening the head & hands of Gower — afterwas set my accounts in order & am going to bed (8 hours work).

19th Breakfasted in bed. Got up at ½ past 8 & to work by ½ past 9. Painted till 3, laid in the hand & cloak of Wicliff in yellow to paint over grey — and M'Guilph — walked over regents park, dined read a novel & let

---

[8] A professional model, employed also by Rossetti.
[9] Vitruvius, Roman architect of the first century B.C., and famous also for his manual of architecture and building construction. Coulton was a model.
[10] This, or the copy (see n.70) is in a Private Collection. The whereabouts of the other is not known.
[11] Thomas had been commissioned by the Mercers' Company to make three designs for altar-pieces for their chapel, and although approved, financial reasons precluded their execution. Rebuilt after the Great Fire of 1666, the chapel presented on its front elevation in Cheapside the figures of Faith and Hope, surmounted by that of Charity. The Chapel was again destroyed in the Second World War.

my fire go out, went out to Dickinsons place, found it was the wrong night. Called on Mark Anthony, saw his large village festival[12] in progress, called on Lucy (5 hours work).

20th worked from ten till four at the grey gown of Wicliff, laid it in very transparent. Walked over regents park for one houre, dinned, Thomas called & smoked a pipe. About 7 I went to Maddox street worked an hour & three quarters, old Paris there gobbling away making a fool of himself. Walked home with Lucy, had some rennet ale & chease on the way. Came back to my study read a novel & went to bed (7 hours work).

21st Breakfasted in bed. Got up at 10 & to work by eleven drew in the head of Chaucer from myself in two looking Glasses, altered that of Gower & reduced one of Chaucer's hands – four oclock went out for one hours walk in the park – dined, read, smoked & went to Maddox St. Came back with Lucy set to work about 11 till ¼ to 12 reduced the other hand & redrew the Sleeve (7 hours work).

22nd Got up at ¼ to 8, had my studio entirely cleaned out. Set to work by ½ past eleven painted in the sleeves & upper part of Chaucer's gown (*a premier coup*). Shall not want to retouch it much I expect. Worked till 4, walked out up & down Oxford st. Made some purchases, bears green[13] etc. Came back dined off one Mutton chop, toast & butter, a very little wiskey & water & one cup of Coffee, have one chop at lunch & toast for Breakfast – after dinner read a novel & smoked. Out to work again by ½ past 7, worked till ½ past 9 had tea at ½ past ten, to work again till a quarter past eleven, laid in the hand of Chaucer & Gower. Washed my brushes. Am going to settle my accounts after this, 12 o'clock (7 hours work).

23rd Sunday got up at ½ past 9 & to work by ½ past 11 painted in the skirt of Chaucer's dress & laid in his legs – left off at ¼ to four walked over the park, went & bought a newspaper to keep up my connexion with the outer world come back, dined, read my paper & had tea, about 9 began working at the outline of John of Gaunt till 11 (6 hours work).

24th Breakfasted in bed, got up at ½ past 10 drew again at the outline of John of Gt. till four. Walked round the park, dined, & went to madox St. Come back with Lucy, met Thomas, set to work again at the outline from ½ past 10 till ½ past 11 (5 hours work).

25th painted or rather laid in the head of Gower & the hands of John of Gaunt. Made one too small & the other too large, left off by 3½ to go & see

---

[12] *Landscape and Figures, Village Green* won scant praise when exhibited at the Suffolk Street Gallery, though in scale and subject it was Anthony's most ambitious work to date.
[13] Hair pomade for men.

what Thomas has been doing – came back & dined smoked, read, luxuriated & went to Madox Street. Making a good drawing of it went home with Lucy (6 hours work).

26th Wednesday Got up at ½ past 8 went out for a walk found it too cold went & bespoke Miss Ashley[14] & come back. Miss Ashley came at 11 stopped till four let the fire out 3 times & talked all day, will never do – in the evening I work at the head of the female drawing it in, in water colors, could not succeed (4 hours work).

27th I breakfasted in bed & got up at ¼ to 9, set to work about ½ past 9 drew at the head of the female then drew in the head of sleeping child & laid it in, left off at ¼ to four. Walked out to the park, skating going on, called on my aunt Brown tired & went to Maddox street & home with Lucy (7 hours work).

28th Yates came & I made a drawing of his head for chaucer from ½ past 10 till 12. Afternoon drew at the head of Chaucer till Miss Ashley came, when I painted in the head of the female & left off. Afterwards retouched it by lamp light after she was gone, succeeded. Mark Anthony came in gave me a ticket for Professor Anwells [Ansted] Lecture in Geology. Went to Madox Street, Lucy came back & supper with me (5 hours work).

29th Mrs Yates came at ½ past 10. I made a drawing of her hand & her child till ½ past 12, afterwards painted in the hand of Chaucer (rather too dark) & put in White led with a Pallet Knife for a ground for his scarlet hood. Packed up my bag & after dining in the strand went and spent the evening at Blackheath & slept there.

30 went to Foots Cray to see how Aunt Madox is, found her better, saw my uncle & Henry Barraud.[15]

31st Came up By couch & rained. Went to my taylor to endeavour to get my bill – come back to my Studio had lunche & set to work at the hands of the female, drew them in – dined, went to Madox Street, model did not come – went to Suffolk St to hear professor Anstead tell us that the colour of the air is blue & that of Mist grey etc etc – this they call geology[16] (2 hours work).

---

[14] A model. Mrs Ashley by 13 Oct.
[15] Harry Barraud (1811-75), sporting and genre painter whose most popular pictures were *We Praise Thee, O God* and *Lord's Cricket Ground*. He had an older brother William (1810-60), also a painter.
[16] The first lecture in a series delivered by D.T. Ansted (1814-80), Professor of Geology at King's College, London. "The Atmosphere" was the subject of the lecture.

1st feby. Got up at ½ past 10 breakfasted & read in bed. Set to work about 12 worked about 2 hours laid in the hands of the female & child – went to grays in Lane to Seddon to get his "Shaw's furniture" thence to Mark Anthony's to get the dictionary of architecture.[17] Come back, dined, Thomas called in we looked over the works & jawed about architecture & Phylosophy. I afterwards set about composing the furniture for my paint-ing – did not do much (2 hours work). Got a note from Helen Bromley enclosing one from Miss Ensgrubber[18] to her to ask my poor wifes address, O! dear, her's has been for upwards 19 months the Cemetary of Highgate, mine this rascally barn of a studio, to think that We once had a home together! in Paris how different & even in Rome how different, bless you my poor child.

2nd Got up at 8 worked from 10 till four at compsing the chair of John of Gaunt, dined, dressed & went to Mr Bamfords, dansed till 3 in the morning. Got to bed at ½ past 5 (6 hours work).

3rd breakfasted in bed & went to sleep again till 1 o'clock, got up & called upon Lucy then upon Thomas – came back to my studio at 5, dined & wrote a note to Helen & one to John Marshall. Going to set to work for about 3 hours at the chair. Did little good what a Muff I am (3 hours work).

4th Breakfasted in bed, set to work about 10 recomposed the chair & composed the letterm & began painting it. Worked till ½ past 4 walked round the park, set to work again at 7 when Thomas & John Marshall came in. I did no more work. Thomas accused Marshall of having spoken about our London University Project at the Colledge, Marshall dinied it but said that he had heard that an other body of Artists had preposed the same thing about a year ago.[19] Thomas stopped till 11 & we drank two glasses of grog each! (6 hours work).

5th Breakfasted in bed, set to work about half past 9 worked at the lettern altered it, painted at it till 4, dined etc a wet day did not go out, began work again at 7 till 8 & from 9 till ½ past 11 painting at the lettern what snobbish[20] work (9 hours work). Forgot to go to Highgate alas! my poor wife.

---

[17] The Seddon furniture firm and manufactury was in Gray's Inn Road where Thomas Seddon, Senior, was also listed as house agent and undertaker. (The Royal Free Hospital stood next door.) The book in question was *Specimens of Ancient Furniture*, published by Henry Shaw, 1836. The Dictionary may have been J.H. Parker, *Companion to . . . a Glossary of Terms used in Gothic Architecture*, 1846, or John Britton's *Dictionary of the Architecture and Archaeology of the Middle Ages*, 1838.

[18] According to W.M. Rossetti this was a friend of Brown's first wife, of whom nothing further is known.

[19] Probably some form of decoration for the interior of the College had been suggested.

[20] The early meaning of the word was "Having no pretensions to rank or gentility". Brown considered this work to be of a lowly order.

6th Got up at ¼ to 10 Sunday, to work by half past 11 painted till ½ past 4 walked round the park bought a news paper, dined & read then had tea set to work again from 9 till 12. Laid in the Lettern (8 hours work).

7th Monday got up at ¼ to 8. Breakfasted & went to Highgate had Iron stakes put to the standard roses. Called on Lucy went to the London university to see about Capbells [Campbell] bust of Potter. John Marshall on behalf of the Comittee commissioned me to make drawing of it for which I'm to receive 5 Geoneus.[21] Dined, set to at my accounts. Thomas called in to know if I would accompony him tomorrow to a meeting of the free masons of the church to hear a lecture on beauty by a baronet M.P. He for the first time explained to me his views on beauty & the explanation thereof. Wonderful fellow I hardly know what to make of him his talents are so wonderful & varied. Stopped till ½ past 11.

8th Got up at ½ past 8 went to the british institution, saw a wonderful peice of light by Inskip a beautiful marine by Domby [Danby] a calm after a storm with a heavy ground swell. I stopped one ½ hour looking at this picture. Lance, Frost, Copley Fielding,[22] etc. Afterwards I went to the university & began the drawing of the bust came back after 2½ hours work, dined, Sam Bamford called in, then Thomas when we went to hear a most absurd lecture by a bart[23] – beside whom was seated the duke of Northumberland – after which some antiquarian controversy. I went home to Thomas to Supper & smoked with old Thomas (2½ hours work).

9th got up at 8, went to the university by 10 worked till half past 4 dined with John Marshall. Sam Bamford spent the evening with me (6 hours work).

10th got up at ¼ to 8. At ½ past 8 walked out over the park, afterwards came back dressed & went to the university, drew at the head till ½4 finished it pretty satisfactorily – went to Lucy to show it him. Come home dined, went to sleep, wrote a note (6 hours work).

11th Got up at ½ past 7 went out by ½ past 8 walked over the park set to work by half past 9 till 12 at the head of Potter then wrote a letter to Miss

---

[21] The drawing made from a bust by Thomas Campbell (1790-1858) of J.P. Potter (1818-47), anatomist and house surgeon to University College Hospital, was to be lithographed.
[22] The painting by James Inskipp (1790-1868) was probably *Reaping*. The work so admired by Brown was *A Calm After Heavy Gale* by Francis Danby (1793-1861). George Lance (1802-64), painter of still-life; W.E. Frost (1810-77), painter of portraits and mythological subjects. A.V. Copley Fielding (1787-1855) was distinguished for his marine paintings.
[23] Sir Walter James, Bt, lectured on "The Nature of Beauty and Province of Taste in the Fine Arts".

Ensgrubber. Made me very low & took me till ½ past 4. Dined went with Marshall, Hawart[24] to see about the lithograph of it (2½ hours).

12th Got up at 7, walked round the park, by ½ past 9 set to work to compose the chair of the female did nothing till 12 but brood over it. John Cross & Broadie [Brodie] just come in from Paris, I went with them till Cross's studio in Robert street to see a painting of Broadie's.[25] They returned here & stopped till 5. I dined, then came Thomas & took me away to Sadler's wells to see Miss Addisson in Twelfe night very well got up indeed.[26] Went to see old father Thomas after the play at ½ past 11, stopped till 1!! very bad with a cold or something worse.

13th ill, got up at ½ past 11 set to work by ½ past 12, began composing the chair worked ½ past 4, walked out round the park & bought a newspaper, dined, read my paper till 8 set to work at the chair till 11. Smoked read & drank some grog (7 hours).

14th Got up at 7 set to work by ¼ to 9, painted at the chair till 4, wrote at my accounts & diery till now 5, going to dine – went to Madox Street (7 hours work).

15th Got up at 7, took a walk, set to work by 10 finished the chair. Went to Madox St (8 hours work).

16th walked in the park, come back, employed all day drawing in the arche and composing the moulding for it, in the evening went to see my aunt Brown & the Lucy's (6 hours work).

17th breakfasted in bed. Miss Ashley called in. Composed the chair of John of Gaunt & began it, in the evening went to hear Lesley's first lecture on painting. Twaddle[27] (6 hours work).

18th Painted at the chair from ten till 4 with interruptions, after dinner painted at it with Thomas & Lucy here. (7 hours work).

19th finished the chair began painting the arche (10 hours work).

20th went to Gravesend to see my sweet child. Called on Mark Anthony stayed till 12.

21st get up at ½ past 7, walked over the park, set to work about 10 painting

[24] Probably Frank Howard (1805-66), lithographer, whom Brown had known for a number of years.
[25] John Cross (1819-61), painter of historical subjects, was at Robert Street, Hampstead. J.L. Brodie (fl. 1848-81), known chiefly as a portrait painter.
[26] Shakespeare's *Twelfth Night* at Sadler's Wells was praised, though Miss Laura Addison sustaining the part of Viola had not "entered into the spirit with sufficient penetration".
[27] The first of a course of lectures on "Painting" given by C.R. Leslie (1794-1859), Professor of Painting at the Royal Academy.

at the arch. Got a letter from my uncle Madox asking me to go & speak to him in the City on Business. Left off about 2, went to the City found he wanted to sell his ⅛th of the Tan Yard & if I could sell mine he would get me £700 for it, £200 more than I thought it worth. No unpleasant news. Decided to sell it in order to buy a house.[28] John Bromley made me go to Blackheath for the evening to meet the father of Colingwood Smith. Slept there (4 hours work).

22nd Came back to my studio at 11 found Miss Ashley waiting for me. Made me some beautiful Castor oil pomatum, paid her /3 for it. Painted the neck of the female from her. About 2 set to work at the archeway worked till 4½, set to work at it again at 6 till 11 (7½ hours work).

23rd Got up at ½ past 7, went out by ¼ to 9, walked over the park. Called on Lucy, Marshall, Thomass, and went to Shoolbread's [Shoolbred] to get some gloves, to the butcher & to Lawder [Lauder] to enquire about the free Exhin,[29] could not see him, bought an old stove for /5 to replace this one now going fast. Set to work about ½ past 11 at the arche till 5 & from 8 till 12. Mark Anthony called & Hewlett (7 hours work).

24th Went out by ½ past 8. Raining, called on the coulor man finished painting the arche by 2. Man was to come to set up the stove did nothing more, man set up the stove by 7. Thomass called in & spent the evening (3½ hours work).

25th Got up late. Raining, morning did not go out set to work by 10, French revolution proclaimed,[30] worked at the balustrade & laid in the pavement till 5 when my aunt Brown called & we had tea. In the evening I went to see the papers & to hear professor Anstead lecture on geology. Afterwards went again to get a sight of the paper & went at eleven at night to see Lucy, found him in great excitement about Paris, Fenton his pupil in a sad state about it. We all three have associations with paris.[31] Came back & got to bed by 1 (7 hours work).

26th Got up at ½ past 7 went out before 9, called to see Thomas & talk over the revolution − come back to work. Maitland come in by ½ past 10 worked at laying in the legs of John of Gaunt till ½ past 1. Laid them in

---

[28] The share was not sold. The tanning yard may have had some connection with Ravensbourne Wharf, though the adjacent flour mill seems to negate this supposition.
[29] Shoolbred & Co., substantial linen and woollen drapers, silk mercers and hosiers, were the owners of large premises in Tottenham Court Road. R.S. Lauder (1803-69), the elder of two painter brothers, was the first President of the National Institution (originally Free Exhibition) when it opened at the Portland Gallery, Regent Street, in 1850.
[30] The abdication and flight of King Louis Philippe had occurred with unexpected suddenness on 24 Feb.: a Republic was proclaimed.
[31] Lucy and Brown had studied and worked in Paris where Roger Fenton (1819-69), later a noted photographer in the Crimean War, had trained under Delaroche.

light yellow, used cadmium. Afterwards I could do nothing more but went to see the newspapers. Called on Marshall, & Lucy & Thomass came & took me to an artists conversazione at the bricklayers Arms. Saw Schaff [Scharf], Collinwood Smith & Oliver there,[32] had some more information about the free Exhibition. Art Union has joined & members must be proposed & seconded – went in & had supper with Thomas (3 hours work).

27th Got up at 9, set to work by 10 worked at the two figures of pages in the corner chalked at them all day did nothing (5 hours work). Writing this going to diner, walk & spend the evening at Fenton's.

28th Got up at 9 wrote to Casey to Elliott & My uncle Madox. Composed one of the figures for the spandrils over again, & young girl instead of a child to impersonate the Protestant faith. Determined to make the figures fill up the whole of the spandrils with out tracery work. After diner composed the other figure of the Romish faith, a figure holding a chained up bible & a torch – with a hood like the penitants at catholic funeras showing only the eyes, with burning fagots & a weel of torture for accessories. At ½ past 8 Mrs Lucy called to see me & at 9 Mr. They stopped till 11½ did no more work (6 hours).

29th Got up at ½ past 8 to work by 10 painted at the moaldings of the spandrils, at 1 my uncle Madox called to speak to me about the Tan Yard. I went to see Elliots picture advised him etc – came back tired, read the news about the french revolution dined & set to work at the moaldings till about ½ past 9. Hewlet & Thomas called he stopped till 11 I did no more work (6 hours work).

1st March Got up at ½ past 7 went out by ½ past 8, went to my washerwoman's, to the buchers to give orders for chops, to Mrs Murcotts to see how she was getting on poor wretch had be ill gave her some money – came back set to work about 10 painted at the moaldings with interruptions till 4, finished them – walked over Regents park beautiful eveng called on Lucy & on my aunt Brown – dined & set to work at 8 till ½ past 11 drew the letters in at the bottom (7 hours work).

2nd Got up at ½ past 7 went out by ½ past 8 went to Briggs & Barbe's to see about a lay figure. Hired one, went to Lucy's to see about the head of his son, found a letter there about free Exn. Came back found young Sam

---

[32]A *conversazione* was a gathering, sometimes social, at which artists showed their works; on this occasion it was held at a public house of which there were a number of this name. William Oliver (1804-53), water-colour landscapist. (Sir) George Scharf (1820-95), later Director of the National Gallery; his main preoccupation was the illustration of books of an archaelogical interest.

Bamford, Lunched with me. Set to work about 12 at arranging the lay figure for Gower. Begun painting at the head, about 1 Phill Ealing[33] called on me, I painted at it till 5, painted the sleeves of her gown. Dined went to Rowney's & Brown for colors, had tea set to work at 8 till 12 drew in the ornaments between the letters & painted the stone part round it (8 hours work).

3rd Got up at ¼ past 7. Went out at ½ past 8 came back at ¼ to 10 set to work at Gower's head. My aunt Brown called, worked at hood & gown till ½ past 5 dined, cogitated on my picture wrote a letter to the secretary of the free Exn. Set to work again at ¼ to 9 till 12 painting in the letters (10 hours work).

4th Got up 7, set to work by ½ past 8 painted at the Gown of Gower till 11 & the hood. Fog came on, breakfasted, waisted some time, cleared up, set to work about 12 aranging the hood of Chaucer, did not begin painting it till 2, worked till ½ past 5 dined went out to the costume shop & ordered the ermine clook for Monday, came back had tea & set to work by 9 till 12 at the letters (10½ hours work).

5th Sunday got up at ¼ past 7 set to work by ¼ past 9. Painted at the head of chaucer till 11, set to work at 12 at the scetch altering the effect. Painted at it till ½ past 4 dined went to sleep had tea & set to work again at 20 minutes to 8. Worked at the letters till 20 minutes past 11 finished laying them in (10 hours ¼).

6th Got up at ¼ past 7, waisted the morning had a letter from old Dan Casey, all safe. Cloak did not come till 12, aranged it & began painting it by ½ past 1 till 5. Did not do much nor much good. Waisted the evening with Charles Lucy (5 hours work).

7th Got up at 7 & to work by 9. Painted at the ermine all day, did not finish it sad work & slow – dined went out came & set to work by seven to make a lay figure for the child. At 9 began drawing in the spandrils till half past 10 then thought of what I had to do (10 hours work).

8th Got up at ¼ past 7, finished the Cloak began the womans head dress. My aunt Brown called in. Walked out to the strand & trafalgar Sqr to the scene of the riots,[34] come back by 9, Thomas called in. Began one of the flowers in the spandril (9 hours work).

9th got up at ¼ past 7 to work by ½ past 8, worked at the female hood till

---

[33] A model.
[34] The previous day there had been a demonstration against the income tax recently introduced by Sir Robert Peel. "A mob", according to the *Times*, "none of whom judging by appearance were subject to the tax they were assembled to oppose."

½ past 10 then set the lay figure for her cloak & fur stomacker. Painted it and laid in the Cloak. Went out to see Lucy, came back with him. By 8 set to work at making Lions & flower's de luce of Paper for the Jupon of John of Gaunt[35] – till 12 (8 hours).

10th Got up at 7. Set to work sewing on the arms on to his coat, did nothing when smith came all day but paint the two crimson damask sleeves & badly too – Set to work again about 9 at the Gothic flower (8 hours work 3 preparation).

11th Got up at ½ past 7 & to work by 9, altered the hands of John of Gaunt – began painting the Cloak of the lady, interruptions of all kinds – Mrs Murcott, Mrs Lucy, Richard Bromley. Arranged the lay figure I had made of the child, took up much time – did nothing more. Walked back to Tudor Lodge with Mrs Lucy. Came back to Studio at 7, Bury[36] did not come, began work at 8 painted at the spandril till 12. Lucy called in (5 hours work 2 arranging).

12th Got up at ½ past 9 to work by 11. Painted the childs dress yellow to Glaze green, painted the skirt of the females dress green, did not do, rubbed it out – dined, wrote a note. William Bamford came in waisted my evening doing nothing. Traced one of the flowers for the spandrils (6 hours work).

13th Got up at ¼ to 7 ready to work by 8. Smith did not come. Glazed the Childs Dress painted at the green petticoat, interruption, walked out in the evening, worked at the spandril (8 hours work).

14th Got up at 8 painted the hassoc, the childs sleeves, the sripe in the Cloak & the childs head. Walked to Bryanston square after White, did not find him. Came back painted 4 hours at the spandril (10 hours).

15th Got up at ¼ past 7, arranged the lay figure for John of Gaunt's jupon. Began painting it at ¼ to 10. Left off at ½ past 3. If I can not better it by Lamp light must rub it out. Thomas & Hewlett called set to work at ¼ to 10 till 12 at the same (9 hours).

16th ¼ past 7 to work by ½ past 8 till ½ past 12 at the same. Maitland came, found I had nothing to do from him, paid him & sent him off. Scraped out the Jupon of John of Gaunt began painting the sky yellow (white & cadmium) arranged some ivy & painted part of it till ½ past 5 –

[35] Brown refers severally to jupon, the surcoat, the cote hardie. This was the short close-fitting tunic with tight sleeves from which depended the long white streamers, or tippets, which fell to the ground. John of Gaunt, whose arms bore the French heraldic lilies in recognition of his father's title to King of France, also bore the arms of his wife, daughter of the King of Castile and Leon.
[36] A model.

at 8 till 12 finished laying in the yellow for the sky (11 hours work).

17th Got up at ¼ past 7 to work by ¼ to 9. Painted at the Ivy till ¼ past 2 & from ½ 3 till 6 at the Damask back of the chair. Aranged the Lay figure for John of Gaunt. From ½ past 7 till 10 painted in the ground afresh for the jupon (yellow for the blue & white for the red). Nothing like a good coating of White to get bright sunny colour (9 hours work 2½ arranging).

18th Got up at 7 to work by ½ past 8, found the yelloy was not dry, did not know what to do, waisted time, began it at ¼ to 10 after covering it with copal warnish. Painted at the surcoat till ½ past 5, did all above the girdle liked it rather but not quite the thing, went out & bought some real Ultra-marine ½ a drachm. Heard that Goodall[37] had had several drachms this month, must be painting something very blue, came back in time for model at 7, did not come, painted four hours at the lions & flower's de luce, the girdle & the border of the Lady's Mantle (11½ hours).

19th Sunday got up at 8 ready by 9. Began by ¼ to 10 painted till 6 at the sky, hard day's work, pretty tol[38] – but not quite the thing (11 hours). In the evening from ½ past 7 till ½ past 11 composing the Pages.

20th Got up at 7 to work by 9, till 1 at the back ground & clouds. At 1 Miss Ashley for 4½ hours at the head & neck of the female, spoiled it from 7 till 8 retouching it – from ½ past 8 till ten making a drawing of one of the pages, from ½ past 10 till ½ past 11 at the head again (11 hours).

21st Got up at 7. To work by 9 painted at the head of the female. Out & in & out & in, & the head of the child & one hand of the female & the head of chaucer & part of the back ground. Scheff [Scharf] called – went to the frame maker after diner – from 9 till 20 minutes past ten drew in the page holding the books from model – wrote two notes, am doing this, am going to plan a frame (11 hours).

22nd rose at 7 to work by 9, painted in the page with the books all but the sleeves, head very sucessful rubbed out the legs – from 7 till 9 at Moulding of frame, from ½ past 10 till two modelling ornaments for do. (10 & 3 pre-paring).

23rd Got up at 7. To work by 9 till 12 at the head of page with sword, could make nothing of it. From 12 till 2 at neck of John of Gaunt from Model, from ½ past 2 till four at head again – from 4 till 6 at hands & legs – from 10 till 12 at correcting head of Wicliff & J of Gaunt & sundries. Martin, Lucy & frame Makers called ordered frame £6 (11 hours).

---

[37] Probably Frederick Goodall (1822-1904), one of a family of artists.
[38] "Tol-lol" until the late 1850s signified "pretty good". "Tolerable" from the end of the 1850s.

24th Got up at ¼ past 7 to work by 9 painted the head & one hand of John of Gaunt. My eyes so dim & weak I could hardly go on with it, painted till ½ past 2, went out to the city came back painted the cap of J. of Gt. dined went & spent the evening at the Lucy's to rest myself (5 hours).

25th Got up at 7 to work by 9, painted till 12 at the head of fair page. Maitland came painted the hose of John of G. did not do, rubbed it out again, had interruptions, Elliott, Thomas & Rossetti[39] called, the latter my first pupil. Curious enough he wrote to ask me to give him lessons, from his opinion of my *high Talents* knew every work I had exhibited & all about — will see what we can make of him. Worked from ten till 12 at correcting the arms of Wicliff (9 hours).

26th Got up at 9, to work by 10 did not do much all day. Painted the legs of both the pages & the yellow sleeves & the books & drew in the steps. Dined set to work about 9 to compose the symbollic figures in the spandrils. Sketch the female pretty well but could make nothing of the Monck (9 hours work).

27th Got up at 8 to work. Half past 9 till 6 painted the water behind the pages etc & the heads of the two boys with part of the railing heads in shadow, very difficult — dined & walked out & wrote two notes. Set to work by 9 designing ornamental work for the spandrils & also the figures of Catholicism much to my satisfaction, till 11 oclock writing this & mean to work one hour more at the spandrils (11 hours work).

28th got up at 7¼, to work by half past 9, painted till 6 at the draperies of Wicliff, nearly finished them, dined & went out after Miss Wild. Worked from ½ past 9 till ½ past 12 at the ornaments of the spandril, recomposed it & painted in one compartment. Going to take out the flower (11 hours).

29th Got up at 7. After breakfasting set to work. About ½ past 8 till 6 painted the cap of Wicliff, his book & that of Chaucer, worked at the general effect, the dresses of Gower, Chaucer Wicliff & the female also the lettern & sundries. From ½ past 8 till ½ 9 drawing from model for the figure of Catholicism, from 11 till ½ past 12 painted in some stripes in white on the hose of John of Gt. ready to paint tomorrow (12 hours work).

---

[39] D.G. Rossetti (1828-82), of Anglo-Italian parentage, was one of the leaders of the Pre-Raphaelite Brotherhood. From King's College School he enrolled at the age of fourteen at Sass's Academy, Bloomsbury. In 1846 he was at the Royal Academy Schools. Greatly admiring Brown's work he wrote asking to be taken on as a pupil (Appendix I). Brown thinking it might be some kind of a hoax called at the Rossetti's house in Charlotte Street (now Hallam Street), a stone's-throw from Clipstone Street, carrying a stout stick with him. This meeting resulted in a deep and lasting friendship.

30th Got up at 7, to work by ½ past 8 painted the shoes of John of Gaunt, & the head of Gower till ½ past 1 from Maitland. Afterwards the cote hardie & tippet of John of Gaunt. From ¼ to 7 till ½ past 9 from Miss Wild at the cartoon for the figure of Protestantism & afterwards at the draperies. After setting them drew the figure all but the hands (13 hours work).

31st up at 7. After breakfast painted the skirt of the cote hardie of John of Gt, touched his hair & shoulder, painted all the rest of the day at his chair. In the evening from 9 till 11 at the Protestantism (10½ hours).

1st April Got up at ½ past 7, after breakfast to work by ½ past 8. Painted at the legs of John of Gaunt from Maitland. Orange & violet (*abominable*) stripes till 4 then made a drawing of his head in the cartoon for Catholicisn till 5. Went out & dined walked to the regents Canal to look for rushes – went & saw Lucy's picture almost finished. Came back & set to work at a hand [for] the cartoon of Protestantism & one of Catholicism hand. Going to do the other. Finished the hands (12 hours work).

2nd do. Got up at 7. To work by 9, till 12 at the head of John of Gaunt from Smith (bad). Glazed a sleeve & the blue velvet of the same. Painted at the head of Chaucer from Hewlet from 3 till 6 (bad), worked from 9 till 10 at setting the lay figure for the monks draperies, drew part of them till ¼ to 12 (11 hours work).

3rd Got up at 6, worked till ¼ to 10 at the Cartoon of the Monk, finished it, drew in the pavement, finished it, painted over again the legs of John of Gt rather better. Painted his shoes, began one of Gowers, dined walked out began work again at ½ past 8. Squared the monk & drew him in on the Canvas till 10. John Marshall Called did nothing more (11 hours work).

4th Got up at 7. Went out after Models & to see Lucy's picture, going in day for the Accademy – began work at 10 worked till 6 painted the four hands of the pages & the legs of Chaucer & somewhat to the steps, began work again at 9 till 11 at the legs of Chaucer – corrected those of the page drew in the cinque foils of two remaining compartments of the spandrils (9½ hours).

5th Got up at 6. To work by 7 till ten at the shoes of Gower & the steps, from ½ past 10 till ½ past one at the head of Wicliff from Kröne.[40] Eyes so dizzy obliged to leave off – went for a walk bathed my eyes, began again at 3 till 6, not the thing. Dined, went to sleep. Mr & Mrs Lucy called in, set to

[40] A model.

work at 10 at one of the Cinque foil ornaments, have not yet finished it by 12 oclock must finish it before I go to bed – finished it by 1 (12½ hours work).

6th Got up at ½ past 6, to work by ¼ to 8 till one at the figure of Wicliff. Glazed his gown & part of his Cloak & repainted a long time at the head. Eyes very bad walked out over the park. Began again at the head 2 till 3 then painted till 6 at the hands of John of Gaunt. Lucy came in & drew in the figure with Lily in the spandrils. I began to work again at 9 at one of the cinquefoils, finished it by 11 – must try & do the other & last one, did nothing more (11 hours).

7th Got up at ¼ past 7. To work by ½ past 8 at the third head of Chaucer. Made it worse than before, had Mrs Yates for it worked till 11 at it quite horrible, afterwars painted the two hands rather well, then painted the hands [of] Gower & one foot of Wicliff pretty well. John Marshall called in talked a great deal about the approaching revolution,[41] what is to be the upshot of it. Thomas called in. I set to work again at ½ past nine till 11, drew in the figure in the spandril with the lily (10 hours work).

8th Got up at ½ past 7 to work ½ past 8 till 11 at the legs & arms of the child. From 11 till 4 at the hands of Wicliff from then till 6 at the child arms & the females hands – in the evening painted in the head of Chaucer in white from 9 till 11 (11 hours work).

9th Got up at ¼ to 8 to work by 9 till 12 at one foot of Wicliff & the hands of the child & female. Afterwards repainted the heads of the child & female. Went out for a walk. Cook[42] came in to gild the spandrils has done it very badly. Worked at the head of Chaucer from 11 till ½ past 12. Corrected it in white (9½ hours, 3 superintending).

9th [10th] Got up at 6 to work by ½ past 9, corrected the head of Chaucer. Painted that of Wicliff over with white & his hands. Painted the head & hands of John of Gaunt till 6. Walked out, met Lucy, set to work again by 9 till ¼ to 1 at the head of Chaucer & that of the monk in the spandrils (11 hours work).

11th Got up at ½ past 7 to work by 9, painted at the head of Chaucer till 1 then at the hands of Wicliff till 5. Afterwards did little but fill up the last cinquefoil of the spandrils. Worked till 12 (8 hours work) bad day.

12th Got up at ½ past 7 to work by half past 8, painted at the leggs of the pages & those of Chaucer. Glazed the pages & painted a pair of legs for

---

[41] The London Chartist demonstrations were planned for 10 Apr.
[42] Perhaps Absolom, or Gabriel, Cook, carvers and gilders of Upper Marylebone Street and Nottingham Place.

John of Gt on tracing paper to try them. In the evening painted the female head in the spandril till 1 (12 hours work).

13th Got up at 7, to work by ½ past 8. Scraped out the hose & shoes of John of Gt & laid them in a fresh very pale yelloy & Lilac. Hewlet worked all day at the brass lettern. I painted at the archway till 6, at 8 began the monk – calls all day, Lucy, Seddon, Thomas, my aunt, people from the free Exhibition etc etc (12 hours).

14th Up at 7 to work by 8, painted the head of Wicliff till ½ past 10 from old Coulton. My uncle Madox called at 12, began retouching the arch worked at it till 6, went to the free Exhibition. Began painting the petticote in the spandril at 9, worked till ½ past 12 (11 hours).

15th Got up at ½ past 7. To work by ½ past 8 painted at the stone work of the arch till 4, finished it for Glazing, painted at the monk till 6, rubbed white over his head. Began work again by 8, laid in the book & lily painted the shoes & golden fillet of John of Gt, did something to the pages sword (12 hours work).

16th My birth day, 27 to day alas! got up at 7 to work by 8 painted the red cross & rosary of chaucer then the hose of the duke. Muddled at them could not succeed, in despair rubbed them out again partly & made them an other coular, yellow & Grey will do, *must* do but not very well – Glazed the arch way & began marking in the stones did a little to the cloak of Wicliff & the hassock of the female, began work again by 8 till 2 in the morning painted a hoste of little ods & ends (15 hours).

17th Got up at 6 to work by half past 8 – finished the pages & Chaucer & Gower & Wickliff. Painted the Green rushes, finished the ground, the reading desk & the females chair. In the evening painted at the letters from 9 till 11. Then again at the female & the mosaic work till 4 in the morning (17 hours).

18th Got up at 6 to work by ½ past 7, repainted the whole of the flesh. Glazed the shadows with yellow lakes & madder & repainted the lights with their white tint. At 3 began again at the General effect. Miss Barrauds[43] & Thomas called, worked till ½ past 6 then again till 3 at the Mosaic work & sundries (18 hours).

19th Got up at 6 set off with my picture to the Gallery, hyde Park Corner. Got there by 9. 10 oclock before framed & that did not fit, thought I had all day to work but found we were all to decamp at 10. Got leave to wait till the sweeping was done & set to work again at 12 till 6, improved the g e n e r a l

---

[43] Unidentified. Perhaps "Messrs" is intended (see p.27, n.15).

appearance much by Glazing etc. Slept next door at a tavern to be able to be at work next morning at 6 to finish it before the private view (6 hours).

20th up at ¼ to 6, to work by ½ past. Painted at the hose of John of Gt & put in some trees too green — breakfasted & went to get my hair cut & to call on Mrs Mosa [Moser] — then fetched Thomas for the private view — afterwards spent the evening & slept at Bamfords (4 hours).

21st went to the Gallery at about 11 repainted at the trees till 2, dined with Bamford & spent the evening with John Bromley (3 hours work).

22nd free Exhibition.[44] Greenwich. Mrs Lucys.

23rd Called on the Boddy's,[45] went to Highgate.

24th Went to Gravesend.

25th still there — Agueish.

27th went to London & came back aguing.

28th went to Chatham to see John James Bromley.[46]

29th Gravesend.

30th do.

31st Going to Foots' Cray by Erith.

1st May went to Royal Accademy, dined with Lucy, Thomas & Marshall.

2nd went to National Gallery & Old water colour & to see M'creadrey in Lear.[47]

3rd went to see new water colour & Suffolk St.

4th had my pupil rosetti hear. Worked for about 6 houres on a head to show him[48] (6 hours).

---

[44] Private view day. Daily opening hours were from 9 to 6 and from 7 to 10 when the Gallery was "brilliantly illuminated by gas". The *Athenaeum* commended Brown's work for being one of the very few of "high excellence" but tempered its enthusiasm by remarking that the "punctilious accuracy in costume subjects its author to the imputation of pedantry".

[45] Unidentified. They later appear under the guise of Baddeis.

[46] Presumably another cousin; he also had an address at Greenwich.

[47] The exhibition at the Old Water-Colour Society, whose premises were at Pall Mall East, had opened the previous day. The galleries of the New Water-Colour Society at 53 Pall Mall had opened their exhibition on 17th Apr., and the Suffolk Street Gallery on 3 Apr. The tragedian W.C. Macready (1793-1873) was appearing at the Marylebone Theatre in Shakespeare repertory.

[48]Rossetti had been accepted as a pupil at Clipstone Street. Brown had resumed his *Chaucer* picture.

5th went in the evening to free exhibition.

6th Got up at ½ past 6 began work at 9 till 5 from Maitland. Began a study of his head in sunlight & painted the black silk legs for Shakespear & Milton (8 hours).

7th got up at 8, to work by 9 till 4. Did little but a drawing of his head for the courtier next to the one in the yellow hood in the fourground, for which also is the study in oil[49] (6 hours).

8th Got up at ½ past 7 to work by 9, drew the necles for the black prince, the page on the fourground & the courtier last named (4½ hours).

9th Got up at ½ past 5, at Madox st by 6. Boy did not come till 7 to open the door. Began a study of Maitlands head, dined & spent the better part of the day with Lucy (1½ hours).

10th up at ½ past 5, Maitland did not come till 7. Laid in the head of Maitland. Had Maitland & made a Drawing of the surcoat of black Prince (6½ hours).

11th got up at ½ past 5. Maitland did not come.

12th Idem.

13th up at 5 worked at a study of Mrs Yates. Dined (2 hours).

14th Spent the whole day with Thomas & dined with him.

15th Got up at 5 worked at the head of Mrs Yates went to highgate with Lucy (2 hours).

16th up at 5, worked 2 hours at the head and the rest of the day at the outlining of R Burns (8 hours).

17th up at 8. Laid in the hed of R Burns too Large (6 hours work).

17th [?] up at 5, 6 till 8 at the study of Mrs Yates. The rest of the day made alterations in the figure & head of Lord Byron (18 hours).

18th up at 5, 6 till 8 at Mrs Yates. Walked till 11 with Thomas. Had an argument, tried to persuade him that to imitate the true *tone* of the model it must be painted so that when held up beside it it would not be like it in *coulor* – did nothing but try to write down what I had been speaking of, afterwards went to see Lucy –

19th & 20th at Gravesend with my sweet child she had a bad could & the ear ake.

---

[49] The yellow hood study is at Manchester.

22nd up at ½ past 8 to work by 11, altered the head of Burn's & drew in that of Pope. Walked over the parks with Thomas (5 hours work).

23rd up at 5, painted till 8 at the study, then from 9 till 12 Laid in the head of pope. Went to Richmond (5 hours work).

24th up at 5, walked to see houses with Mark Anthony. Painted at Pope (5 hours).

25th up at ½ past 8. Went to see houses with Mark Anthony till 2. Did nothing.

26th up at 5 worked till 8 at the study of Mrs Yates, finished it such as it is, went to the city on business & called on John Bromley – in the evening called on the Lucy's.

27th up at ½ past 8, talked till 1, went to see Hancock the sculptor[50] & Thomas. Dined. Went to see my aunt Brown & Marshall.

28th walked out with Thomas. Went to Blackheath.

29th went to Gravesend. Up at 5, began a study of Mendoes[51] (1½ hours work).

30th Drew 3 hands from myself (7 hours work).

31st June [May] up at ½ past 5. Worked at study from Mendoes at ½ past 9 till ½ past 6. Drew 4 hands from Fry the Model (9½ hours).

1st June up at ½ past 8, to work by ½ past 9, drew his head for Shakespear (8 hours work).

2nd up at ½ past 5 worked at Madox st, began at 10. Drew fry's head for Spencer (8 hours work).

3rd went to see fenton, Lucy, & the university. Set to work about 3 at the head of Shaksper (3 hours work).

4th worked at the head of Shakespear about 5 hours.

5th Monday went to Madox St. Model did not come, worked 3 hours at the outline of Shakspere on the Canvas. Went to Museumm & to Mulreadys Exhibition.[52] Went to Madox Street (4 hours work).

---

[50] John Hancock (1825-69) had exhibited a statue of Chaucer at Westminster Hall in 1844.
[51] A model, whose name was probably Mendoza.
[52] The attendance was rather thin though William Mulready (1786-1863), the distinguished genre painter, held the exhibition at the Society of Arts, Adelphi, to promote the formation of a National Gallery of British Art.

6th up at ½ past 5, worked at Madox St from 6 till 8 – and on the picture at the outline of Shakespear about 4 hours, & from 6 till 7 at Madox St. Finished the head of Mrs Yates (7 hours).

7th up at ¼ to 6, worked from ½ past till 8 at the study of Mendoes at Madox St, & about 6 hours at the outline Shakespear & Spencer (7½ hours).

[Book 1 of the Diary ends here and is continued in Book 2. On the inside of the cover of Book 2 Brown has made abbreviated notes which are expanded in the diary to form the entries 17-25 March 1850. Also a simple mathematical sum, rough diagrams, and two experiments in spelling: "sorry sory soar sore".]

8th up at 10 minutes to 6, worked at the study from Mendoes 1½ hours till 8, afterwards worked about 6 hours. Laid in the head of Shakespear & drew at his hands (7½ hours).

9th up at ¼ to 9 set to work at 10, worked about 8 hours drawing at Shakespear & Milton.

10th up at 6, at work at Mendoes from ¼ to 7 till 8 & from 9 till 8 in the evening at Shakspear. Laid in his hands and the upper part of his cloak (10 hours work).

11th Sunday up at ½ past 8 to work by 10. Laid in the Cloak & "remainder of" & one Mask (3 hours).

12th went to madox St from ½ past 6 till 8 – worked about 6 hours laing in the legs of Shakespear (7 hours work).

14th up very late set to work about 12. Laid in the two hands of Byron & other work (6 hours).

15th Cleaned the dog & shaved his head & paws.

16th up at ½ past 5 worked at Madox St from ¼ to 7 till 8. Went to British Museum & to see Powers Greek slave.[53] Set to work about 3 till 8 laid in the head of Spencer (5 hours work).

---

[53] An idealized female nude in marble with her hands chained, executed in Florence in 1843 by the American sculptor Hiram Powers (1805-73). Bought by Captain Grant (now in a Private Collection) for £300 it was shown in the rooms of Graves, the print publisher, in Pall Mall in the spring of 1845 and roused such admiration that Elizabeth Barrett Browning wrote a sonnet in its praise. Lord Ward ordered a copy in 1845 and it may have been this which Brown saw. After the Great Exhibition of 1851, where the original was again on exhibition, reduced replicas, fifteen inches high, were made in Parian Ware by the firms of Minton and Copeland.

17th up at ½ past 5 to Madox st. Mendoes did not come, walked into Regents Park before Breakfast. Began work about 11, interruption, they want to engrave wicliff for the Peoples Journal. Laid in the skirt of Burns gown, worked about 4 hours till 5 oclock. Went & Dressed had my hair cut, called on proprietor of Peoples Journal,[54] supped at Mr Bamfords.

18th Sunday went to Gravesend to see my sweet child quite well.

19th up at ½ past 9 – went into city did nothing.

20th idem.

21st worked & correcting drapery of Lord Byron (6 hours).

22nd went to Royal Accady & free Exhibition.

23rd went to Gravesend.

24th stayed there with dear Lucy – quite well.

25th came back heard of the revolution in Paris – spend the evening with Lucy.

26th up at ½ past 5 to Madox St – did nothing else all day but reflect on my work (2 hours).

17th July Went to Paris to see my old friend Casey & buy a lay figure. Did both, enjoyed myself much, painted a portrait of Casey,[55] worked about 7 hours at it – came back to London on the 6th.* Lucy had been to Hearn [Herne] bay with Mrs Lucy I took her back to her aunts' on the 10th August (8 hours work).

14th [August] worked at the study of the sleeve of R Burns – arranged it & painted it (6 hours).

16th Drew a study of his hand & laid it in on the Canvas & part of his sleeve (7 hours).

17th finished the sleeve & began Laying in the tartan in dead coulars (6 hours work).

*The trip in all cost £1.6.6, sheer madness but que voulez vous the thing is done.

[54] The *People's Journal* was "published for the Proprietors" (name not disclosed) in Warwick Lane. Brown probably saw the editor, John Saunders. *Wycliffe* was reproduced in vi, (1848, facing p.71) with an account of the personages represented in the painting.
[55] Untraced. Two studies for the head exist at Birmingham.

18th worked at the plaid (4 hours).

19th went to the Art union Exhin & to see M. Anthony.

20th walked to Hampstead with Thomas.

21st up at 9, to work by ½ past 11 till 2. Finished Laying in the plaid (2½ hours) afterwards went to see J. Madox & to Highgate.

22nd Laid in one hand of R Burns and I forget.

23rd Lucy's boy was christened.

24th Altered one hand of Shakespear & his head (5 hours).

25th had the studio cleaned & the coffee & tea pots & the Lamp.

26th Idem & walked to foots Cray.

28th Came up from foots cray, set to work about ½ past 2 till 6 at the architecture & the Byron compartment. Afterwards at the same by lamp light, Thomas has begun working by night in my studio.

29th Went to consult Solly[56] in the City & to see John Bromley & divers – set to work about 3 till 6, had tea & am writing this – went to studio, Thomas there, Sam Bamford came in. Worked at the architecture only one hour (4 hours).

30th walked out over the park then to see Lucy he told me of an other kick-up at the school of Designe. Had been applying for one himself. I began to think of it.[57] Called to see Thomas & talked the matter over, worked but little at the architecture (3 hours).

31st set to work about 12 till 2 & from 3 till 4 at the architecture. Rosetti called with Hunt,[58] a clever young man (3 hours work).

1st worked or rather tried to compose.

2nd had a model & made some sketches of her with a child.

3rd did nothing but call on the Baddeis.

4th went to Gravesend to see my child Lucy.

---

[56] Probably W. Sully, stock and share broker, Old Broad Street.
[57] The London Government School of Design at Somerset House was going through a bad patch, the masters changing frequently. Walter Deverell (1827-54), the promising young painter and associate of the P.R.B., was appointed assistant master this year.
[58] W. Holman Hunt (1827-1910) was one of the original P.R.B. when it was formed in the following month. Rossetti, wearied by the discipline of Brown's instruction, removed himself to Holman Hunt's studio in Cleveland Street, Fitzroy Square, at the end of August.

5th Made a helmet out of the lay figure's head for Lord Byron & painted it (6 hours).

6th & 7th worked at designing but did no good.

8th walked to national gallery & print shops.

9th to Solly & did little else. Spent the evening with Thomas who has been dissapointed of his works for the Art union.

10th Read Keats[59] & spent the day with Thomas.

11th ill in bed with a bad cold. Lucy called.

12th in all day reading with a bad cold. Mr & Mrs Lucy & Miss Lucy called, also Marshall.

13th up late could not get to sleep, out to see Thomas, cold not well yet, who knows it may be the death of me. Damned wretched but only because not occupied.

21st Started for the Lakes of Cumberland in company with Lucy. Saw the Exbn of Manchester.[60]

25th Begun painting a veiw of Wendermere,[61] worked 6 days at about 4 hours a day, Last day in the rain under an umbrella.

2nd Started on foot for Patterdale then over the mountains past the Greenside Leadmine to Keswick.

3rd through the borrodale pass to Wass Water.

4th rain all day, stopped there.

5th Started in the rain over the mountains by Eskdale to Windermere.

6th by rail to Liverpool saw my Wicliff there[62] up high, looked damned bad.

---

[59] Probably, *Life, Letters and Literary Remains of John Keats*, 2 vols., ed. R. Monckton Milnes, published by Moxon, 1848, and perhaps recommended to Brown by Rossetti who had been reading it in August. Keats was a favourite poet of the P.R.B.
[60] The Royal Manchester Institute Exhibition of Modern paintings had opened a few weeks earlier.
[61] *Windermere* (Port Sunlight, Plate 6); a view looking south down the lake. From there Brown proceeded north to Keswick and the next day south-west to Wast Water.
[62] The Liverpool Academy of Arts had flourished independently for over twenty years for the promotion of the arts and held an annual exhibition of paintings and sculpture. A prize of £50 was offered to a non-resident artist, which was to be won by Brown in 1854.

5. *The Young Mother*, Wightwick Manor, Wolverhampton (National Trust)

7th to Chester thence to Birmingham saw Exn.[63] & back to London that night.

8th went to Gravesend to see my Darling.

9th went to City aferward painted at my view of Windermere at the sky (2 hours work).

10th all day writing a letter to Builder about Thomas.[64]

11th to City about money. Bought a Coat Called on Clara.[65]

12th began a pourtrait of R. Bromley's dauter (4 hours).

13th Portrait not dry enough to go on with. Sent for Mrs Ashley & child & began a scetch of them for a little picture of a mother and child.[66] Made a scetch in the evening in black & white of the view of Windermere (3 hours work).

14th Laid in the view of Windermere with a thin coating of asphaltum & white for the high lights, drying oil & Copal. After diner scetched the outline of a small scetch for Mother & child. After tea worked at the helmet & sword of Lord Byron (8 hours work).

15th Painted a scetch of the mother & child. In the evening worked at the Byron's sword (7 hours).

16th worked at the portrait of Julia Bromley about 4 hours. Swollan swolen. [An exercise in spelling; irrelevant to the text.]

17th worked at the portrait about 3 hours.

18th went out with Rosetti to see his picture[67] afterwards painted at the curtain of portrait (1 hour).

19th worked at the portrait about 2 hours and in the evening 3 at the shield of Lord Byron (5 hours).

20th Made a Drawing of the head of Mrs Ashley & worked a little at the portrait (5 hours).

[63] The annual Birmingham Society of Arts Exhibition, where the following year his *Wycliffe* was to hang.
[64] Cave Thomas had written three papers for the *Builder* (9, 16, 23 Sep.on "The Influences which tend to retard progress of the Fine Arts".
[65] Clara Bromley, wife of Richard (see p.24, n.4).
[66] *The Young Mother*, known alternatively as *The Infant's Repast*, *Mother and Child* (untraced). A sketch exists (Birmingham) and a duplicate was made (National Trust, Wightwick Manor, Wolverhampton, Plate 5).
[67] *The Girlhood of Mary Virgin* (Tate), Rossetti's first exhibited picture bearing the P.R.B. initials.

21st Drew at the cartoon for Mother & child and painted the dress of portrait.

22nd Painted in the sky of the copy of the view of Windermeer with copal & drying oil. It dryed to quick, made a mess of it. In the evening called on Cross & Lucy (5 hours).

23rd Painted the dress of child's portrait with asphaltum & prussian Blue over yellow – afterwards worked at Byron's shield & in the evening (9 hours).

24th repainted the head of little portrait with M'Gilp & copal & Lemon yellow (4 hours).

25th to Greenwich – to Gravesend & to see old Bamford.

26th painted same coular one arm of portrait, then drew a study of childs head sucking, for little picture – in the evening worked at Shield (6 hours).

27th painted at the view of Windermere & in the evening at the shield with copal & MGilp (6 hours).

28th painted other arm of Julia Bromley (2 hours) & in the evening wrote a defence of Thomas's lecture for Builder.[68]

29th wrote all day & in the evening went to black heath.

30th worked 4 hours from Mrs Ashley & child, made drawing of the Legs & arm etc. Called upon Lucy & Marshall. Came home & wrote (4 hours).

31st wrote all day at the letter to builder.

1st paid [?painted] the Lady [word illegible] portrait & finished it (5 hours)

2nd Nov to Highgate – to City & to see Anthony.

3rd worked a little at Landscape of Windermere. Toothache & Thomas in the evening (4 hours).

4th Tooth all day. In the evening wrote about Influences of Antiquity in Italy.[69]

5th Tooth ach better, painted at the view of Windermere in the [evening] went to see Thomas (4 hours).

6th up late, worked from Mrs Ashley made Designe of her arm. In the evening Traced in the outline on Panel (7 hours).

---

[68] Published 4 Nov. under the title "Modern versus Ancient Art" and signed "An Artist".
[69] Published in the *Builder*, 2 Dec., and signed "An Artist".

7th Painted on the Windermere & in the evening outline in Pencil (7 hours).

8th Laid in the head & arm of Mother in Little white & grey picture. In the evening wrote about Influences of antique art (4 hours).

9th Laid in the child all in white & grey. Painted at the Lake (5 hours), writting in the evening.

10th wasted the whole day cleaning & varnishing some gilt Leather. In the evening wrote.

11th wasted the better part of the day & in the evening.

12th Did very little, painted a copy of Lucy's head[70] (2 hours).

13th Drew a pourtrait of Mrs Ashleys Baby & wrote in the evening on Italy & Art (3 hours).

14th Wrote all day.

15th went out all day & spent the evening with Seddon.

16th worked at the little picture, laid in the back ground & altered the Legs of the child in the evening. Thought a great deal about a subject (4 hours).

17th wasted half the day & composed Lear & cordelia.[71]

18th went to Pratt's & subscribed for armour & old furniture.[72] Tried to work but did little. Lowes Dickinson came to see me and in the evening brought his brother with him, Thomas & Lucy came also.

19th began work late composed Lear & Cordelia (6 hours).

20th wrote an answer to "Amateur" in the builder[73] & started for Gravesend.

21st came home by 8 p.m. Drew at scetch of Lear (3 hours).

22nd went to Pratt's, set to work at 1 till ½ past 3 at the mirror, spent the evening studying grammar (3½ hours).

23rd began work at 10 till ½ past 3 at mirror & gilt-leather – asphaltum, Cadmium, Lemon yellow, ivory, black, sienna etc, magilp & copal. In the evening worked at the composition of Lear & Cordelia (6 hours work).

---

[70] See no.10 above.
[71] *Lear and Cordelia* (Tate, Plate 7).
[72] Samuel Pratt, of New Bond Street, importer of armour and ancient furniture who seems to have hired out his goods to subscribers.
[73] This may have been sent but was not printed.

6. *Windermere*, Lady Lever Art Gallery, Port Sunlight

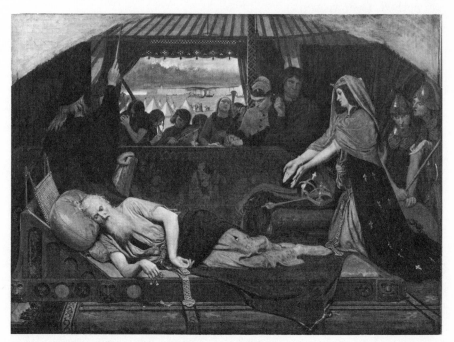

7. *Lear and Cordelia*, Tate Gallery, London

24th got up at 8½, got to work by ¼ to 11 worked till ¼ to 4 at the gilt-leather in the little picture of mother and child; copal and magilp etc. In the evening at Lear and Cordelia, 3 hours (7 hours work).

25th up late, to work by 11 till 1 at the gilt leather – John Marshall came in, did little more but arrange a bunch of keys and begin them, in the evening worked at the Lear but have not yet settled it (5 hours).

26th up at ½ past 8 to work by 11. Painted the keys and finished the mirror and began the cupboard door. In the evening worked 4½ hours at Lear, going on well (9 hours).

27th up at ½ past 8, went to Pratt's abut the oak paneling, came back and painted it. Till one at the gilt-leather of the cupboard door and from 2 till 4 at the upper shelf and bottles etc. In the evening wrote three notes and worked from 7 till 8 at Lear finished the outline of the scetch (5 hours).

28th Seddon called on me, stayed till 12, I then painted till 4. Did a good part of the scetch of Lear & in the evening went to the play with Seddon to hear Sims Reaves in Lucia di Lamer.[74] Supped afterwards, head very bad, overworked. (4 hours work).

29th nothing but idle, spent the evening with Lucy. Fenton there – Head very quere.

30th painted at the scetch, went with Lucy to see Elliott's picture & Rosetti's (4 hours).

1st Dec Repainted at the scetch (3 hours).

2nd did no work, called on Fenton.

3rd spent the day looking at my picture & reading.

4th went to see my uncle Madox & stopped at Bamfords.

5th Spent the day in divers ways. Bought a large oak door & scraped it with Glass & varnished it, in the evening composed the panels of the little picture (3 hours work).

6th had a King charles spaniel[75] paid /4.6 for it, painted it in 3 hours. Evening began chalking the outline of lear on canvas (7 hours work).

---

[74] Sims Reeves (1818-1900), the celebrated tenor, was singing in Donizetti's *Lucia di Lammermoor* at the Theatre Royal, Covent Garden.
[75] For *The Young Mother*, where the dog seated on the right gazes up at the mother and child. Later, when interpreting the work, Brown remarked that "doggy is jealous" and that the picture needed no other explanation.

7th painted at the panel 5 hours in the evening. Had a Model to draw the nude of Cordelia (7½ hours).

8th painted at panel 5 hours. Model in eveng. (7 hours).

9th finished panel, begin sofa. Spent evening at Thomas (5 hours).

10th finished Laying in Sofa, white & Lake to Glaze (5 hours).

11th Painted all day at the petticoat & rubbed it out (4 hours).

12th painted at the petticoat, did a small peice of it at one painting, emerald green, bitumen, cobalt, carmine Sienna, black, white, Lemon yellow M'glilp & copal. Evening to fenton till 2, could not sleep till 5 (5 hours work).

13th up at 11 painted a bit of petticoat & went to sup with Lowes Dickinson till 2 (4 hours work).

14th up at 2 did not sleep till 6. Morning, evening with Lucy.

15th cleaned out studio. Robertson[76] of Paris called, evening to play.

16th up at 10 to work by ½ past 11 till ½ past 3 at petticoat, afterwards finished it by lamp light & drew childs frock (7 hours).

17th Sunday painted utrech velvet sofa, touched the dog. Evening to Lucy's (4 hours work).

18th painted childs frock, corol & shoe (5 hours).

19th bought mittens & a rose & made a fan, arranged it & began the gown. In the evening Maitland for two hours, scetched the figure of Lear (7 hours).

20th painted at the dress & in the evening (6 hours).

21st idem, in the evening finished sofa (6 hours).

22nd reception day – in the evening painted the leopard skin mat & the oak floor (4 hours).

23rd painted the stripes of the Dress (5 hours).

24th went to Gravesend to spend Xmas with my dear child Lucy, quite well, left her on Tuesday.

26th and walked from Erith to Foot's Cray to see my aunt Madox, stayed there till Thursday morn.

---

[76] Unidentified.

28th against my will, came home went to Highgate & to see Lucy. In the evening worked at the outline of Lear (4 hours).

29th Reception day. Nobody came, worked from 11 till ½ past 3, painted at the petticoat and the Roses. In the evening Maitland for 2 hours (6 hours).

30th Drew at the outline of Lear till 3 then left for Foot's Cray to a party at uncle Madox (5 hours).

31st at Foots Cray.

1849

1st Jany/49 came up from Foot's Cray began work about 12 at the outline again, again a little in the evening & then the remainder at Thomas (5 hours).

2nd at the outline about 8 hours work.

3rd idem. In the evening to Lucy's to a party (5 hours).

4th idem. In the evening Maitland 3½ hours (8 hours).

5th Mrs Ashley came late, began painting hair from her in little picture. After she went rubbed it out again and painted it in red, liked it better. In the evening Maitland 4 hours, drew in Jester & Musicians in Lear on to the canvas direct (7 hours work).

6th Mrs Ashley late, painted the head & rubbed it out again. Worked but very little at the outline of Lear (5 hours).

7th Mrs Ashley missed, did little in consequence. Painted at the hair & round the head & the floor & the fan. In the evening Maitland from 5 till 9 for the Lear (6 hours).

8th Mrs Ashley missed, ran about for Models, retouched the gown. In the evening drew at the outline of Cordelia from Model two hours (3 hours).

9th painted the basket, brush, powder box & puff & the nightgown. In the eveng drew in background of Lear (9 hours).

10th painted the head of the mother from Mrs Ashley & drew in the tent of Lear in the evening (9 hours).

11th painted the sea, cliffs, shipps & tents in Lear, in the evening painted the 4 little figures & drew in the nude of warrior resting upon his shield from Maitland (4 hours).

12th Mrs Ashley & child, painted in the child's head & arm. In the evening Maitland, drew in nude of warrior whispering (5½ hours).

13th Miss Stone,[1] began a drawing for the head of Cordelia. Painted in the bosom in little picture & the legs & hand of the child from Mrs A & child. No work eveng. (5½ hours).

14th Miss Stone, finished study for Cordelia, & painted the hand & arm in little picture from Mrs A. (6 hours).

15th Miss Stone, drew two hands for Cordelia, & painted sleeve of dress in little picture from Mrs A. (5½ hours).

16th up till 4 night before supped with Lucy & Mark Anthony at an oyster shop. Began work at 1 till 4, painted bodey of dress from Mrs Ashley. In the evening rubbed it out & drew 4 hour at the head of Cordelia, Made it beastly (7 hours work).

17th Arranged the dress in the lay figure & painted in the body again, toned down the basket & nightgown. In the eveng drew at the head of Cordelia & laid it in with emerald green, white & umber (16 hours work).

18th up at ½ past 8 to work by 11. Worked all over the little picture, toned & settled the back ground & retouched the mothers head, made the expression rather more satisfactory, walked over the park – set to work again at 7 till 12 at the head of Lear, drew it (10 hours).

19th Cleaned the studio, set to work at 2, painted in the sky in the lear. Elliott called then Lucy – spent the evening with him (2 hours).

20th began work late painted in the open-work part of the tent & began the mast – Thomas called round. I set to work again, finished the Mast & made a Jesters cap after 9 & painted it in by 12 (9 hours work).

21st Sunday up at 9 to work by 11 painted in one of the background curtains & nearly the other. Spent the evening with Lucy at Mark Anthony's (6 hours).

22nd finished the curtain & painted the tent etc. In the evening painted the drapery of Kent (12 hours).

23rd Slept at Studio, up at 8. Laid in two hands, finished drapery of Kent & painted in one sleeve of phisician. In the evening Sam Bamford called & I rubbed it out (7 hours).

24th up at 10. Seddon called & rosetti. Began work about 12 painted in the sleeve again & went with Anthony to Hampstead conversazione (4 hours).

25th up late to work by 12 painted in the rest of Phisician's gown & his

---

[1] A model.

book. In the evening the Jesters cape & sleeves, small peice of the mast, part of iron work. To bed (9 hours work).

26th painted in the six musicians (11 hours).

27th Laid in the Jesters hands and repainted the flesh of the child in little picture, in the evening laid in the head of the fool from Rosetti (7 hours).

28th repainted one arm & hand of Mother in the little picture & retouched it generally. In the eveng. laid in one hand of the physician and retouched the expression of Jester (8 hours).

29th retouched little picture all over — eveng worked at Cordelia's head (white & green) & laid in the hands (10 hours).

30th painted the mirror in little picture & divers, & repainted the head of Mother & one hand from Model, eveng retouched it again, painted in physician's cap & drew in the head of Lear (10 hours work).

31st Laid in the head of Lear from a cast of Dante's and a drawing of Coulton. Called on Lucy & ordered a frame in the even. Again in the eveng (8 hours).

1st feby worked all day at the head of Cordelia from Model, in the eveng rubbed it out & retouched the head of Lear, found a dog in the rain & brought him home with me (7 hours).

2nd painted in the head & hands of physician from Krone. Drew at the bed in the even (9 hours).

3rd painted green curtain behind him & painted at the bed (7 hours).

4th all day at the head & hands of Cordelia from Model, eveng painted at bed (9 hours).

5th repainted heads & arms & hands of little picture, too white, retouched mothers head again at night — & painted at Bed (9 hours).

6th finished the little picture & evening the bed (9 hours).

7th arranged the curtain behind Cordelia & began it & finished the bed (9 hours).

8th finished the curtain & began arranging the lay figure for Cordelia. Eveng at Lucy's (5 hours).

9th all day arranging lay figure. In the eveng painted in two helmets and composed wariors armour (8 hours).

10th up late through foolery the night before. Began the veil of Cordelia, only laid in a part of it when a girl as loves me came in & disturbed me[2] (3 hours).

11th To work late, quite upset, finished laying in the coverchief of Cordelia, laid in the ground for the tapistry & drew in the chair & crown (5 hours).

12th Laid in the Cloak, & paint in chair & crown (10 hours).

13th Tuesday went to a phrenologist's & got a head of Dr Broussais.[3] Set to work Late, painted in part of white Tunic of Cordelia & in the even painted her hair & girdle (7 hours).

14th painted in a part of cloak & altered one hand, eveng laid in the head of Kent (8 hours).

15th up early to work by 9, painted in the cloak, Couverchief, & finished tunic. In the evening altered the head of Cordelia (12 hours).

16th Painted in the two arms & hands of Lear. Eveng. laid in one warior & sundries & altered the head of Cordelia (11 hours).

17th altered the head of Cordelia, painted in head of Lear & head & hand of Kent, evening retouched hands of Kent & jester & Cordelia (11 hours).

18th Sunday painted in the head of Cordelia from Model & one hand, evening at Lucy's (7 hours).

19th Made the cushion of Lear's head & painted it with a model, altered one arm of Lear, & finished cushion & painted blue ball & white garment (7 hours).

20th painted in the upper part of Lears gown, in the even scraped it out again & painted in the mascled armour[4] of one warior (9 hours).

21st painted in the heads, hands and arms of the two Wariors from Maitland, in the evening painted in the shield & bipennis[5] etc (11 hours).

22nd painted in the wings in wariors helmet and the two hands of Jester

---

[2] Very probably Emma Hill whom he was later to marry. Though not mentioned by name she may have made her appearance as a model at the end of 1848. There exists a study of her head for Cordelia dated "Xmas/48" (Birmingham).

[3] Brown may have seen a likeness to his own head and temperament in that of the French Doctor F.J.V. Broussais (1772-1838) whose reasoning powers were said to have been very develcped and whose faculty of judgment was said to have been so pronounced that it formed a protruberance on his forehead (H. de Montègre, *Notice historique sur F.J.V. Broussais*, 1839). Brown may have been inspired to buy the bust through an interest in phrenology – a common interest at that time.

[4] A coat of mail made up of lozenge-shaped pieces of iron or steel resembling the meshes of net. Illustrated and described in *Knight's Pictorial History*, p.639.

[5] A double-headed axe.

from Model & drew head of Cordelia. Again in the even retouched and finished the two warriors & powdered the cloak of Cordelia with fleurs de lis (9 hours).

23rd arranged the yellow leather for one corner of the mattress & painted it, arranged the Drapery of Lear, could not get it right, tried at it till three oclock, then Miss Stone came in & I did nothing more. Went with Lucy to see Elliott's picture. Set to work in eveng drew in the outline of the figure in the tapistry (6 hours).

24th Tooth ache — set to work about 11, rearranged the drapery & began painting it over Lears legs. John Marshall called in, went to see Lucy's picture,[6] going on well (Tooth ache) (5 hours).

25th finished peice of Drapery over the legs & begin Laying in the Cloak. Evening *swelled* face (5 hours).

26th Letters. To work about 12, passed a feverish night, finished the Drapery Laying in (6 hours). painted over the chair, cloak, septer, crown etc (9 hours).

27th painted the tapistry in the even, finished it.

28th finished Lears cloak by transparent lake & painted the ends of boards (6 hours).

1st March painted the head of the jester from Danté Rosetti & the hands from Mrs Ashley, so muddled away the day. In the evening Bell Smith[7] of free Exhibition called to inforrm me I might keep it till private view, also of secret Machinations to form a fresh society & so get rid of the muff (7 hours).

2nd went to Greenwich & then to free Exhibition to ballot for places. Eveng at Thomas'.

3rd repainted Lears cloak, dragged blue & white over it, finished sundries to bed & cordelias girdle (6 hours).

4th Poor Thomas has been done out of his competition for Art Union Bassreliev[8] by Hancock &, as I imagine, an inferior work. Painted the uper part of Lears' gown & girdle. Even, Lucy's (6 hours).

---

[6] *Mrs Claypole, Cromwell's Favourite Daughter . . . at Hampton Court . . . A.D. 1659*, R.A. 1849.
[7] Hon. Secretary of the Free Exhibition, also an artist.
[8] *Christ's Entry into Jerusalem* won the Art Union prize of £100.

5th went to see Sleeping beauty of M'Clise at Phillips Auction rooms,[9] did little in consequence. Lucy called, has a chance of selling his puritans, want it sadly. Painted the Lear & the ornaments to Lears gown & began the carpet. Evening went with Thomas to Sadlers wells & saw King John,[10] admirable (3 hours).

6th Kröne, model for phisician, painted his hands & head & gown & Lears hair & beard (7 hours).

7th repainted the chair, crown, septer etc – worked at the back ground generally (6 hours).

8th repainted the landskip part & some of the figures of musicians – spoiled one head & scraped it out. Marshall called (7 hours).

9th Maitland all day, repainted the two wariors & sundries, eveng painted Lears girdle (10 hours).

10th finished the musicians & tent, went with Lucy to see Mr M'Ians picture[11] & free exhibition. Even foolery & to see Thomas (5 hours).

11th repainted head of Lear from Model (3 hours).

12th repainted arms & one hand of Lear & hair & beard from Model. Even to Lucy's (6 hours).

13th repainted one hand of Lear (bad) & his head (not too good), a bad day. Evening, carpet (8 hours).

14th repainted Kents head & draperies & the Jesters head. Draperies (7 hours).

15th painted one hand of Kent & his head again & one hand of Lear, retouched the head of Cordelia (7 hours).

16th repainted the head & hands of Cordelia from Model & part of the draperies (7 hours).

17th repainted head & beard of Lear, touched his hand & draperies, finished the draperies of Cordelia & began her pleated sleeves (8 hours)

18th finished the sleeves of Cordelia repainted her head from model & her

---

[9] *Sleeping Beauty*, lot 36, 6 Mar. 1849; sold for 620 guineas at Phillip's Auction Rooms, 73 New Bond Street.
[10] The leading parts were taken by Phelps and Miss Glyn (an actress much admired by Rossetti) who in the rôle of Constance "rose into sublime of emotion and the terrible of passion". The bill concluded with *The London Lady*. For Lucy's "puritans" see p.17, n.42.
[11] R.R. McIan (1803-56) a Scottish actor turned painter of historical genre, was showing *Highland Girls Winnowing Corn* at the Free Exhibition where it earned praise for its truth to nature.

hands, found I had spoiled the head, rubbed out part of it in the evening & made a mess of it (7 hours).

19th repainted at the head of Cordelia and at the head of Lear, painted at the tapistry and divers. Lucy & Fenton called in, did not like her (8 hours).

20th painted at lear's head again from Model & all over the picture odd's & ends (8 hours).

21st repainted & finished the head of Cordelia at Last. Painted the carpet & flowers & shield & divers (8 hours).

22nd took Lear to the free Exhin. Found a Large white sky come directly beneath it, kicked up a row & got it taken away then worked at the picture at divers (3 hours).

23rd repainted the sky & touched many things & finished it definitely (6 hours).

24th went to Private view, pictures much liked,[12] started for Gravesend. My child in bed.

28th went to see Baily's graces at his studio & Nichols sculpture for the pediment of the Hall of Comerce Manchester,[13] bad but effective. Also to see some magnificent Dutch pictures at Mr Theobald's.[14] In the afternoon dined with Seddon at the factory and Daubed away at a Medalion he is painting for a ceiling. In the evening with him to see how Lucy was getting on.

29th went to see young Hunt & then to see Millais picture Isabella,[15] wonderfully painted full of expression, sentiment, & colour & extreme good painting but somewhat exagerated in caracter & careless in Drawing. Thence to City to my uncle Madox & to see the Bass relief of the art union,

[12] Brown had been working at *Lear and Cordelia* until the day before the Private View. It was generally praised, the *Athenaeum* finding it a work "wherein powers of imagination are sustained by perception of fact", and the characters and minor details given with "intelligence and erudition". Brown's *The Young Mother* was also hung, as was Rossetti's *The Girlhood of Mary Virgin*.

[13] E.H. Baily (1788-1867), the successful sculptor, worked at 17 Newman Street. His marble group of *The Graces* was shown this summer at the R.A. W.G. Nicholl (1796-1871) had his studio at Grafton Street, Tottenham Court Road, and the sculpture seen by Brown was probably for the pediment of St George's Hall, Liverpool, representing Britannia with Commerce and the Arts. The pediment was designed by Cockerell, executed by Nicholl in Caen stone, and uncovered in 1850. There was never a Hall of Commerce at Manchester though the Free Trade Hall of brick and without a pediment was erected in 1843.

[14] Unidentified.

[15] From Holman Hunt's studio in Cleveland Street, Brown proceeded to Gower Street where Millais (1829-96), the youthful prodigy and one of the P.R.B., was preparing his *Lorenzo and Isabella* (Liverpool) for the R.A. exhibition.

thence to Thomass's studio, Thomas poëtising & *intending* to paint a large picture – in the evening tried to settle my money accounts & afterwards to see Lucy with Thomas.

30th wrote two letters & then to studio, spent much time setting it to rights, found it too late to begin at my view of Windermere. Went out to see British institution, too late, went to fenton & saw his picture.[16]

31st Painted at the view of Windermere, even went to see the beggars opera[17] (4 hours).

1st April painted at Windermere (6 hours).

2nd Called on Lucy & Millais & thence to call on Truefit & with him to Archtects institution (Truefit will get on, Clever), afterward to British institution. Evening spent at Rosetti's. Saw his designs and his brother, all up & in his little room 5th storey.[18]

3rd painted at windermere, evening at Lucys (5 hours).

4th Walked over the park, called on Fenton. Painted at Windermere, went with Thomas to Theatre [illegible][19] (5 hours).

5th Painted at windermere cows & foreground, bad cold (5 hours).

6th Painted at idem, Horses etc (5 hours).

7th Idem (cold very bad on the chest). (4 hours).

8th Sunday painted at trees etc & in the eveng (6 hours).

9th painted at idem (6 hours).

---

[16] The annual exhibition at the British Institute had opened in early February and was to close in May. Fenton was painting *You Must Wake and Call Me Early* for the R.A. exhibition.

[17] Brown had taken up the *Windermere* in preparation for the R.A. exhibition. *The Beggar's Opera* at the Princess's was given together with *Lucia di Lammermoor*.

[18] After walking from Gower Street to George Truefitt (1824-1902), the architect, in Bloomsbury Square, Brown would have turned west to the Royal Institute of British Architects in Grosvenor Street. Rossetti's younger brother William Michael (1829-1919), diarist and art-critic, was present at this visit of Brown's to the Rossetti house. Originally Gabriele Rossetti's dressing-room, the small room "quite at the top of the house" had been appropriated by his son, and here the brothers spent many hours, "small, bare and uncared-for" though the room was, sitting over its "scanty fireplace" (W.M. Rossetti *D.G. Rossetti, Letters and Memoir*, 1895, i, p.117). Having completed *The Girlhood of Mary Virgin* and wearying of Holman Hunt's tutelage as he had done of Brown's, Rossetti removed his property from Holman Hunt's studio and in November took a studio at 72 Newman Street.

[19] Possibly the name of the play.

10th painted in the day time & in the evening from 9 till 11, finished it & carried to the Royal accad.[20] (7 hours work).

11th painted at restoring a picture of John Bromley's (3 hours work). Went to a party at the Barrauds.

12th painted at the same (4 hours).

14th went to Gravesend.

16th my birth day, 28 years old, spent it with my child.

17th came up from gravesend.

27th worked at the outline of Poets', drew in the page in the fourground from natur[21] (4 hours).

28th again & at the back figure in the hood, drew in the nude again (3 hours).

1st May again at the same & the Courtier in extasium (8 hours).

5th worked at the water colour scetch, begun repainting it in oil (4 hours).

8th do. (3 hours).

10th do. (4 hours).

13th do. (2 hours).

18th do. (4 hours).

19th do. (4 hours).

23rd 3 hours

24th 5 hours.

25th drew two human heads for John Marshall (3 hours).

26th Idem (2½ hours).

28th painted at the scetch 3 hours.

1st June idem 4 hours.

2nd idem 6 hours

3rd walked to Charlton & Woolwich

[20] The *Windermere* was not accepted.
[21] *Chaucer* was taken up again.

4th painted at the scetch, afterwards to Greenwich (3 hours).

5th idem (4 hours).

6th Idem (4 hours).

7th Idem (5 hours).

8th began painting on the center compartment of the picture. Painted at the yellow hood in the foreground, painted in the head of [blank in MS.] (up at first) lemon, crome, cadmium, & yellow lake *with copal*, vehicle copal & drying oil (5 hours).

9th idem (5 hours).

10th to Gravesend.

11th finished the hood (8 hours).

14th began the Green gown, rubed in the shadows with vermillion & copal, when dry painted it all up at once (verdigris, emeral, crome, lemon, yellow lake, Bitumen, white etc, same vehicle), finished the sleeve (7 hours).

15th repainted at the same (5 hours).

16th painted the part covering the legs (6 hours).

17th painted all day at the same (8 hours).

18th finished idem (6 hours).

19th Maitland, painted the two hands of yellow hood, afterwards the sleeves (10 hours).

20th Drew in the courtier in admiration, from Maitland (8 hours).

21st painted in one hand & the head, laying in the shadows with emerald green & white & *much copal* & the lights with pure white & copal, the outlining drawn with water colours much hatched (10 hours).

22nd painted in one hand from Maitland in sun light, find I can put the models in the sun (3 hours).

23rd painted in the neck & hair & draperies of the admiring courtier also one hand of the fourground page, always laying in the flesh with pure white (8 hours).

24th to Hampton court to see Richard.

25th painted a study of the head of Maitland from[22] the black prince, and the head of page from young Deverell (7 hours).

[22] In the diary manuscript W.M. Rossetti has cancelled the word "from" and substituted "for".

26th to Collingwood to see abut the scetching club & to vernon gallery.[23] Evening with Seddon.

27th walked about town & to get some silk hose, afterwards painted at the scetch (4 hours).

28th painted in one leg of the party colored hose of the page from Maitland (8 hours).

29th painted in the other leg, touched the pages head & painted in the Jester's from John Marshall (9 hours).

30th painted in the Jester's hood (4 hours).

1st July to Gravesend. Lucy has the Hooping cough.

2nd Set off to Thorp [Shorn] ridgway, found some fine scenery overlooking the Thames & Essex. Began a study of it for my background to Chaucer[24] (3 hours).

3rd Windey bad weather could not go on with it, sketched some trees (3½ hours).

4th Idem. Scetched & horsechesnut trees (3 hours).

5h nothing, Idle.

6th idem.

7th Tidied up the studio, had Maitland all day making a stand to be able to wheel about the large center picture. Fitted up fresh blinds to admit the sun if necessary. Made extensive olterations.

8th Cleaned Brushes — waited in vain for E[25] to come back from the coundtry. Began work after diner, scetched in some of the females preparatory for next day (5 hours).

9th Miss Wild. Painted in one of the female heads in sun light & the red silk headress of the one speaking to her[26] (5 hours work).

10th Miss wild, did nothing in consequence of forgetting the time &

---

[23] The Vernon collection of one hundred and fifty-seven works by contemporary British artists had been presented to the nation in 1847 by Robert Vernon, a patron of the arts who had amassed a fortune by horse dealing. The pictures were being shown at the National Gallery.
[24] (Private Collection.) Brown repeated this landscape, in reverse, for the background of the *Chaucer*.
[25] Presumably "Emma".
[26] On the left Julia Wild (see p.24, n.5 and diary entry p.74) with head turned round to the front, wearing a headress as illustrated in *Knight's Pictorial History*, p.867.

walking too long in the park. After diner Emma came back, went to the play.

11th Emma came by 12, painted in the veil & afterwards the face from Emma (the ladye with ye red Head Dress) (7 hours work).

12th went to see some copies of the old Masters by some french artist,[27] dined & went to meet Emma in the fields by Highgate (2 hours work).

13th Seddon came to work in my studio. I began the blue cloak of the above mentioned figure, did nothing in the afternoon (3 hours).

14th went with Bishop[28] to have his phiz dageureoutiped, diner in my studio with him, afterwards to Dickinsons till 3 morning.

15th painted at the veil & blue cloak (3 hours).

16th fooled away much time, scetched in the out line of the Grey velvet cloak (3 hours).

17th out on business, painted at the Cloak (3 hours).

18th Painted at Idem (6 hours).

19th My sweet Lucy 6 years old. To Gravesend.

20th Seddon in my studio painting from Miss Stone. Worked at the cloak (4 hours).

21st painted at the cloak (6 hours).

22nd Walked about all day with E[mma].

23rd Seddon painting again, I at the cloak (6 hours).

24th painted at the Cloak (4 hours). Then to R. Acad & to Surrey Zoologicall.[29]

25th Got some rushes from a man, painted at this after arranging them (4 hours).

26th all day at the rushes (6 hours).

Painted 6 days more at the Rushes (3 hours).

---

[27] Monsieur Colin had executed a series of copies of celebrated pictures by the great masters, and was showing sixty of these in Francis Street, Bedford Square.
[28] Unidentified, but might be W.J. Bishop (1805-88), Liverpool genre and landscape painter.
[29] A series of promenade concerts and a spectacle of "The Storming of Badajoz" were being held at the Surrey Zoological Gardens which encompassed fifteen acres of ground and three of water, at the junction of Kennington Lane and Newington Butts. A large conservatory contained cages for animals.

Painted about 12 days at the picture of King Lear, altered the head of Cordelia, shortened her hands & arms, enlarged the head – thickened the figure (60 hours). Painted 4 days at the little Picture of mother & child before sending it home (20 hours).

Painted 3 days at the scetch of it (15 hours).

Painted one day at the view of Windermere (6 hours).

Painted 3 days at the view of Shorn (15 hours).

Spent one day arranging the cap of the page.

Painted 2 days at it & the hair (12 hours).

Spent 3 days arranging the sleeve of the Page. Went to Margate with my daughter & stayed there 2 weeks during [which time] had three sittings for her portrait[30] (9 hours).

Went to Ramsgate for one week with Emma. Came back on 24th Septer.

26th rearranged the sleeve, began it (4 hours).

27th Painted at it (5 hours).

28th & 29th idem (11 hours).

30th idem (2 hours). Cleaned lamp.

1st Octr idem (4 hours). Cleaned lamp.

2nd [no entry]

3rd went to see after a stove.

[4th] found one & fitted up (3 hours).

5th Begun a portrait of Mr Seddon to be painted & that of Mrs Seddon, for a sofa.[31] Went to Conversatione with thomas.

6th Made a drawing of Maitlands legs (3 hours).

7th worked at the Pages legs (3 hours).

8th Studio floor taken up to discover stench.

9th painted all day at the legs of the page (5 hours)

10th portrait of Mr Seddon (3 hours).

[30] Private Collection.
[31] In exchange for the portraits (Private Collection), Mr Seddon was to give Brown a sofa from his own works.

11th all day looking after some silk. Even arranged lay figure.

12th worked all day at the figure in scarlet gown drew it in & painted ermine[32] (8 hours).

13th painted swan's-down & red sattin, even drew in & Laid in the white cowl (8 hours).

14th to Richmond. Even cleaned pallets & brushes.

15th Mr Seddon 3 hours, painted at the ermine (5 hours).

16th all day at the red sattin (6 hours).

17th foot-cray.

18th Gravesend.

19th Painted at the Red satin (3 hours).

20th idem 5 hours, eveng painted in the camp stool (7 hours).

21st repainted & improved the red sattin (4 hours).

22nd Mr Seddon portrait (5 hours).

24th Red Dress etc (5 hours).

25th Mr Seddon (3 hours).

26th The red dress & stool & ermine (4 hours).

27th Mr Seddon (3 hours) Coat. Spoil swandown (5 hours).

28th worked at the ermine, swansdown, spoilt (3 hours).

29th yellow sleeve next to Red dress (6 hours).

30th Painted at the swandown, the yellow sleeve & white cowl (5 hours).

31st Mr Seddon. Painted coat & waistcoat (3 hours).

1st Nov painted at the white cowl (3 hours).

2nd finished white cowl (3 hours).

3rd Mr Seddon, painted at head & curtain (4½ hours). Finished Mr Seddons Portrait. Drew in the Jester & painted his hands, sleeves etc. Drew at other parts. Composed a subject from Beauty & the Beast — one from [?Potter].[33] Drew a figure of Beauty from nature — wasted about 2 months

---

[32] The woman in the "sideless" dress of p.12.
[33] A charcoal sketch for (the untraced) *Beauty Before She Became Acquainted with the Beast* is said to have been bought by John James Ruskin in 1857 for £10. A chalk drawing of Potter (presumably the Potter of p.29) is untraced.

changing into a new studio.[34] Began the Portrait of Shakespear for the Dickinsons. Painted a scetch of it, made a drawing of the head, and a study from Mr Barker for it.[35] Drew a cartoon of it, had the Dress made up. Drew a figure of the Lord Jesus for the Dickinsons.[36]

[34] Brown moved into his new studio at 17 Newman Street on 12 Jan. 1850.
[35] The portrait of Shakespeare (Manchester) commissioned for £50 by the Dickinson Brothers for lithographic reproduction was a conflation of the then accepted likenesses of the dramatist. Barker was a professional model who posed for the fireman in Millais' painting *The Rescue* (National Gallery of Victoria, Melbourne), exhibited at the R.A. in 1855.
[36] A study in pen and ink for the head of *The Lord Jesus* is in a Private Collection.

1850

2nd March worked at it & the cartoon of Shakespear today (4½). In the evening three hours at the Lord Jesus (border work).

3rd March Sunday Laid in the whole of Shakespear in Burnt Siena, asphaltum & umber, medium turpentine & copal (ground white) 4 hours.

4th wasted the day, worked at the ornamental border of the Lord Jesus then to see Popworths panarama,[1] then to meet S.C. Hall at Lucy's Meeting of the comittee of the North London School of Drawing & Modelling[2] (2 hours).

5th Painted in part of the tapistry of Shakespear (8 hours).

6th Painted at the forehead and Hair of Shakespear and drew the border of thorns of the Christ (8 hours).

7th Muddled – Drew the thorns and corn (8 hours).

8th Drew the corn and the vine (8 hours).

---

[1] The "panarama" is unidentified. E.P. Papworth (1809-66), sculptor and pupil of E.H. Baily, whose daughter Caroline he married, exhibited a "panorama of Rome at a Gallery in Great Portland Strteet, in about 1844" (F. Boase, *Modern English Biography*, 1965). The "Gallery" seems likely to have been at No. 60, the premises of Joseph Hogarth, print mounter, who within the next couple of years moved to the Haymarket where he was well-known as a printseller and framemaker.

[2] Samuel Carter Hall (1800-89), editor of the *Art Union Monthly* (later *Art Journal*), known more familiarly by Brown's nickname for him, "Shirt-collar Hall" owing to the correctness of his attire, took the chair at a public meeting in April, held at St Pancras National School Rooms off Euston Road, to promote the establishment of the Drawing School. The original idea of such a school was due to Thomas Seddon and its purpose was to instruct "in the true knowledge of form" workmen engaged in masonry, carving, plastering, cabinet-making, casting and chasing of metals. The school opened on 1 May, under the patronage of the Prince Consort, in Mary's Terrace, Camden Town. The committee consisted of E.H. Baily, Brown, Roger Fenton, S.C. Hall, Thomas Seddon, George Truefitt and Charles Lucy. The last-named also directed the women's classes, held on alternate days from 6 to 8 p.m. The Drawing and Modelling Master was Cave Thomas and the Hon. Secretary was J. Neville Warren, a civil engineer. The students were limited in number to two hundred and classes were held from 8 to 10 p.m. Admission fee was one shilling and sixpence a month.

9th Drew at the vine, painted three hours at the face of Shakespear (8 hours).

10th Drew at the christ (5 hours).

11th Idem (8 hours).

12th Idem & went to a committee meeting of the North London School (6 hours).

13th Idem went to Fenton to paint his dead child[3] (6 hours).

14th to Fenton's, finished the head – & back to work. Finished this, all except retouching head. Eveng altered head (11 hours).

15th finished altering head (4 hours).

16th painted at the head of Shakespear and background and drew at the Cordelia for Etching (16 hours).

17th Sunday painted part of the tapistry of Shakespear & drew at the Cordelia for etching (12 hours).

18th Monday all day at head of Shakesper. Eveng, drawing (12 hours).

19th all day & part of eveng painting flouers. Eveng, drawing (14 hours).

20th Painted at face & painted flouers. Eveng drew (12 hours).

21st drew at the etching, painted draperies of Shakespear (12 hours).

22nd Painted forhead, the draperies, began etching (14 hours).

23rd to city about money, etched (11 hours).

Sunday Herbert for draperies 3 hours, etched 10 (13).

Monday Lambert[4] 3 hours at face, Herbert 3 hours draperies.

[3] The Fentons lived at Albert Terrace, Primrose Hill. It has not been possible to discover any record of their child's death (or birth).
[4] Four days later, Lambert, a professional model, sat to Rossetti for the head of the archangel in *Ecce Ancilla Domini!* Herbert was presumably also a model.

1854

Diary resumed on the 16th August 1854

Idle morning spent musing in bed afternoon walked out with Emma & Katty.[1] Evening garden & dim reflections. Much study of Blue book of Department of Art & science impudently called of "Science & Art".[2] In the interval which this diary shows to the best of my recollection I painted in the year /50 (still in Newman St) first the remainder of the Shakespear portrait for which I was paid 60 guineas, then I finished the Etching for the Germ[3] which cost me 31.6 & brought me in nothing. Afterwards I designed a card for Dickinson Exhibition of Shakespear[4] on which I worked several days for no remunoration. The drawing of the Lord Jesus was paid me £2. They afterwards lithographed it in shameful stile so as to cause me much annoyance. For the remainder of the year I worked at the Large picture of Chaucer & studies of Landskip for it, one of which I afterwards finished up & gave to Seddon.[5] In 1851 I finished the centre compartment of the "Fruits of English poetry" having determined to abandon the wings. To get this part finished for the accademy I had to labour very hard & at the last worked three whole nights in one week, only lying down with my cloaths on

[1] Rossetti and Thomas Seddon were witnesses to Brown's marriage to Emma Matilda Hill (1829?-90) at St Dunstan's-in-the-West, Fleet Street, on 5 Apr. 1853 (Plates 8 and 9). At about the time of the last diary entries (Mar. 1850) Emma conceived a child, Catherine (Katty, Cathy), who was born on 11 Nov. 1850 and was baptized at Old St Pancras Church, 18 Apr. 1852. In 1872 Catherine married Franz Hueffer. Ford Madox Hueffer (later Ford) was their child.

[2] Published in June, this was the *First Report of the Department of Science and Art*: "This ponderous volume of 642 pages contains a great deal of mighty matter — we say it in earnest and not in jest" (*Athenaeum*, p.754).

[3] *Lear and Cordelia* was published in the third issue of *The Germ*, March 1850 to illustrate W.M. Rossetti's poetic contribution *Cordelia*. The composition, according to Hueffer, was based on earlier designs made in Paris, and represents the parting of Cordelia from her sisters. It differs slightly in treatment from Brown's oil sketch of the same subject, *The Parting of Cordelia and her Sisters*, 1854 (Private Collection).

[4] The invitation card (Birmingham) shows the figure of Shakespeare, with above and to the left thirteen lines in red, mostly in Gothic scripst, within a trellis border.

[5] *The Medway* (Private Collection).

8. D.G. Rossetti, *Ford Madox Brown*, National Portrait Gallery, London

for a couple of hours. Emma sat for the Princess which was done in two sittings of two hours each. Gabriel Rossetti sat for Chaucer beginning at 11 at night, he sitting up beside me on the scaffolding scetching while I worked. We finished about four in the morning & the head was never subsequently touched. His brother William was the troubadour. Elliot [Elliott] a pupil of Lucy's, the cardinal. John Marshall of University Hospital was the Jester. Miss Gregson since *Mrs Lee*[6] was the fair princess behind the Black Prince. Her friend Miss Byne sat for the dark one but much altered. The scoundrel & afterwards thief Maitland then under Marshalls hands for an operation, sat for the Black prince. The fine woman below looking round was a portrait of Julia Wild celebrated as model & prostitute also for black eyes, the boys were mostly portraits, but the other heads Ideal chiefly. I sold this picture to Dickinson for 85 per cent of whatever he might afterwards sell it for to be paid after he should have received the money. I have since urged him to put it up to Auction which he has done but no one would buy it. So he still has it – this year /54 he paid me £20 on account of it which was all I ever had for it. After Finishing this picture (which I forgot to say the Accademitians hung in such a way as to shine all over & *without the frame*[7]) I took a house at Stockwell.[8] I went for three days to the Isle of Wight with Anthony & Hunt. The first day we marched for 5 hours in the rain. The second & third revelled in the enjoyment liberty, novelty of scene, fine weather & huge appetite – the forth we returned home.

At Stockwell this year I painted one month at the sketch for the Chaucer begin on paper & water colar, Anthony was to give me a work for this but I afterwards asked him to give me 12 Guineas instead which he did. I then began my picture of the Baä Lambs[9] which I finished in five months of Hard Labour during which time I was very hard up generally owing to McCracken not paying me all at once for the picture of Wickliff which he purchased of me at this time for 50 Guineas & a very bad Deighton,[10] a do in fact. During this time I painted Mrs Seddon's portrait which turned out bad & a curse. This was the second portrait for the sofa which they valued at 13 guineas cost price. During this time I also finished the Lanskip study of Shorn[11] which I gave to Tom Seddon he having kindly lent me money

[6] A model who married Mr Lee, secretary of the Clipstone Street Artists Society, where life classes were held. Miss Byne was also a model.
[7] To Brown's great annoyance the Academy discarded the frame; only the narrow mount remained. In 1855 the picture dealer D.T. White acquired the painting for £50.
[8] South of the river, then in the parish of Lambeth, where he lived with Emma and their child.
[9] Birmingham.
[10] Probably W.E. Dighton (1822-53), landscape painter. Francis MacCracken, of a Belfast firm of shippers, was a purchaser of early Pre-Raphaelite work.
[11] See p.72, n.5.

9. *Emma Brown*, City Art Gallery, Birmingham

about this time £12. I think £5 of which I borrowed to lend Lucy. But Seddon was the first to borrow of me £10 once to get his uncle George out of prison.

At this time I also finished the sketche of Wickliff & the *first* of Chaucer[12] (since given to John Marshall), about a days work between the two. The baa lamb picture was painted almost entirely in sunlight which twice gave me a fever while painting. I used to take the lay figure out every morning & bring it in at night or if it rained. My painting room being on a level with the garden, Emma sat for the lady & Kate for the child. The Lambs & sheep used to be brought every morning from Clappam common in a truck. One of them eat up all the flowers one morning in the garden where they used to behave very ill. The back ground was painted on the common. The medium I used was Robersons undrying copal (Flake White). After getting rid of these works I went to Foots Cray for Mickelmas with my daughter Lucy where I painted my picture of "Pauls Cray church" in ten days. This I have sent to Robinsons Auction a few months since and it fetched £2.8 inclusion of Frame. It was exhibited at Grundy's and Liverpool in /52.[13]

After these works I Began my picture of Christ washing Peter's feet,[14] painting this one at my painting Rooms in Newman St. At the same time I began the study for the small picture of "Waiting"[15] working at it in the three evengs a week I used to sleep in Stockwell. The other three being passed at the studio to save time. Twelve days before sending in the Christ picture I had given it up in despair, none of the heads being yet done, so I returned to stockwell to ater the head in the Baa Lambs picture being dissatisfied with it.[16] I afterwards took up the Christ again at the instigation of Millais & painted the heads of Peter, Christ & John (this one the only one laid in) also *all the other figures of* apostles in 10 days & sent it in. This picture was painted in four months the flesh painted on *wet white* at Millais' lying instigation, Roberson's Medium, which I think dangerous like Millais' advice.

Having got rid of these pictures which were hung one above the line so as to shine all over the other against the window in the octogon room, I

[12] The "first Chaucer", *The Seeds and Fruits of English Poetry*. For Wycliffe see n.27 below.
[13] The (untraced) painting was sold at George Robinson, Auctioneers, 21 Old Bond Street and exhibited at J.L. Grundy's Winter Exhibition, Regent Street, in Jan. 1852. The Liverpool exhibition followed later in the year.
[14] Tate, Plate 10. Later, the half-naked figure of Christ was fully clothed in deference to public opinion.
[15] This sketch which served as a study for the oil painting *Waiting* (Private Collection) was reworked and renamed *An English Fireside of 1854-5* (Untraced).
[16] Brown showed three pictures at the R.A. in 1852: *Christ Washing Peter's Feet*, *The Pretty Baa-Lambs* and *Waiting*.

10. *Christ Washing Peter's Feet*, Tate Gallery, London

immediately began the picture of "waiting",[17] from Miss Ryan the head, the remainder coppied from the study painted at night. I all but finished this little picture before leaving our house at Stockwell, 10 weeks work at least. During the winter I painted the study from Emma with the head back laughing[18] at night in Newman St. All this while Rossetti was staying at Newman St with me – keeping me up talking till 4 A.M., painting some-times all night making the whole place miserable and filthy, translating sonnets at breakfast working very hard & doing nothing.[19]

In June I left Stockwell and newman St for Hampstead, Emma going to Dover for the summer. At Hampstead I remained one year & nine months most of the time intensely miserable very hard up & a little mad. During this time I was head master of the North London Drawing school for nearly a year.[20] I once received £5 from the secretary as a loan which I returned to him a short time after; this was all I ever saw of my salary of £60 a year. The first work I undertook at Hampstead was the designe for my picture of "work"[21] still unfinished save the background. I also made a small copy of the Baa Lambs & painted two small portraits[22] one for nothing not even thanks, the other for £5. I began the background for "Work" in the streets of Hampstead painting there all day for two months having spent much time in inventing & making an apparatus.[23] This and finishing the paint-ing of waiting took up till the beginning of Octr when I commenced the Landscape of English Autumn Afternoon[24] which I had to give up after a months work in consequence of Mrs Coats' being ill & her bedroom being required. Having given this up about the End of Octr & decided that I should not have time to finish the "Work" for the next acady Exhn I

[17] Miss Ryan was a professional model.
[18] Begun as a portrait of Emma, modified later when the canvas was enlarged, left unfinished, and named *Take Your Son, Sir!* (Tate).
[19] In May 1851 Rossetti had accepted Brown's offer to share his studio and this arrange-ment lasted until Nov. 1852 when Rossetti moved to rooms of his own at 14 Chatham Place, Blackfriars. Brown is here referring to the winter of 1851-2.
[20] Brown took over the Drawing School (see p.70, n.2) from Cave Thomas. During this time Brown had a painting room in the lodging-house of a Mrs Coates, High Street, Hampstead. He suffered greatly from depression brought on by extreme poverty and lack of recognition. Emma and their baby were living elsewhere and he became morose and almost inaccessible.
[21] Manchester, Plate 11. Completed in 1865 this great social document is arguably Brown's outstanding achievement.
[22] Unidentified and untraced. The small scale repetition of *Pretty Baa-Lambs* is in the Ashmolean.
[23] The site for the composition of *Work* is still easily recognizable on the west side of Heath Street, Hampstead. According to Brown he painted from a "truck fitted up by myself" (Hueffer, p.91). Holman Hunt was more explicit: "For an easel he constructed a rack on the tray on a costermonger's barrow; above the canvas were rods with curtains suspended which could be turned on a hinge, so that they shrouded the artist while working" (W. Holman Hunt *Pre-Raphaelitism and the Pre-Raphaelite Brotherhood* 1905, ii, pp.96-7).
[24] Birmingham, Plate 12. A view from Brown's back window looking towards Hampstead Heath.

11. *Work*, City Art Gallery, Manchester

12. *An English Autumn Afternoon*, City Art Gallery, Birmingham

designed the subject of "The Last of England"[25] at the colored sketch & cartoon of which I worked till Xmas. During this period I worked about 10 days at the cartoon of "Oure Ladye etc"[26] & the picture of the Baa lambs. About this time also I got the 12 guineas from Anthony & sold the sketch of the Wickliff to McCracken for 10 guineas. Also the scetch of the "Infant's repast" to some scoundrel at Bristol for £5.[27] At the beginning of /53 I worked for about 6 weeks at the picture of "Last of England", Emma coming to sit to me in the most inhuman weather from Highgate. This work representing an out door scene without sun light I painted at it chiefly out of doors when the snow was lieing on the ground. The madder ribons of the bonnet took me 4 weeks to paint. At length finding that at this rate I could not get it done for the Acady I gave it up in much disgust & began repainting the sketch of Chaucer to give to John Marshall. On this I worked about 2 months. Also a little at the painted scetch of Cordelia from the Etching in the Germ. About this time I lost many days through interruptions of a domestic nature but resumed work again about the 15th May at the picture of "King Lear" & Baa Lambs, doing about 2 months work to the King Lear which I sent to Manchester along with the "waiting" and perhaps 5 weeks work to the Baa Lambs, for Glascoe[28] all of which returned unsold. During this period we were residing at Hendon till the 1st Sepr 53 when when we removed here at Church End.[29] About the 15 sep I recommenced painting on the "English Autumn" Picture & finished the view from the back window about the 20th October. From this period till the 10 of June 1854 I must have wasted 4 weeks through Lucys Hollidays – 2 through Nervous dissorder of the Brain – and about 1 through Emma's illness. Of the remaining time about 2 months was taken up again repainting the "King Lear", one month on the Picture of the Last of England – 3 days on repainting the picture of Winandermere[30] (since sold to White for £5), 10 days on a lithograth of Winandermere (a failure), nearly a month

[25] Birmingham, Plate 13. The genesis of this picture was suggested by the emigration to Australia of Thomas Woolner (1825-92), sculptor and occasional poet, and one of the original members of the P.R.B. Son of a Suffolk post-office sorter he was seeking his fortune in the gold-rush. Brown, Holman Hunt and Rossetti had gone to Gravesend in July 1852 to see him off.

[26] *Our Ladye of Good Children* (Tate). A chalk cartoon executed in 1847 on his return from Italy. Damaged in 1858, water-colour and pastel were added in 1861.

[27] The *Wycliffe* oil sketch was acquired from MacCracken by White, the dealer, and sold to B.G. Windus. (Recently Phillips sale, 20 Apr. 1980, bought by Maas Gallery for £21,000 and now Bradford City Art Gallery). The Bristol purchaser of the (untraced) sketch was Edward Stanley.

[28] The exhibitions at the Royal Manchester Institution and the Glasgow Royal Institute of Fine Arts, were held in September.

[29] 1 Grove Villas, Church End, Finchley, for which Brown paid fifteen shillings a quarter in rates, was to be their house for the next two years. Here the prodigy son "Nolly" was born; Christina and Gabriel Rossetti and Elizabeth Siddal stayed; and Brown painted *The Last of England* and took up his picture of *Work*.

[30] Private Collection. Brown's alternative name for the picture.

13. *The Last of England*, City Art Gallery, Birmingham

on an etching of King Lear, yet unfinished, 6 days on a Lythotint of "Baby" (a failure) and the rest of the time on "English Autumn Afternoon" which last took me about 6 months was sold at Phillips Auction for 9 guineas to Dickinson, the frame having cost 4. He has since sold it to Charles Seddon for 20 pound and declares he will not make any profit by it but put it to my accompt. The King Lear was sold at the same time for 15 Guineas to John P. Seddon having cost 8 months work & the frame £3.10.[31] Shortly after this White[32] who had just purchased the two Whickliffs from McCracken came here & bought the "Cordelia" sketch for £10, Picture of "Waiting" 20, sketch of "Baa Lambs" £5, & "Winandermere" £5 in all £40. Since which I have spent one month in finishing the Cordelia for him along with the others. Having finished these & got the money, I wasted about a week and have since been engaged finishing off a study, two views of the same little girls head painted at South End in /47[33] – one day at this & the rest at making a picture of study of Windermere painted in /48 when with Lucy at the Lakes.

I must now endeavour to keep up this diary more accurately, but have become lazy through discouragement – yet not so much so as some people think – but broken in spirit and but a melancholy copy of what I once was. "Ah what to me shall be the End".

17th august/54. Rose at ¼ before nine – garden after breakfast. Shower Bath before. To work by 11 till one at the view of Windermere. Dined, to work again by 2 till near six worked at sky & all over. Tea & then for a walk with Emma. An umbrella each for a threatening storm which caught us sure as we returned. This even I intended drawing but instead reflected on alterations to be made in the picture of Christ & Peter which I think of sending to Paris with the Chaucer, if the *English Committee accept it*[34] (6 hours). The Christ in its present state I consider to be a failure – too much melo-dramatic sentiment not sufficient dignity & simplicity of pose. What to do with it however I scarce know. To suite the public taste however it should be clothed! to suit my own, not – but then the action suits me not to

[31] Phillips sale, July 1854. Charles Seddon and John Pollard Seddon (1827-1906), architect, were brothers of Thomas Seddon.
[32] D.T. White, more generally referred to as "old White", a picture-dealer with premises at 28 Maddox Street. He was one of the main buyers of Brown's early work, though not a particularly generous one.
[33] The double portrait (Manchester, Plate 14) is of Millie Smith, daughter of Brown's landlord at Southend. Signed and dated "1847" it was begun in 1846 (Mary Bennett, *Burlington*, Feb. 1973, p.74).
[34] The English Committee of the Universal Exhibition, Paris, 1855, was under the superintendence of Henry Cole. The handing committee numbered Redgrave, Hurlstone and Creswick among others. The contributors to the exhibition were required to enter details by 30 Nov. of the nature and number of their pictures and the space which they would occupy in height and breadth.

alter which would be more trouble than to cloath the figure. Auriole they *must* all have. The St John is all right. The Peter would be perfect if the carnation were redder & deeper in tint & the cloak a better green, also a bit of the right arm should be shown; but how? Judas requires a fresh head of hair – his present one having been dabbed in from *feeling* in the last hurry of sending in. Memo, his garment to be a paler yellow. Four of the other apostles require more *religious feeling* which must be done. William & Gabriel Rossetti in particular require veneration to be added to them.[35] The table cloath will require alteration & the tiles of the floor. Health & spirits tolerable to day, nerves quiet.

18th Up at 9 shower bath, to work ½ past 10 till 1 at the view of Windermere altered the trees to the right; dinner & to work at ½ past 2 till 6 altered sky. Tea garnening till 8 – worked from 9 till ½ past ten at the charcoal sketch of "Beauty before she became acquainted with the Beast" (7½). Read Anthony & Cleopatra in bed this morning found it more inter-resting than ever, was deeply affected & strengthened such is the effect of all History reading. The moral it, the play, seems to imply, if any, is that there is in shame and degradation a pitch than which self inflicted death is more to be tolerated. Pity when any one with modern notions of the criminality of such act is driven to it. With poor Haydon it was the only attonement he could make to humanity degraded in his personal conduct.[36] How can degraded beings be still interresting.

20th Up at 9 shower bath, late breakfast, letter, writing this at ¼ to 11 a.m. Yesterday one of degrading idleness did nothing, settle a few accompts before 12, set to work at ½ past. Illustrated news came in read till dinner & after lazed till ½ past 3, then worked for about 2 hours. After

[35] Writing in 1898 F.G. Stephens (see p.154, n.98) identified the apostles from left to right: Judas "a common model, if my memory does not err the man was a bricklayer's labourer" (might he have been employed by Emma's late father, see n.58 below, and introduced by her?); W.M. Rossetti, his head already partially bald; the third figure, now thought to be Holman Hunt, Stephen describes as D.G. Rossetti, and "most decidedly not Mr Holman Hunt, whose hair and skin were both fair whereas those of D.G. Rossetti were both dark, and his eyes unlike Mr Holman Hunt's, were very dark" (Stephens was undoubtedly mistaken in his identification). The fourth figure he identified as Holman Hunt's father, the fifth as W.B. Scott. No. 5 is now more generally thought to be Holman Hunt senior; No. 4 bears some resemblance to Thomas Seddon and D.G. Rossetti is No. 7. The identity of the sitter for St John on the extreme right and behind St Peter is uncertain. Stephens was under the impression that it was Christina Rossetti "until she herself explicitly told me she had not sat for it. It is certainly not a portrait of Deverell . . . I took his portrait and knew him intimately for many years. Nevertheless he, and several others, may have sat to Brown for it, but it is not like him . . . if Walter Deverell sat for it, or any part of it, as I myself might have done, it is not like either of us" (the figure does in fact seem strongly to resemble Deverell). Stephens sat for the Christ while St Peter is unknown (unpublished letters from F.G. Stephens to Mrs M.P. Brocklebank. Private Collection).
[36] As a result of professional disappointments and the consequent pecuniary difficulties, Haydon took his own life in 1846.

out for a longish walk with Emma, came home tired dejected & nervous, tried to work at drawing of Beauty for about 1 hour, contemptible state (3 hours). This morning have written notice of sending Chaucer, King L., and Christ to Paris (will the committee permit!?!?!?!?!?!). To work by 12 till 1, dinner, and at work from 2 to ½ past 5, at the study for the picture of "waiting", retouched with fine brush all the right hand side of the picture which had been painted in coarsely by lamp light (6 hours). In the eveng 1 and ½ hour at Beauty (Sunday).

22nd St Albans. Yesterday non entry. We intended visiting the British Mus — but I was taken with a certain desire for running away which might have rendered the trip unpleasant not to say dangerous so gave it up. Emma went in to London sola & called on the Rossettis.[37] I worked at the little picture till 6 or half past — repainted the childs hands from the studie & the head from feeling till I became thouroughly disgusted with the work as I have with the Windermere. Both are now put by till the inspiration comes on again. When nothing hurries this is the best plan. In the evening too lazy to work (6 hours). This morning I felt incontrolably disgusted with every thing, could literally do nothing not even summon energy to go into London when Emma started the bright idea that we should go to St Albans. As soon as dinner over we started on foot for Colney Hatch station with Katty & Sarah[38] whom we then sent back with the bribe of a bun to secure a quiet parting. The rail only goes to Hatfield we found, but then got a ride on the top of the bus here in the most lovely weather. Emma in a state of boyant enjoyment. We should have thought more of the fields no doubt were we not so much used to them of late. However one field of turnips against the afternoon sky did surprise us into exclamation with its wonderful emerald tints. And then we passed a strange sight; two tall chimneys standing seperately in a small space of ground about a rod I suppose, the rest covered with black looking rubbish some of it smoking, some children looking at it. This the day before had been a house the home of a young couple married some three months, the man a wheel right. Fire surprised them in bed the previous night it would seem and they had to escape as they were in their bed cloaths. And here lay all that they possessed flattened down in to black ashes. I broke a tooth a day or two ago and the gap seemed for some days hard to reconcile with my impressions of what forms sought to surround my tongue. If so it is with the remains of a decayed tooth, the gap caused by the loss of all one has must be harder still to realise at first. However they are young and no life was lost and as the man is not an artist there is yet hope of prosperity in store for them.

---

[37] The Rossetti family, with the exception of Gabriel, was living at 45 Upper Albany Street, Regent's Park (later renumbered 166 Albany Street).
[38] The servant who was dismissed a few days later for insolence.

And now we are at the *Pea hen* and Emma is just gone to bed and I am writing God knows to what purpose (but vanity) and we have spent 6 shillings getting here which is sheer madness in the present state of our prospects – besides one bob wasted on a description of the Abey, certainly the sillyest little book that fool ever penned – the most complete do that ever I was subjected to – fifty pages of the most complete vacuity that ever small-country-town-bred numscull without a shade of learning, ingenuity or imagination could possibly have put into circulation. And now to bed – not even one line of the Battles of St Albans[39] the excrement.

23rd we arose at 20 minutes past 7 and bullied the chamber maid for not waking us, at least I did. Breakfasted & off to the Abbey. Bill at the Pea-hen most gloriously small by the way, we expected at least 16 shillings, it was only 9; Bed /1.6, no wax lights, what meekness on the part of this woman of the Peahen; a woman keeps it.[40] We paid /1 for two tickets to the abby, not to go up the Tower which would have been 2 bob. Emma's tender state made it a matter of prudence more than economy not to go & well we did not pay the other shilling for! mark the sequel. We two, nothing buckram about us as yet, went & found ourselves opposed by one abby door which would not open – then one rectors maid servant came towards us two & said that it did not open till 10 – & moreover that service began at half past & that if we wished to see the place she had better go for the verger. Well we two being there quite in the dark as to what all this meant naturally concluded that the rector, his maid, the verger & the whole conclave were of a plot to rob us, so we declined the offer saying it was scandalous conduct & that we would go to the verger. So having got there a stout woman told us plainly no verger should open the door before 10 o'clock. So seeing there was no remedy we wandered forth to spend the time somehow and at 10 we got in, bullied the verger who confessed they had been shown up but a short while before in the papers. I of course promised a most venomus letter to the "times" but somehow looking over the these workings up & scrapings down of so many centuries, our little tif about half an hour ago was forgotten & before we saw half the wonders of the place we were excellent friends. However venerable masonry many hundred years old may look, be it free stone or rubble, plaster or roman tile, some how the stones of these are like the stones of now, only a little time-eaten, but there was a thigh bone & scul belonging to the Good Duke

[39] In the first of the two battles of the Wars of the Roses, the Lancastrians were defeated and Henry VI was taken prisoner by the Yorkists. In the second battle the Lancastrians were successful and the King set free.
[40] Situated in the High Street, the "Peahen", a posting house and coach office, was kept by Mrs Mary Marks.

Humphrey[41] that seemed to me more speaking in its age than all the rest. It might have been any one else for all we could tell, but we toke it (on trus) and there good heavens, is a part of the man we read of in history who was too good for this country 400 years ago, who was therefor got rid of & the Duchess made to walk in her shift – a great grandson of Edward III, brother to Henry V, Protector of England & an honest man, and it is not a dream for this is the thigh bone – this is more interresting than stones & mortar after all. How I could have wished for a little more of the same, but no – next in interrest were puritanical mutilations[42] – comical in their concistency – but lifelike. I had been here with Mark Anthony some years ago so it was not new. Bus to Hatfield, ruins still smoldering but cold in interrest already; rail to Barnet, walk home, Lazy; sad, nervous, stupid state again, hopes gone, unspeakably flown, onions for supper.

[Book 2 of the Diary ends here and is continued in Book 3]

26th I hope I shall keep this one more regularly up than hitherto. Having now recommenced, must in earnest one would think after such a pause. Should every one keep a record of his daily acts & sentiments, the history of the world would be made out in a way that no historian could distort however illiberal or enthusiastic in his nature. However stupid a man might be could he be persuaded to set down what he thought or did, something would accrue from it. To judge by myself however many would have day after day to record blank. I have had a trouble to remember if it is one or two days that I have omitted to fill in for want of a book & now I know it to be two. I can remember yesterday but not the one before. I know them both to have been idle ones. A loathing of my vocation has seized me. I must rest. Work, work, work for ever muddles a mans brain and mine at times is none of the clearest. What have I done today – worked in the garden & weeded the back yard. Yesterday I turned a servant out of doors and we walked far enquiring for another. The day before I forget, I only know I did not work. About this girl turned out of doors let me record the fact and if wrong confess if not attone. We took her from Barnet Union,[43] she was hard working and resonably good in her behaviour. But she seemed to be cursed with the devils own temper which made her incontrolobly surly at times – also at times insufferably insolent. Once

---

[41] At the beginning of the fifteenth century the Abbey came under the patronage of Humphrey, Duke of Gloucester (1391-1447), son of Henry IV, remembered more for his liberal support of scholars, than for his political ineptitude. His remains are buried in a vault beneath the chantry chapel.

[42] Brown is probably referring to the figures on St Alban's shrine which at the Reformation were partly destroyed.

[43] The workhouse organization which concerned itself with the parochial able-bodied poor. The parish of Finchley came under the Barnet authority.

before I had given her warning to leave – but let her remain. Since this I had again told her to look out for a place because she insisted most impudently that *8 weeks* made *two months*. This time however I told her I would not force her to leave till she had a place. Yesterday we were going into London and she was to take Katty for a walk while we were absent. On account of the Cholera now every where[44] I cautioned her *not* to take the child into any house. She answered "I wont take the child out at all." She stuck to this, I to the fact that servants must do what they are told or leave, she was obstinate, I told her she should leave the house that minute. She said she would not leave till the next morning, I told her the police should be called to take her out. The result was that before one she was gone. I gave her wages up to the day and one month clear. So she went off with /12.6, her wages were £5 a year every thing found her. If this is poor wages for a girl – I myself am very poor & cannot help it. She had a good place in all except wages but wanted sence to keep it. Where she is gone I know not. And now for my share, was I right? Custom says yes – Conssience says no – Discretion says what would it had come at last had you put up with such rebellion in one instance, Charity says better put up with it a dozen times than turn a poor girl out because she is a fool by nature – with /12.6 in her pocket. I feel like a scoundrel. Yet it was her own fault – I was not even cross with her to draw forth her insolence. I dont know what to think of it, I must endeavour to forbear passion in future & all haste – had I not been angered I might have found some way to adjust matters without proceeding to Extremities. I have just killed a wasp.

30th Worked to day 5½ hours at the "Windermere", and 2½ at Beauty this even from 9 to ½ past 11. Yesterday for one hour in the eveng at beauty (1 hour). Sunday I did not work nor go to church, but laid the stair-carpet down (8 hours) (heat intense). After about 5 P.M. had a shower bath & dressed & so spent the afternoon & eve loving Emma, the poor dear tired with no servant & char-woman not to be had in the neighburhood – getting very stout in the waist also now.[45] Monday 28th I went into London early walking to Hampstead. Called on old *White* a serious & too long deferred visit. He says he'll come & buy the "Lady of saturday Night" Cartoon for £20. This will save our bacon for a little time longer, I do begin to think that the run of ill luck is out for this time & that good will continue to be the order. Saw there Etty's "Robinson Crusoe",[46] one of his 4 or 5 really fine works. Saw a little picture of Millais quite recent – a waterfall with a little lady & gent & a child in the back ground.[47] The figurs very

[44] The severe cholera epidemic resulted in the loss of about nine thousand lives.
[45] Emma was about four months pregnant.
[46] *The Shipwrecked Mariner*, 1831.
[47] *The Kingfisher's Haunt* (destroyed in the Second World War).

pretty. The foliage & foreground icy cold & raw in color, the greens unripe enough to cause indigestion. Thence the B. Mus about french Bible – thence to see Cave Thomas. He showed me a study of a Rushian Merchant[48] that quite astonished me, a most noble painting equal to any thing modern or ancient, Thomas will paint great works yet I am now convinced. Afterwards dined at Tom's Coffee House,[49] then Blackfriars, Rossetti out, so I came home very tired & exhausted & did not work yesterday in consequence but lay the greater part of the day on the sofa in a state of fish out of water. The new servant came Monday promisses well, splendid black eyes & brows & colour to paint. To day I been industrious & hope to remain so for a time. Heat still intense.

1st September yesterday, up at 7 shower bath & out by ¼ to 8 to examine the river Brent at Hendon, a mere brooklet running in most dainty sinuosity under overshadowing oaks and all manner of leafgrass. Many beauties & hard to chuse amongst for I had determined to make a little picture of it. However nature that at first sight appears so lovely is on consideration almost always incomplete, moreover there is no painting intertangled foliage without lossing half its beauties. If imitated exactly it can only be done as seen from one eye & quite flat & confused therefore. Came back for breakfast, missed it & set to work on the female head of the emigrant picture from Emma, a complete pourtrait – after six did nothing more except prepare for this morning being very tired & sleepy (6 hours).

[2nd] This morning up at ½ past 7 shower bath & out by ½ past 9 to the river Brent; after trouble selected the place & began work[50] till ½ past 1 – home to dinner slept after, strangely lazy now after dinner. Woke up and determined on walking to find an other subject – wandered far could not please my taste, home by ½ past 6, eveng pallet & "Beauty" (4 hours).

5th On Saturday up at 8 shower bath. At the Brent by ½ past 9 till ½ past one. Rossetti came in the middle of the most broiling sun, I knew he must have come to get something. He wanted costumes to paint a water coulor of the "Passover", this instead of setting to work on the picture for which he has been commissioned by McCrack since 12 months. His aunt has moreover

[48] The "French Bible" is presumably an illuminated MS. Thomas' studio was a backroom on the ground floor of 72 Newman Street, in what had been a Dancing Academy in 1851 when, for a short period, Rossetti had occupied a studio immediately above it. In the depth of winter, and before the outbreak of the war in the Crimea, Thomas had undertaken a hazardous journey to St Petersburg with a large sum of money in gold on behalf of a mercantile firm. This would have given him the idea for his painting *The Russian Dealer of the Gostvinordor* on which he was now engaged.
[49] Cowper's Court, Cornhill.
[50] *The Brent at Hendon* (Tate, Plate 15).

14. *Two Studies of Girl's Head*, City Art Gallery, Manchester

15. *The Brent at Hendon*, Tate Gallery, London

given him £30 so that it is not for want of money.[51] However whatever he does it is sure to be beautiful but the rage for strangeness disfigures his ideas. After dinner He & I & Emma walked into Hampstead & took bus for London. He went to his studio — I with Emma to buy her two dresses the duck. Afterwards grumbled at her for inducing me thus to spend in all £1 when we had only £8 left & Whites promiss of £20 for "Saturday Night" (4 hours). On Sunday I began work about 11½ scraped out the Head of the man in the Emigrant picture because it had cracked all over. This is the first time a head has ever served me so. 3 days work gone smash because of the cursed zink white I laid over the ground. The female head has healed. Drew in the man again & worked at the expression of the female till ½ past 6. In the evening at beauty (8 hours). Monday up late shower bath — to work at Brent by 10 till ½ past one — Idimum & sleepy. About 3 out to a field to laying the outline of a small landscape,[52] found it of surpassing lovelyness, Corn shocks in long perspective, farm, hayricks, & steeple seen between them, foreground of turnips, blue sky & afternoon sun. By the time I had drawn in the outline they had carted half my wheat, by to day all I had drawn in was gone. At night "Beauty" till 11 (7 hours). This morning up late the fleas this weather will not let me sleep I pass wretched night trying to catch them — my skin is so nervous & thin that a flea is torture to me. To work by ¼ to Eleven having had to go to the surgeons for Ruth[53] who has the cholera. Left the Brent at half past, after dinner contrived an apparatus for slinging my work round my neck while at painting. Set off with it, began a little langdscape in a hurry & fluster attempting to paint corn sheaves & cart while they were going, I fear it will not repay the trouble for I cannot paint in a hurry. Lazy to night (6 hours).

10th Sunday Wednesday girl ill — worked at the Brent before dinner about 2½ hours — after at the landscape eveng beauty (6 hours).

Thursday Morning spent in going to the Doctors about the girl — & getting a char woman for Emma. Afternoon at the Landscape (3 hours).

Friday Morning Brent — afternoon sky of Landscape at home (8 hours).

Saturday Idem. Evening Emma had a sick fit gave her medicine & sat up to watch her. At Beauty till ½ past 7 a.m. (3 hours).

Sunday Got up to day at ¼ to nine, Emma slept well the child, servant & self well. Cholera all round. Worked all day at stretching the charcoal of

---

[51] *The Passover in the Holy Family*, 1856 (Tate), was bought by John Ruskin but remained unfinished. MacCracken's Commission was for *Found* (Wilmington). Rossetti's benefactor was his aunt Charlotte Polidori.
[52] *Carrying Corn* (Tate, Plate 16).
[53] Nicknamed "Ruth the Ruthless" by Rossetti, she had taken the place of the insolent Sarah.

Beauty, twice missed it, at last all right. About 4 P.M. set some accessories & drew them in this evening, at it for about 2 hours, all well yet (5 hours). On last friday some frames[54] came home & I passed the eveng in great glee putting in the pictures, all old rubbishy things saved to sell to dealers or others. The study for Waiting finished into a picture. The study of a little girls head positioned in two views at Southend in 46, on a table napkin — now lined & retouched. The drawing for the "Emigrants" & the Charcoal of beauty.

12th yesterday up at 9 no bath, feeling queer inside but to work at the Brent by 11 a.m. Emma & the child brought me my dinner there at 2 — in a little basket. Hot Hashed mutton & potatoes in a basin, cold rice pudding & a little bottle of rum & water, beer being bad for cholera. Very delightful & very great appetite. Set to work again by ½ past 2 till ½ past 6. In the eveng tired & lazy (7 hours). This morning up at 8 shower bath, to the Brent by ½ past ten worked till ¼ to 2. After dinner from 3 till 6 at the corn field picture. This eveng worked at the kitten in Beauty for which Emma & I went out after dark & stole one yesterday. White commeth not, only £5 in the monney box, this is all till the quarters rent of the wharf comes in £26 — not for 5 or 6 weeks yet, whats to be done I scarce know. I ought to go & take Lucy a pounds worth of things & can't — I ought to buy shoes & can't — We ought to send monney to Emma's Mother — Tomorrow Emma means to send her a parcel of things by the Carrier with five bob as a breather — this is all can be done just at present (7½ hours).

14th yesterday up at 8 no shower bath, rain, over to Hendon to order the things of the grocer for Emma's mother, got them here & sent off by carrier by 11 a.m. Rain cleared off, to the Brent from half past 11 till ½ past 2. After dinner to the corn field, but it came on to rain so I had to return. Worked at Beauty and again in the eveng, all well — letter to say Lucy well thank God (7 hours). This morning up at ½ past 8 no bath, think my head felt oppressed in consequence — rain all day so worked at the confounded charcoal of "Beauty" which seems as though it never could get done. No doubt people would accuse me of folly for wasting so much time over it — but work to the best of one's power is never waste. I am true to my intention of finishing every thing I have begun to the best of my power — and moreover whatever an artist works at with pleasure to himself must be good if he is worth any thing. It is near done, thank goodness, & the figure & face of "Beauty" pleases me, though I shall not paint the picture, the Idea is now safe & intelligible. I intend it for what the story is, a jumble of Louis XV and Orientalism. The glories of eastern luxurience mix't with household

---

[54] It is not known at what date Brown started to employ Green of Charles Street to make frames from his own designs, but probably by 1853 at which date Green was packing and despatching Brown's work (*Letters*, pp.124, 126).

common appurtenances to tickel the fancy at both ends, nothing serious yet nothing without purpose. Works of this kind should be intentionally full of anacronism. To endeavour after unity is to injure the subject & not illustrate it (10½ hours).

15th Up frightfully late after breakfasting in bed. Shower bath, at the Brent by 11½ worked till 2½ pretty successfully. Home to dinner, after too gloomy to work satisfactorily at the corn field so back to the Brent from 4½ till ¼ to 6, too dark to do any good consequently I did harm to the work. Emma irritable & head bad after tea & gone to bed. Set to work at "Beauty" from 8 till 11. Scraped out puss & put in one with a more satisfactory miow; finished it all over but the general effect is spotty so must work over it yet (7½ hours).

17th Sunday Up at ½ past 8 Shower Bath Breakfast found the charcoal of "Beauty" quite spoiled through my having wet it to fix it, not understanding the steaming process. It is all cockled – tomorrow I must iron it out & make hot cockles of it if nothing better. To Church with Emma who turning faint had to bring her out after the Litterny. After dinner we went as far as Millhill with the maid & child and at dusk had tea in some gardens there & so home, not an aristocratic proceeding but pleasant & healthful. The scenery is very beautiful & paintable about this part & I suppose the finest round London. One bit in particular pleased us, it was looking down from a hill in a deep hollow surrounded on all sides by beautiful trees lay part of a road already small by the perspective; through the foliage at the top in the extreme distance was Hendon church with large foreground figures on the hill in front. It would have made a most admirable picture for perspective depth, everything alas! can not be painted however. Yesterday I worked at the "Brent" from 10 till 1½ & from 3½ till 6, beginning to make some show, must up early to it tomorrow. In the eveng I worked at Beauty, finished it & then spoiled it again through wetting it at the back, but a work of art is never spoiled it can be done again (8 hours).

18th Monday up at ½ past 8 to work at the Brent by 10. Emma brought me my dinner, so I staid at it till 6 P.M. In the Eveng ironed out "Beauty" but with no good effect, so had paste made & stretching a clean sheet of paper pasted it down (8 hours).

Thursday 19th Rain so had out the picture of "The last of England" & scraped at the head of the female, afterwards worked at it 2 hours without model & four hours with – using zink white. Afterwards retouched "Beauty" which with constant wetting was much blurred – in the eveng fixed it in frame, lettered it, & pasted loosse drawing in my big book (7½ hours).

20th Wedy Lazy & disgracefully inclined. Up with difficulty to go down &

breakfast with Emma who was up in spite of condition. Did not wash till after so got to the "Brent" late at 11 – worked till one when it was raining pretty freely – I endeavoured to work through it but the big drops piercing the foliage over head I had to give over, spent 20 minutes under a thicket of leafage – tried to begin again when the rain was a little cleared off, but found the weight of water quite displaced the different branches from their normal possition making confusion, so came home to dinner, felt my head very oppressed while there & extremely & unusually nervous before setting to work, is this from smoking again? After dinner worked at drawing in the outline of the male head in "the Last of England" – then reflected on it till near five, settled that I would paint the woman in Emma's shepherd plaid shawl instead of the large blue & green plaid as in the sketch. This is a serious affair settled which has caused me much perplexity. After this I worked till tea time at scraping away the ground of Zink white which I had laid myself for the picture at Hampstead. I found that the head of the man had cracked all over since I painted it, so had to scrape it out – his coat also has crack in it, a bad thing in a coat in particular, so I will have no more of this zink confound it. There is nothing like *tin* for a foundation to go upon, in this system will I work henceforth. After tea I worked at altering the little laydy reading a letter in the "Brent" which had rubbed in from Emma the other day, I have made it more sentimental. After this I cleaned my pallet & brushes & am now writing this. I must now leave off to begin the lettering of the "Cartoon" & painted scetch of "the Last of England" – only did the scetch 11 p.m. (6½ hours).

21st up at ¼ to 8 bath, to the Brent by ½ past 9, worked well till ½ past 1, begins to look bravely & beautiful color but still requires all my energy & attention to master the difficulties attending a style of work I have not been bred to. Weathr very cold, north wind which it is to be hoped will take off the Cholera. After dinner to the corn field for about 3 hours – interrupted by a shower & somehow did very little – altogether these little landscapes take up too much time to be proffitable. This even wasted 2 hours with Emma trying to make out an error of sixpence in our accoumpts in which I succeeded at last. I meant to have done so much to night & so have done nothing. I cannot help it but somehow whatever I am about I must go through with to extremity. This if the work happens to be of importance is a most happy quality, but on the other hand it is a most unprofitable mania when the occasion that calls it forth is trivial as in the present case, such as an error of sixpence, weeding a piece of garden or such like. The only thing I can never bring myself to do with ease is writing. This has always I know not wherefor appeared to me as base & mechanical and in some way I am sure to make it disgraceful, either I spell it wrong, & this I cant help & never could manage, or else I get a bad pen & so blotch &

scribble it that it is not readable, or else I get sleepy & fill it up with itterations or faults of prosody which must make me appear like a most illiterate ass which however I am not. O! for Woolners precision rare in a man of art (6½ hours).

22nd Up at 8 Shower bath, at the "Brent" by 10 worked till 2, after dinner at the corn field − about 2 hours. In the evening I lettered the drawing of the last of England and hung the Beauty (6½ hours).

23rd Saturday to the Brent by ½ past 10 (shower bath) worked ¼ to 2, scraped at the zink ground of "Last of England" before & after dinner. To the corn field from 3 to 6. In the eveng newspaper and scraped at the zink from 9 till ½ past 12 (6 hours).

24th Sunday up at 9 bath & to Church by *myself*. After church stayed at home with Emma, worked some 2 hours at dressing up the lay figure for the man in "the Last of England". In the eveng wrote a letter, cast up accounts, wrote in this book the two entries above. Afterwards worked at the "Ladye of Saturday Night" Cartoon which White has promised to buy but has not yet performed, two pounds and the pawn shop is all that now remains us. No debts however except about £14 in all to my tailor my lawyer & my frame maker whose account is not sent in so I do not owe above £8 − & have one hundred a year still. This week I have worked steadily on neither sunday but 42 hours in the week which is 7 hours per diem *pure work* for I only put down the time I actually work at art, not the time lost in preparations. I am in reallity employed at *business* all my time from the moment I get up till I go to bed − but I am dreamy & slow in my movements (1 hour).

25th Monday bath − to the Brent by ½ past 10 till 2, home to lunch & at the field from 3 to ½ past 5, home to dinner at 6, at work on Whites Cartoon from 8 till 11. This is fair working (9 hours).

26th Tuesday up at 8 bath to the Brent by 10 worked till 1 − finished the landscape part as much as I can do to it from nature − went to see the river as far as the Decoy farm,[55] found none of it so beatiful as I had painted − home to lunch after a splendid walk in a broiling sun. Afternoon to the corn field − dinner at 6, eveg no art work, tired, odd jobs (5½ hours).

27th Wednesday Up late − worked at filling up the holes made over the parlour window from which I had knocked away three hideous grinning heads that formed part of the house. After twelve worked at the cartoon about 2 hours then at the cornfield − eveng cartoon, no good (6½ hours).

---

[55] Situated at what is now the junction of the Edgware and North Circular Roads, it was occupied by John Bland, the farm bailiff.

29th [28th] Up late shower bath & off to the Chalk farm station on foot, thence to Gravesend by Stepney. Found in the carriage an old acquaintance a certain Miss or Mrs Ashley,[56] who used to sit to me, did not know her at first nor wish to appear to know her. These sort of people recognise one in any company and are bores. She looked very glum, I was sorry afterwards I was not more civil to her. An awful looking snob in the same carriage went off with her arm in arm & took a boat to some ship – coming back with Lucy in the steamboat to Tilbury my snob sidles up to me, with a considerable smirk on his face he wishes to know who the Lady is, having found her "very agreeable sort of person". O ho said I, was you not with her then, no he merely met her in the carriage & saw her speak to me. I did not tell him how she had been long "mrs Ash*ley*" imaginary wife of Mr Ash*ton* & the mother of two boys sitting to artists & God wot. I said I merely knew her casually long ago for a certain Mrs Ashley. Miss Ashley said my snob, very possible said I, it was one or the other. What is she doing looking so smart?

29th up at 8 shower bath worked at the cartoon from 10 till ½ past 12 then out to Hendon with my two daughters to buy them shoes. In the shop if I am not much mistaken was Mrs Coventry Patmore[57] – but she did not recognise me nor I her. Terribly warm could do nothing after I came back, headacky & feeble – ought have been to the field. This evening after dinner no work stupid and lazy – unwell & disgusted – a letter from Emma's Mother pressing very much to see her – in the mean time funds reduced to £1.9.6 (2½ hours).

30th Saturday Up late Shower bath Placed the Lay figure in the back yard & after reading the newspaper worked at the *resumed* coat of the Emigrant from the one I had made on purpose two winters ago at Hampstead & have [?never] worn since then it being horrid vulgar & worked at it from 12 to 2½. Lunch & to the field from 3 to 5½. After tea the cartoon for about 2½ hours, Emma gone to see her mother.[58] Game with the children & cat after tea (7½ hours).

1st October sunday Up at 9, Katty slept with me in the absence of her mother. I meant to have worked at the coat in the morning when the sun is off the backyard & then to have taken Lucy to Church in the afternoon, but heaven put a bar to the Godless intent in the shape of a thick mist with drizle so that we went in the morning. It was Collection morning & I having

---

[56] See p.27, n.14.
[57] Wife of the poet. They were living at Highgate Rise, Kentish Town.
[58] Catherine, widow of Thomas Hill, bricklayer. Now aged about sixty-two, she had opposed her daughter's marriage and had become a financial burden to Brown.

nothing but 3 half crowns, my last, asked Lucy what money she had – which turned out to be an other so no alternative obtaining I gave one of my half crowns – I did this not in imitation of Haydon,[59] but because I did not like to pass the plate at the door so now my enemies will rejoice in the fact. But yet in truth was I pleased at being so forced to give because if I had not given it would have been on principle because I have no right to give when I have deficiency instead of superfluity to take from, but indeed giving is a pleasure & it was for the poor Cholera parentless brats – now my enemies are chop-fallen & say pish! & stuff & humbug. So after this we took Katty a walk in the fields & Katty kept thinking the horses would eat her & teasing after *black-bellies* & biting the acorns I gave her & finally asking to be carried which not answering she ended by running away but we caught her. Dinner at ½ past 4. Reading paper, tea, game with cat & children again. Cartoon after all till Emma came back by ½ past 11 per bus (3 hours).

2nd up at ¼ to 9 shower bath, to work at the coat of the emigrant from 11 till 2, at the corn field from 3 till 5½, at the cartoon in the Eveg. Too much time over little works (8 hours).

3rd Up at ½ past 9 disgraceful – Shower bath – to work from 12 till 2 at the sleeve of Emigrants coat taking the lay figure out into the back yard – a little inclination to rain kept me hesitating before I began & so made me later. Lunch & to work at the corn field from ½ past 3 till ¼ to 6, did next to nothing. It would seem that very small trees in the distance are very difficult objects to paint or else I am not suited to this sort of work for I can make nothing of the small screen of trees though I have pottered over sufficient time to have painted a large landskape, the men of english schools would say. This eveng there were no lamp candles in the house & Emma strongly advised lazyness so I cuddled the children & her on the sofa till tea time it being very cold, after tea I made Lucy play her pieces over, altogether stupid (4½ hours). White does not come, he cannot value my works much one would think as he would show more anxiety to purchase, buying at such prices as I offer at. What chance is there for me out of all the Bodies, Institutions, Art unions & accademies & Commissions of this country, Classes sects or cotteries, Nobles dealers patrons rich men or

[59] A reference to a passage in Haydon's *Autobiography*. At St George's Hanover Square on 18 June 1843, Haydon placed a sovereign in the offertory plate. This he did in reparation for having neglected to do so at an earlier time when he had but one sovereign left in his pocket. On this present occasion he was aware of having "expatiated my neglect" and felt "the most refreshing assurance of protection and victory". Brown's astonishment at its being "Collection morning" is puzzling. St Mary's congregation was a wealthy one and a collection was taken up each Sunday morning. That on this occasion it was made for the orphans of the cholera epidemic is irrelevant, what is perplexing is his implicit astonishment at there being a collection at all, for which he was quite unprepared.

friends. Which one takes an interest in me or my works. Is it encouraging to go on? Is it not rather a clear affirmation of my not being required by the British Public and yet — patience is the only motto — we shall see what we shall see. I only wish to be allowed to go on to be permitted to work — Ill sensation — by the next generation. Emma brought me home 8/6 of her money, unspent funds at present 10 shillings.

4th Shower bath, to work at the sleeve from 10 till 2, finished it, at the corn field from 3 to 5½ worked over the screen of trees again & began the turnips at length. Eveng no work (6 hours).

5th Took Lucy back to school calling on the Rossettis in the way. They well, no cholera in Camden Town, Gabriel supposed to be at work at Blackfriars & William returned from Cornwall & Ostend.[60] Heard from Christina the first news of the fall of Sebastopol — What times we live in, it would seem that the Allied armies were quite determined to show the irrisistable supremacy of the Western nations this time, how fearfully humiliated must feel the Emperor of Rushia what a merited lesson. Perhaps most of all this is owing to the genius of one man — Omer Pasha.[61] Forty years ago the Rushian armies of Serfs used to fight drawn battles with the conquering legions of the 1st Napoleon — Twenty five years ago the Turks were hopelessly their prey and could not make a stand against them.[62] One man furnished only with a lively & keen perception of the real state of things, perplexes & retards the Pedantic Rushian Generals till he makes their troops doubt their own prowes, they who come to conquer & submerge — while his own wild ruffians at length believe themselves invincible wherever he will allow them to fight. He does all this in spite of the brutish obtuseness of his own generals, who where there is a chance left them of blundering do it. The Pashas being as incompitent as the wild troops are naturally brave. Then follows the ever memorable defence of Silistria,[63] where some eight thousand Turks headed by a brave man, & assisted by two young Englishmen, left to themselves for six weeks, while upwards of

[60] Accompanied by B.H. Paul, a chemist (later the author of a manual on *Industrial Chemistry* based on a translation from the French), W.M. Rossetti had been on a walking holiday in Cornwall and Devon. He returned to London in the middle of September and spent another fortnight in Belgium.
[61] Commander of the Turkish forces in the Crimean War.
[62] The Russo-Turkish War of 1827-9.
[63] At the beginning of May the Turkish fortress of Silistria on the Danube had undergone a fortnight's bombardment by the Russians. The garrison's commander, the brave and energetic Mussà Pasha, had been killed and the remaining officers were mainly ignorant and negligent. The Turks had fought gallantly but their spirit was beginning to weaken when two young British officers, in the service of the Honourable East India Company, Captain Butler and Lieutenant Nasmyth on their way home from India, stopped at Silistria and threw themselves into the defence of the fort. Gaining the confidence of the Turks, though unable to speak their language, they advised and directed operations with skill and courage, and forbade any suggestion of surrender.

one hundred and fifty thousand English French & Turkish soldiers are *doing nothing*, not 50 miles distant, and by defeating the efforts of forty thousand Rushians to take the place by storm or bribery, much to the inexpectancy of all parties it is wispered (oh dark & hideous suspicion) & cause the rushians crestfallen to abandon Turkey. For, say they, if a Turkish rabble can serve us thus what were we pitted against French & English – again say French & English soldiers if Turks can handle them thus what must be expected of us – and so the huge reputation shrinks up like the decline of an accademician or any other Titled, decorated, and legallized humbug and nothing remains but bitterness & the necessity through long habit of speaking pomposly. To what pitch is England destined to soar in the History of the world. Externally a far shining glory to all the Earth and an example, internally a prey to snobbishness and the worship of gold & tinsel – a place chiefly for sneaks and lacqueys, and any who can fawn or clutch, or dress clean at church, & connive. The deepest pondering alas brings me back to old & nothing original conclusions that the Aristocracy of this Country presses with Torpedo influence on all classes of men and works, commerce allone is free from their intermeddling and thoroughly successful. In all else be it war, literature, art, or science we are great if great, in *spite* of them – and the depressing influence of established authority taking the precedence of merit & justice. And yet every one would avert revolutions as still worse. Abroad somehow things are managed with more of the feeling of modern improvement & commonsence justice; even, amid the crash of breaking up governments & violations of personal liberties & rights. Here the Government with our boasted nobility the greatest in the world takes the lead in all that is dullest & stupidest, and the genius of the nation with utmost effort can allone force the improvements of art & the dictates of commonsence on it long long after date, after patience is exhausted & frequently not before a press feeling has again sprung up, and yet such is the vital energy of the nation & the stubborn irristable patience of Englishmen that improvements keep pace almost with other nations in all except such branches of art as are especially government reared, such as architecture, sculture, music & High art. Alas for the latter. Yet has the nation forced even some of that on it, witness Dyce. [64] Our troops are decidedly victorious in spite of the utmost obtuseness of feeling at the Horse Gards with respect both to improvements & the causes of promotion. It would seem as if it were impossible to set an Englishman to a duty that he does not fulfil with ability of some degree – but were the Napoleonic spirit of promoting and evoking merit the rule with us in lieu of *family interrests* what heighth should we attain to

---

[64] William Dyce (1806-64), variously gifted as an artist and administrator of the Government Schools of Design, came early under the influence of the Nazarenes in Rome. In sympathy with the P.R.B., he gained Ruskin's support for them in 1850.

in the scale of glory & the worlds wonder, but the world is a mere mouse-trap – a trap baited to catch poor greedy selfish stupid man, who thinks himself so precious clever while damming his soul to feed his guts. A most cunningly devised trap forsooth, where the utmost circumspection & wisdom, aided by the purest intentions shall hardly serve to keep a mans heels free. Alas the poor selfish man is baited on all sides – Gluttony, leachirry, glory were the least chances of destruction, where a wretch may serve two ends the safety of a nation & his own damnation or thinks still more cunningly to save his selfish soul by selfish religion and giving up of man for God & thinking to win Gods notice & refuge by forced marches, leaving all others behind – alas! man shall forget himself in the community of being. Woe to the temerity that would call down the searching eye on his individuality. Therefor is the Eternal shrouded in impenetrable mistery otherwise who but themselves would be first to seek him. Whoever feels a tenderness for a fellow being worships God in the act, nay a kind of feeling for a dog or a cat shall not pass unnoticed, but woe to the selfseeker & him who despises the poor

> "Whose belly with thy treasure hid
> Thou fillest: they children have
> In plenty; of their goods the rest
> They to their children leave.
>
> But as for me, I thine own face
> In richousness will see
> And with thy likeness when I wake
> I satisfied shall bee."[65]

6th Up late shower bath off to the field, rain, wasted abut an hour and a half under an umbrella at the sweeds – rain drove me off came home & dined at ½ past 3, prepared all our plate (6 teaspoons), all the Jewelry, my watch, oppera glas & bronzes to take into London to the Pawnbroker, stayed unconsciously too long at dinner. After dinner it rained so furiously that I hesitated & finally remitted the expedition so I have the pleasant task for the morning. Funds reduced to 3 shillings & two more that Lucy has left behind (2 hours).

7th Walked into London. Raised £11. Bought Lucy some things & self a Pr shoes. Called on Thomas. Heard from him some curious details of the Cholera which raged furiously round his two streets but did not molest

---

[65] A metrical version of Psalm XVII, vv.13, 14, as used by the Church of Scotland, published in 1850 (for "richousness", v.14, read "righteousness").

them.[66] Bodies taken from Middlesex Hospitals in *vans*. In the pest-stricken street groops of women & children frantic for their relations taken off. Police & others with stretchers running about. Undertakers as common as other people in the streets, running about with coffin like lamplighters. Herses with coffins *outside* as well as in. People following in cabs – one funeral consisted of a Cab with coffin a'top & people inside. Thomas & family all well, one brother frightened into much loosiness in the bowels! Heard of the Taking of Sebastopol being all a lie so my flaming up to Epic pitch was unnecessary & unwaranted "Sic transit gloria etc". However let me before it be too late to Prophesy declare it my conviction that the allies acted imbeciles to allow the Austrians to take the princi-pallities without first having *fought* the Rushians – so – next our govern-ment acted like imbeciles to Imagine the Emperor of Russia would with-draw his troops without force – & so waste precious time. Next the govern-ment has acted with pusilanimity in not requiring more of Dundas in the Black sea. Next it is disgraceful to the nation that while all the powerful places of the baltic & Black sea have been hithertoo unmolested, some unfortunate Laplandes in the White sea should be murdered in their houses & ruined to no earthly purpose under the pretext of war. Surely, surely, this nation is powerful enought to enable them to do grace to the poor inhabitants of the Frozen Ocean. What a pity Captain Lyons cannot be exchanged with Admiral Dundas.[67] In the regions were nature shows itself so cruel man should (fear of the Almighty would suggest) be awed into charity – & so the capital of Lapland combining antiquity of most strange & foriegn character with mysterious remoteness almost unearthly, is reduced to a heap of ashes by a set of semy-barbarous sailors – very likely that neither Captain Lyons nor any of his crew are elevated in Literary knowledge, feeling for art, morals, or the worlds best interrests much above the rank of shopkeepers or any other mechanically civilized savages. The men whatever or wherever set to do, will do their work, this certain, but they are uneaqually officerd – & the want of vigour & unanimity & vigour at home is very sadly apparant. Lord John[68] would perhaps sniff &

[66] William Cave Thomas does not appear in the London directories during these years, but until 1856 his R.A. exhibits are catalogued in *Graves* under his studio address, 72 Newman Street. However, as early as 1850 "Cafe Thomas, jun." and "Cafe Thomas Smith", both artists, are listed as residing at 80 Newman Street and are no doubt the family in question, William Cave Thomas having dropped the final "Smith" and Welsh pronunciation probably being responsible for the incorrect spelling.

[67] The Russians had occupied territory around Archangel in the summer and British forces, failing to drive the enemy from their batteries or have the flag of truce recognized, later made a successful assault upon them. They then proceeded to attack Kola, the capital of Russian Lapland, and destroyed the town. Admiral Dundas was in command of the British Fleet in the Crimea. He was thought to be incompetent and was succeeded later in the year by his second in command, Captain (later Admiral Lord) Lyons.

[68] Lord John Russell (1792-1878), Whig statesman and Prime Minister, had held many influential Governments posts and had been mainly instrumental in passing the Reform Bill of 1832. At this time he was President of the Council.

snort could he read this — & what in sooth *can* I know about the matter yet sure it is that men of genius & vigour have been in politics & it wants no ghost to tell us Austria is false at Heart & Rushia in want of a vigorous licking. Called on Dante Rossetti saw Miss Siddall[69] looking thinner & more deathlike & more beautiful & more ragged than ever, a real artist, a woman without parralel for many a long year. Gabriel as usual diffuse & inconsequent in his work. Drawing wonderful & lovely "Guggums" one after an other each one a fresh charm each one stamped with immortality, and his picture never advancing.[70] However he is at the wall & I am to get him a White Calf & a cart to paint here, would he but study the *golden one* a little more. Poor Gabriello — Came home after walking some twenty miles — nothing else but rest.

8th Sunday all day Idle no work nor religion scarce anything but sleep like a hog, a little "Montaigne" a little "Accounts", this writing & nothing more.

9th Up at ½ past 7 shower Bath, to the corn field, at the sweeds from 10 till 2 and from ½ past 3 to ½ past 5; eveng from 8 till 12 at the "Saturday Night" (10 hours).

10th up at ½ past 7 Bath, at the sweeds from 10 till ½ past 5 at one spell. This eveng nothing but accounts for 2 or 3 hours. Emma suffering severely from cramp (7 hours). I hope Sebastopol is done, I hope also White will come & be done

> Could I but see him here once more
> That shining Bald pate deep old file
> O how I'd meet him at my door
> And greet him with a pleasant smile.
>
> His blarney soft I'd suck it in
> Nor let his comments stir my bile
> And when my hand once grasped his tin
> How kindly on him would I smile.
>
> And as he strained my hand, full fain
> My daubs were in his cab the while
> And promised soon to come again —
> Oh! how I'd smile him back his smile.

[69] Elizabeth Siddal (1834-62) had sat to Rossetti since 1850. There was an "understanding" if not a definite engagement between them. Her beauty and grace, and the pathos emphasized by her ill-health informed nearly all Rossetti's work until her death. "Gug", "Guggums", were pet-names they conferred on one another. Brown, who used the earlier spelling of her surname (though the final "l" was discarded by others at Rossetti's insistence), was always her champion and admired her imaginative and melancholy drawings.
[70] *Found.*

11th The field again, sun shine when I did not want it, cold & wind when it went. Worked at the trees & improved them, found the turnips too difficult to do anything with of a serious kind. I dont know if it would be possible to paint them well, they change from day to day. An unpleasant profitless day (8 hours).

12th Up latish, bath, saw my turnips were all false in color ruminated over this disgrace & tried to retrieve it; put it in some shape ready to take out this afternoon — set to work at the coat from lay figure in back yard. very cold — worked till 4 at it then to the sweeds. Found the gate nailed up & brambled, had to go round by "detour" but in & set to work but not much good tried to get the main tree more in harmony, a little to the sweeds, men in the field pulling them. At night the cartoon (7 hours).

13th beautiful day meant to walk to Hampstead feeling strangley idle. Emma being better of her cramp came for a walk instead, exquisite day, hedges all gold rubies & emeralds defying all white grounds to yield the like. About 1 to work at the coat from self in a glass, back yard, altered the folds of day before, made it all right, nearly done. Afterwards to the field for the last time thank heaven. I am sick of it, I have now only to work at home at it to put it a little in harmony. A labourer came and looked and stuttering fearfully expressed admiration which ended in his supposing he *could not beg half a pint of beer*, one whom I used to look upon as a respectable man. I gave the degraded wretch twopence & scorn (5 hours).

14th to day one of fearful Idleness self abasement & disgust. Emma got up, I went down to breakfast with her unwashed & only half dressed. I intended working at the coat then walking to Hampstead to purchase flannel for Emma & baby cloaths. I sat down to write to Gabriel a few lines about his calf & like an ass must write in verse — bad rhimes.[71] Spent till one oclock & lunched still unwashed then read the paper still unwashed till ¼ past 4. "Oh that it should be so", then dressed & took Katty out — then we dined then read the paper to Emma, the dear is poorly & nervous. This is the true & particular history of a day a pitious thing to tell of.

15th Sunday worked at the coat out in the yard then indoors driven in by fog, then fine & out again, five hours in all. Evening worked at "Saturday night" (6 hours).

16th a long walk over the fields from "Five Bells", by the Spaniard's[72] to Hampstead, bought flannel for baby cloathes paid bills, then to Hendon

[71] In his reply (18 Oct.) Rossetti complained to Brown that his "inopportune poetic furor has rather foggified your note" (*Letters*, p.228).
[72] The "Five Bells" (still in existence) at East End, a large village a mile east of Finchley, was a popular tavern and a resort of pugilists. The "Spaniards Inn" stands to the north of Hampstead Heath, on the road to Highgate.

for do. Home & to work by 3 at placing draperies on lay figure & I alter the robe of the Lady of saturday night – drew a little at it in the eveng, reflected seriously on my money position found I should have 4 weeks money & the same credit, after which something must be done if White does not come – decided on going the next day to collect my rent at Greenwich & to look up acquantances in London to see what might turn up (3 hours).

17th walked to Holloway, but to city, rail to Greenwich & back, got my quarters rent. Called on Robert Dickinson, tried to find John Seddon, called on my poor old aunt Brown & on the Rossettis, heard of Woolner's return.[73]

18th a complete blank. Have done nothing all day but sit by the fire with Emma & try to think of ways towards means – ineffectual – could think of any thing else but that, romped with Katty – a pitiable day –

19th to Gravesend to take my daughter her winter things & a trunk. Met Shenton who had forgot his purse – lent him half a crown saw his art union Print of Coeur de Lion – not very good, has taken I think 6 years. Find that he lives at Hendon & is great friends with the old rascally vicar there whom we nicknamed Judas from his iniquitus looks & conduct especially towards cats.[74] Helen Bromleys eldest daughter very sadly ill. Mine quite well. Walked home from the Camden Station, walked altoghether 17 miles, spent £1.12. Read a number of Thackeray's Newcomes[75] – good, females equal to Shakespear, in all worldliness perfect, his artists all asses & his knowledge on that head about at zero.

20th Up late no bath still lazy, dreamy, & incompitent. Worked at the draperies of "Our Ladye" about 2 hours, head aches (2 hours).

21st wrote reluctantly to White – but with some appearance of a reason, the infamous scoundrel Reynolds having published in his miscellany the wood cut that was formerly in the peoples journal of Wickliff[76]. Worked at the draperies about 4 hours. A letter from old Bamford to ask me to make a portrait from the one I formerly painted of his son, since just lost in the Lady Nugent.[77] Some sort of tin tumbling in & the old saying of an ill wind very truly exemplified (5 hours).

---

[73] Woolner had landed in England on his return from Australia on 13 Oct.

[74] H.C. Shenton (1803-66), engraver. The original painting by John Cross was destined for the House of Lords. His friend, the Rev. Theodore Williams, had been incumbent of St Mary's, Hendon since 1812.

[75] Part No. 13 of *The Newcomes* was published on 30 Sep., price one shilling.

[76] *Reynolds's Miscellany* was owned by G.W.M. Reynolds, Cleasby Villa, Hornsey. The woodcut was published on 21 Oct. 1854, p.193, with a commentary on the personages represented (for the *Peoples Journal* woodcut see p.44, n.54).

[77] Having at some earlier date made a portrait of James Bamford's son, Brown was now asked to undertake a copy for the bereaved father. In May, Edward Bamford, aged about

22nd Sunday up at ½ past 8 bath, worked well all day at the Lady of Saturday, finished the drapery & began spoiling the heads.

23rd up at ½ past 9 no bath, to work at the Ladye, found part of the drapery bad, rubbed it out, hightened the seat she sits on mended the heads again, did a great deel but not finished yet. Any one might be surprised to read how I work whole days on an old drawing done many years since and which I have twice worked over since it was rejected from the Royal acady in /47 – and now under promiss of sale to White for £20 – but I cannot help it. When I see a work going out of my hands it is but natural if I see some little defect that I should try to mend it, and what follows is out of my power to direct – if I give one touch to a head I give my self 3 days work & spoil it half a dozen times over, this is invariable – is it so with every one? Alas! – this eveng spent fixing the Ladye in her frame with corks *carefully*, then arranging the packing case to send for poor Ned Bamford – & writing to old do. Now at this work (7 hours).

24th Morning lost with workmen for house, out to London by ½ past 12. Bought things for coming baby & Katty & the servant, bought colors, vehicles etc, called on divers beings, out. Came home in the rain. Spoiled my cloaths so save eighteen pence.

25th Not having the portrait to copy I wasted great part of the day & painted about 3 hours at the Brent. Cleaning of specks of dirt, little nothings (3 hours).

26th Worked at the mans head in the emigrants, then out after Emma to buy things for the comming one. Evening at drawing in the copy of poor Ned (7 hours).

27th At the emigrants, evening Ned (6 hours).

28th All day at the portrait, eveng prepared panels white (7 hours).

29th To dine with the Rossettis to meet Woolner, found him very strangely altered.[78]

30th The portrait (8½ hours).

31st At the portrait again. The evening Rossetti came (7 hours).

twenty-eight, a staff officer in the 25th Madras Light Infantry, was aboard the troopship *Lady Nugent* which was conveying reinforcements from Madras to Rangoon. A hurricane swept the Bay of Bengal for several days during which time the ship foundered. Nothing further was heard of her and by September hope of any survivors was abandoned.

[78] Rossetti found him "rather broader and stouter... but unaltered otherwise" (*Letters*, p.225). Woolner had made some reputation for himself as a sculptor during his two years in Australia and may have shown a self-confidence which Brown found distasteful. That he had become self-assertive there seems to be no question.

1st November Up by 9, sat up talking to Gabriel about poetry till 2 in the morning, he read me an imitation of an old scotch Ballad which is extremely beautiful – with critique of it done by Allingham, who cuts it up very neatly & cleverly with some truth & error.[79] This morning Gabriel was not down to breakfast till 2 hours after me so waiting for him I read the "Angel in the house" by Patmore which is deplorably tame & tiring. Afterwards Master Gabriel came down & we blathered at some length about Allingham, Patmore, Tennisson [Tennyson] etc, I maintaining that Longfellow & Smith,[80] were incomparably the best men except for Tennisson. Gabriel sais he has studied the matter all his life & should know best, I say that he belongs to a party & is prejudiced against all others. We went after his calf & succeeded to a miracle. He is gone to Ruskins for this eveng.[81] Tomorrow he returns. After he has talked as much as his strength will bear he beomes spiteful & crusty denying everything & when chaffed he at length grows bitterly sarcastic in his way, but never quite unpleasant nor ever umbearable.

2nd worked at the portrait about 2½ hours, set work at ½ past 11 till Gabriel returned at ½ past 12. Spent till ½ past 3 getting him off & going to see him begin. Eveng Jaw chiefly (2½ hours).

3rd friday Gabriel went off about 11 to his calf, I had a cold in my head worked at the portrait all day (6 hours).

4th Saturday dreadful cold or influenza – one hours work only (1 hour).

---

[79] Rossetti was staying with the Browns while painting the calf into his picture *Found* (Brown was said to have been one of the various models for the farmer; no study of him exists nor does the diarist mention it but what seems to be a reference occurs in *Letters*, p.229). Rossetti's ballad *Stratton Water* was published in *Poems*, 1870. In October he had written to his intimate friend, William Allingham (1824-89), the Irish poet, that he had finished a ballad "professedly modern-antique... I'll copy it for you... asking your *severest* criticism", and again the next month: "Many thanks for your minute criticism on my ballad" (*Letters*, pp.227, 232).

[80] Allingham had published *Poems* in 1850 and *Day and Night Songs*, 1854. Coventry Patmore (1823-96), poet, had been a contributor to *The Germ*, 1850, and in 1851 had drawn Ruskin's attention to the excellence of the P.R.B. exhibits at the R.A. and had persuaded him to write to the *Times* in their defence (9 and 26 May). *The Angel in the House* was his remarkable poem in celebration of married love. Alexander Smith (1830-67), one of the so-called "Spasmodic" school of poets, had published *Poems* in 1853, and jointly with S.T. Dobell *Sonnets on the Crimean War* in 1855. Rossetti lacked Brown's admiration for the work of Henry W. Longfellow (1807-82), the American poet.

[81] This is Brown's first mention of John Ruskin (1819-1900), art critic, author and social reformer, whom he had disliked intensely ever since the 1852 R.A. exhibition when Ruskin failed to say a word in praise of *Christ Washing Peter's Feet*. The Working Men's College had opened on 31 Oct. and Ruskin took his first class on 2 Nov. It is most likely that on this evening, 1 Nov., he urged Rossetti to do likewise. "He and I had a long confab. about plans for teaching", Rossetti wrote to Allingham in November. "He is most enthusiastic about it, and has so infected me that I think of offering an evening weekly for the same purpose" (*Letters*, p.231).

5th Sunday all day to portrait, finish this eveng. Last night I cleaned my old lamp which I have not used since I left Clapham, to night I enjoy the result of it. This eveng I have altered the flower in the study of little girl in two views to satisfy Gabriel (10 hours).

6th Worked at Emmas head in "the Last of England" (5 hours).

7th do, chiefly from *feeling*. Evening draw in the groups (16 hours).

8th worked at my own head in the same – had a baby to put in the infants hand, made a mess of it – worked at the head again till dark & all the eveng from feeling – Gabriel do. at his calves head (10 hours).

9th all day at the same, eveng drew in the man's head from self (8 hours).

10th all day placing the shawl on the lay figure, eveg idle (5 hours).

11th still lazy – began the shepheards plaid shawl, drawing the pattern in pencil on a pure white ground till dusk & then till *2 P.M.* [A.M.] (8 hours).

12th dreadfully lazy, breakfast & newspaper in bed, worked the same as yesterday. This eveng accoumpts & filling up this since last Monday. Gabriel gone to town to see Miss Siddall, getting on slowly with his calf he paints it in all like Albert Durer hair by hair & seems incapable of any breadth – but this he will get by going over it from feeling at home. From want of habit I see nature bothers him – but it is sweetly drawn & felt.[82] I ment to work on my shawl only 2½ hours today as yet (8 hours).

2nd December today no work. Woolner dined here last night & this morning Rossetti took a walk with him & me & then went into London with him. I walked out with Emma & then over to Hendon to arrange with Smart our grocer[83] about not paying him & getting credit. Yesterday I worked on the tarpauling over the Ladies' knees in the last of England (3 hours). Woolner who ought to know likes it well, also the subject for which I painted the background at Hampstead – called "Work". Since the 12th Gabriel has still been here & I have omitted filling up in consequence, not choosing he should know of this. To the best of my recollection I have worked as follows, 13th 14th 15th 16th & 17th pattern of shawl in pencil on a zink white ground, day & evening by lamplight, in doors & comfortable (40 hours). 18th saturday to London to buy things for Emma

[82] Meanwhile Rossetti was writing to Allingham: "As for the calf, he kicks and fights all the time he remains tied up, which is five or six hours daily, and the view of life induced at his early age by experience in art appears to be so melancholy that he punctually attempts suicide by hanging himself daily at 3½ daily P.M. At these times I have to cut him down and then shake him up and lick him like blazes" (*Letters*, p.231).
[83] John Smart, grocer and provision dealer, Brent Street.

on account of an invitation to Mrs Seddon's, Emma being ill furnished with dress poor Emma. 19th & 20th Shawl pattern again. 21st to Gravesend – letters (12 hours). 22nd to London to get the money for Bamfords portrait & to Seddons in the Eveng. Emma did not go not finding herself small enough to go. 23rd Up disgracefully late – placed the tarpauling over the Lady's knees in the Eveng drew at the shawl. 24th Drew Both (14 hours). 25th rain, finished drawing the shawl, rubbed in the tarpauling with yellow transparant color, worked till late (11 hours). 26th began painting the tarpauling out in the back yard – having arranged bars to the chair in which the lay figure sits like a Guy (4 hours). 27th out to buy pewter spoons in honor of William Rossetti coming to dinner[84] one being broken by Katty & two melted by Ruth so as to have but one servicable out of 4. Saw Gabriels calf, very beautiful but takes a long time. Endless emendations no perceptebel progress from day to day & all the time he wearing my great coat which I want & a pair of my breeches, besides food & an unlimited supply of turpentine. Worked at the tarpauling out doors, snow came on. Eveng William Rossetti (2 hours). 28th tarpauling out of doors, wet day, came in worked at covering shawl (5 hours). 29th Wednesday good day at Tarpauling. Eveng shawl, worked till ½ past 2 A.M. with a tint lightly covering the pencil with paint (11 hours). 30th Beautiful day worked well at the shawl in the open air. Now that the pattern is all drawn & covered with a tint I put in the out door effect. To have painted it all out of doors would have taken six weeks of intense cold & suffering & perhaps have failed (5 hours).

1st Decr painted at the tarpauling out of doors till Woolner called.

3rd Up shamefully late, Breakfast in bed shower bath about 12, to work about 2 till ½ past 4 open air, finished tarpauling. After dinner tried to think of ways towards means – could think of any thing else fell asleep – no decision as yet, £8 left – (2½ hours).

4th Up late to work about 9 till four at shawl. Went to the farm[85] with Emma to see Rossettis calf. Coming home he walks on & leaves us – arrived at home we find as usual that he has been frightening Kattie telling her he would put her *in the fire*. Begins to us, on our entering, with "That ass of a child" – I stop him with "I've told you before I don't choose you to call my

---

[84] "Can you fix a day to come and dine with Brown at six", Rossetti wrote to his brother, "or on Sunday earlier if you like? He tells me to ask you. Brown adds, if you come on Sunday you will have the anguish of missing *me*" (*Letters*, p.233). W.M. Rossetti dined at Finchley on a Monday.

[85] Manor Farm, East End, farmed by Bruce Johnson, was about a mile by road from Grove Villas. A convent now stands on the site, facing St Marylebone Cemetery. The farm was an extensive property (its rateable value was £430) and, given Rossetti's known dislike of walking, it is possible that the farmyard could have been approached by a short cut across the fields.

child as ass, it is not gentlemanly to come & abuse persons children to them — If you can't stay here without calling her names you had better go." He did *not go* but was silent for the rest of the eveng I worked at back ground of beauty & spoilt it (5 hours).

5th up at ½ past 8, to town called on Marshall saw his wife in a splendid room without fire[86] — both look starved & pinched — National Gallery — Absurd old pictures bought by Dyce. An Albert Durer however very fine though not painted, rather *mapped*, a Massaccio with fine in it — Bad Rembrandts & a worse Wilkie the Beadle.[87] Altogether it goes from weak to foolish — faults of last year corrected by faults of this. Saw old Glass — talked pollitics.

6th up at 9½ worked from 12 till ½ past 4 open air, painted on the tarpauling & added the water on it then at the shawl. Eveng read & talked abut W.B. Scotts beautiful poems with Gabriel then read his blessed Damozel[88] — pleasant eveng (4½ hours).

7th to work about 11½ — at shawl (open air). Blanket round feet, two coats shawl & gloves on, very cold in spite. Woolner came to see Gabriel about Ruskin in hopes of his helping him towards the statue of Wentworth the Lag.[89] Took him to see Rossetti where he paints in the farm yard. Saw what he is about, done calf and almost cart. Woolner back here, dined & off with Gabl, me writing this & to W.B. Scott about his beauties of poetry (4 hours).

8th worked in doors at retouching the Brent (3 hours).

---

[86] John Marshall had recently moved to 10 George Street, Hanover Square.

[87] Dyce, who came under the patronage of the Prince Consort, may have been influential in the purchase of a group of pictures for the National Gallery in June 1854, the authorship of which have now been mostly reascribed. Bought as a Massaccio, *St Bernard's Vision of the Virgin* is now attributed to Filippo Lippi. *Portrait of a Man* by Baldung was cleaned in 1957, when a false Dürer monogram was removed. *An Elderly Man as St Paul* by Rembrandt and Wilkie's *The Parish Beadle* (Tate) were among the numerous bequests made by Lord Colborne to the National Gallery.

[88] William Bell Scott (1811-90), artist, poet, and at present master in the Newcastle-on-Tyne Government School of Design. His book of verse, *Poems by a Painter*, had lately been published. Rossetti's first version of *The Blessed Damozel* was written before his nineteenth birthday (May 1848) and was published in *The Germ*, 1850.

[89] W.C. Wentworth (1793-1872), Australian politician, had been influential in founding Sydney University. £2000 were subscribed in New South Wales for a statue to commemorate his achievement but the competition was to be held in London. Woolner had made a bronze medallion of Wentworth in Australia (reduced version in the National Portrait Gallery, London), which had been praised, but having been unsuccessful in his goldmining activities Woolner had decided to return to England, hoping to secure the statue commission. Wentworth was laggard in selecting the artist, which may have occasioned the nickname, but more likely it was Rossetti's choice of a slang word, "Lag" being used for a convict in the first part of the century, and Australians at that time being largely descended from transported convicts. Eventually the statue was executed by an Italian.

9th Up at 7 to Gravesend to fetch my daughter Lucy. Yesterday Gabriel told me story of Hunt & one of himself too good to be forgotten. Hunt when about 12 or 14 was placed in care of one of the "League" Bread shops. Becoming acquainted with the topic then in vogue among those sort he takes it in his head to write to one of the leading journals *his* views in the matter. The letter was *printed* & much discussed. *Cobden* called to see him at the shop & very much surprised, talked to him at great length to purswade him he was in error. *Hunt maintained he was in the right* — & still believes himself to be so. This is characteristic. I must remember to ask Hunt when I see him again what the subject of his letter was.[90] The other of Rossetti was that while he was painting the wall in his present picture in a lane at Chisick in the open air — a low fellow came up & after many appologies said that he took a great interest in art & that the moss in the wall (nothing else was done) reminded him of a picture he used much to admire at Dantzik when in Germany. He said it was a celebrated picture of the last Judgement painted by two Brothers their names he forgot, that the female heads were very beautiful in it. Rossetti asked if the name was Van Eyke. He could not remember. Rossetti afterwards consulted a dictionary of art & found that at Dantzick there *is* a celebrated last Judgement by the brothers Van Eyke.[91]

10th up at 9 shower bath, to church with Lucy, came home & worked at the little lady in the Brent 2 hours ½. Idle after (2½ hours).

11th worked at the shawl in open air 5 hours. Eveng scraped out part & redrew it (9 hours).

12th worked at the shawl & in the open air. Eveng Idle, talk with Rossetti (4 hours).

13th Open air work, shower bath again & two days before. In the eveng I worked long at cutting out the frame to fit better the studies of heads painted at Southend, pasted them in, then finished the background of Beauty & lettered it afresh & pasted in frame, then wrote the letter to secretary Mogford of the Sketch Exhn. I have sent this morning "the

---

[90] There seems to be some confusion here. In about 1842 Holman Hunt worked for a short time in the London calico business of Richard Cobden, statesman and reformer. This was at the time of the Anti-Corn-Law league, a movement formed for the abolition of the corn laws, in which Cobden was the moving spirit. Holman Hunt having read the pamphlets of the extremists wrote an anonymous letter in opposition to Cobden's views, which, according to him, was never printed.

[91] A puzzling entry. No moss is apparent on the brick wall either in the finished painting of *Found* or in the oil sketch (Carlisle Art Gallery) on which Rossetti was working at Chiswick in October, but this he may have eliminated at the time the girls's head was introduced (*c.* 1858). The altarpiece of *The Last Judgment* at the Marienkirchen, Danzig, is now ascribed to Memling; it includes no wall and cannot be said to number any beautiful female heads among the souls of the damned or the saved.

Brent" to this place & tomorrow go the studies of Heads & Beauty.[92] Talked about suicide & suicides afterwards with Rossetti – to bed at 5 A.M. (7 hours).

14th up at ½ past 7, only so much sleap, to London to fetch niece Lizzie.[93] Went to National Gallery. Met Woolner, his statue of Wentworth the lag not a safe bill yet. Poor Woolner, the lag has some idea of being done by some greater artist – & going down to posterity more beautiful. Walked home from the archway with a bad foot. Evening suffered severely.

15th up at 8, foot bad, boil on the 4th toe of the left foot.

16th Worked at the Landscape of the turnip field, took off dirt & inequalities of surface & retouched the corn part of it, eveng idle & suffering (2 hours).

17th up at 9, foot bad worked at the duplicate of "Waiting", retouched the mothers hand & childs flesh without models, improved the childs head. This morning 16th [17th] Gabriel not yet having done his cart & talking quite freely about *several days yet*, having been here since the first Novr & not seeming to notice any hints, moreover the two children being here & one stupid girl insufficient for so much work Emma being within a week or two of her confinement & he having had his bed made on the floor in the parlour one week now & not getting up till eleven, & moreover making himself infernally disagreeable besides my finances being reduced to £2.12s which must last till 20th January, I told him delicately he must go – or go home at night by the bus – this he said was too expensive. I told him he might ride to his work in the morning & walk home at night, this he said he should never think of. He thinks nothing of putting *us* to trouble or expence so he is gone for the present (2 hours).

18th up at 11, foot getting better still obliged to keep it up, worked at the duplicate of waiting repainted the velvet lining of chair & rubbed out what I had done. This eveng inconceivably dejected & stupid, read newspaper & thought over our melancholy position. Emma about to be confined, £2.10 in the house, Christmas boxes to be *paid out of this* & the children taken back to Gravesend & not one person in the world I would ask to lend me a pound – no one that buys my picters, Damn old White (2 hours).

19th Disagreeable day foot rather better, I lazy & not wishing to work we

[92] Probably John Mogford (1821-85), water-colour painter of coastal scenes. The Winter Exhibition, 121 Pall Mall, opened this month. For the studies of Heads see p.82, n.33 and diary 5 Nov. 1854.
[93] Elizabeth Bromley (1843-75) was the niece of Brown's first wife and bore the same name. Her mother kept the school at Gravesend which Lucy Brown attended; the first cousins were of the same age. Elizabeth Bromley died of apoplexy in St Paul's Churchyard while shopping with her husband.

decided to have the Drugget up, it being at length too disgracefully full of holes — remainder of the evening nothing.

20th wrote a disagreeable letter & put down the carpet & planned & directed the patching thereof. Children assisting in great delight & with Ruth we got it done. Last night also glued sundry chairs etc.

21st Took down the Christ & Peter & scraped it for repainting morning & eveng (6 hours).

22nd Worked at the shawl open air again, very mild delightful day took a walk with the children, they made me very nervous & iritable by getting under my feet in the mud & sticking close to me in spite of all I could do. Eveng worked at "Christ & Peter" (6 hours).

23rd An allarm from Emma, Carruthers[94] thought it very probable that the labour would come on during the day, so we thought best to bundle the poor children back to Gravesend leaving Emma with the servant. We sent the boxes off by the carrier & walked into Hampstead, bus thence to the Camden station, too late for train moreover boxes nowhere, at last Boxes come & at 4 P.M. we started, I took my ticket for Stratford only. I was very nervous however about how the children would get over from Tilbury Fort when a gentn turned up on the platform whom we knew going the same way. I left them at Stratford & started back as far as Islington to see after the nurse who (it was well I went) had not got the letter. I told her to come by the eveng bus & took bus myself to the Archway Highgate in distress of mind at not being able to afford a cab in such an emergency, and so walked home four miles racked with anxiety about Emma the most beautiful duck in existance. With 18/9 in hand to last at least three weeks how *could* I take a cab & this was all that remained me this eveng. As I walked down the Grove & very tired with a weak foot I felt that mysterious assurance that all was right, which I have before felt when nearing some dreaded event that has eventualy turned out all right. I got home at 8 P.M. & found dear Emma still in expectation & statu quo — thank Heaven. I found also (strange coincidence) a letter from William Bamford[95] asking me to do a miniature of him — such a demand I have wished for at other times in vain & not for months & months has any thing of the kind occurred.

24th got up late. Breakfasted in bed felt very tired worked a little at the "Christ" picture wrote letters. This eveng Emma found in her drawer 2

---

[94] The only medical man residing at Finchley or Hendon was a Scotsman, James Corrie, surgeon, who had taken his degree at Edinburgh in 1830. He was also a surgeon to the Barnet Union. Might "Carruthers" be one of Brown's malapropisms?
[95] Unidentified, but see p.9, n.24.

shillings & 3 farthings all in fourpenny pieces, pennys, halfpence, farthings etc left there at different times & forgotten, what a boon. Katty appropriated the 3 farthings. To night I have worked about 4 hours at altering the linnen cloaths round the loins of Christ & correcting the drawing (7 hours).

25th Xmas day up at ½ past 9 Emma still pretty well. I worked about 4½ hours at restoring the erasures I had made in the Christ, I have begun altering the character of the head to severity, lengthening the forearm enlarging the hand, shortening the thyes, enlarging the girdle to be less indecent & planning the glory. Worked comfortably in front parlour, rain pouring down. Katty cut her eyelid with a knife & could not eat Xmas dinner. Emma & I therefor eat ours quite tête à tête. Nurse is next door but one at a sisters house. Finances £1.-/6 (4½ hours).

26th Up at 9 Kattys Eye still bad & so slept with her mother kicking me out into the back room where the draft from the window increased a cold so that I could scarce work to day. To bed by 7 (3 hours).

27th very bad stopped in bed with the fever, got up by 3 P.M. This cold must have been taken on saturday being out so many hours with shoes unsound in wet weather. Dreary, dreary very dreary, Emma still well.

28th day trifled away, Eveng almost do. Emma still well.

29th To Town to see after William Bamfords miniature, the ass wants something for 2 Guineas yet will not decide even on this, so back defeated having spent one bob in busses. Called on Woolner[96] & heard how badly the country was governed – paid to day the Baker 2 weeks lest I should be asked for 3 next week & 3/6 for soling shoes the net result of all which is 4/8 in pocket – O heavens! & little fishes no work. Here endeth Book III.

[Book 3 of the Diary ends here and is continued in Book4.]

---

[96] Woolner was living at 15 Mary Street, Regent's Park.

1855

3rd Jany. Up at 9, shower bath, out with dear Emma for a short walk, got chilled so took one by myself to get warm – to work by 12 at the fringe of the shawl finished it by 1 – triumphantly stripped the lay figure & set the place somewhat to rights & restored poor Emma her shawl which she has done without the half of the winter. The shawl is at length finished thank the powers above. Dinner, then took the little picture of "Waiting" & scraped it preparatory to beginning to retouch in order to fit it for the Great Paris Exh – having received intimation that the board of trade proposes sending it & the great "Chaucer" picture. Scraped & pumisstoned it all over till it looks quite spoiled – prepared my box for tomorrow to go & work at the "Autumn Afternoon" which I propose sending to the British Institution, it is at Charles Seddons.[1] This eveng worked at the designe of the Hampstead picture called "Work". Whenever I set to at designing I feel in the most ethereal & extatic state possible. I do not hurry with it because it is such enjoyment. Tonight I arranged the chief navvy tossing off the beer also the one decending the ladder & improved other parts.

I must try & fill up the other days omitted. Saturday 30th Dec I worked out in the open air at the shawl till ½ past 3 when having fully resolved I took my dress coat trousers & waistcoat & necktie with a silk cape & brooch of Emma's & putting them in the bag walked into Hampstead & took bus to Newroad & discovered the abode of old Williams[2] who used to wash for me & told him to pawn them, which he did for /10. I gave him one, at which he stared in awe & respect – came away 8/5 richer – called on the old folk at Seddon's. Tom[3] expected daily – came home & read (3 hours).

[1] See p.82. The British Institution was to open on 7 Feb.
[2] "Old Williams" was once a policeman in Wales. Known to the Rossettis as a jobbing man who blacked their boots, he had sat for St Joachim in Rossetti's *The Girlhood of Mary Virgin*.
[3] Late in 1853 Thomas Seddon had gone to Cairo, there to await the arrival in the New Year of Holman Hunt, whose pupil he was. In the early summer they had continued to Jerusalem. Old Mr Seddon was particularly fond of Emma. "Do you know", Brown had written to Tom Seddon in Jerusalem, "I seriously suspect that he comes to see Emma, if he is inclined to play the Johnny Millais however he will find me not at all a Ruskin, being neither jellous nor impotent thank God as yet" (Morgan Library).

31st Sunday up latish worked at the shawl, made up my mind to apply for a mastership of one of the government art schools, wrote letters (4 hours).

1st January Shawl out of doors & in Eveng at length wrote the long deferred much dreaded application, to the humbug Henry Cole C.B.[4] It will only be the humiliation for nothing. Afterwards took up the designe of "Work" & enjoyed it — Designed the artist in it again & sundries (7 hours).

2nd up about 9. At 11 took the lay figure out in the yard as usual but this time laid it down on its side in order to paint the fringe blown by the wind, doing so disordered the folds, then it came on to drizzle — then the wind was too high & blew the fringe so that I could not paint it. After wasting much time I brought the lay figure into my room & placed it on the table & after much arrangement painted for about 1½ hours — but it was good — today I finished it & it looks as natural as life (4½ hours). Evening 4½ I worked at the navvies — the pot boy a triumph, the mortarman perfection & the ragged child upsetting the barrow & getting cuffed, all creations — & the whole becoming more & more exciting. Finances reduced again to 6/9 so we drag on . . . . (6 hours).

8th Up at 10 felt ill could eat no breakfast, set to work at the Part of the Little picture of waiting which I set & began last night. Sunday I begun it. Slow work retouching all over having scraped within a hairsbreadth of its existance. Took a long walk at dusk & in the eveng placed the table lamp etc having changed the subject into one of an officers wife thinking of him at Sevastopol. A miniature effect this[5] (8 hours).

4th Thursday I went to Charles Seddon & worked at the "Autumn" piece which is for the British [Institution]. In the even at the designe of "Work" (7 hours).

Friday the same & even do. Very perplexed & low in spirits (7 hours). Saturday I scraped the little picture of Waiting all over with a razor in order to get it up fine for the Paris Exn, after dinner began retouching — in the eveng copied in the background from the study at Hampstead in the designe of work so as to get all quite correct (8 hours). Today I finished the

---

[4] (Sir) Henry Cole had gained his reputation as an energetic civil servant in various government departments, and his efficiency in the management of the Great Exhibition of 1851 had earned him the order of Commander of the Bath and the position of acting commissioner to the Royal Commission for Great Britain at the Exposition Universelle at Paris in 1855. He was joint secretary of the Department of Science and Art at Marlborough House (later becoming the first Director of the South Kensington Museum) and Director of the Government Schools of Design. He was a genial man with many influential friends; perhaps this was the basis of Brown's mistrust and his reluctance in applying to him for a School of Design mastership.

[5] A miniature of a man wearing a red coat is on the table beside her, lying on a sheaf of letters.

miniature, letters etc of last night, then began the table cloath – took a walk & at it again till 12 tonight (9 hours). I have been queerish all day, work & worry begin to try me, 4/10 left in pocket. Emma dearest still up but in pain these three days. Cole C.B. answered me very short saying a certificate was imperative & referred me to Burchett.[6] I wrote again to Cole telling him that as he knew as much about me as any examiner could, that if he thought I could be of use he had better write & let know & then I would go through all formalities. Will he answer? Waking up this morning with a bad head I began to reflect & at length a lucid idea came as to my prospects. It struck me I was doing very foolishly to let myself down in so many ways instead of raising money & going hard at it & conquering. If I do not get a school I will do it.

9th Up at 9½ queerish, to work by 10½ at the table cloath till 4 made a mess of it – did not sens the rest – took a walk; tea & to work at the cloath again from 7 to 9, dispirited, & heavy about the head – funds 4/, Emma the same (7 hours).

10th up at 10. Headache, to work about 12 at the Table Cloath till 4, felt very oppressed about the head owing to anxiety. Emma still going on. This eveng worked at the designe of "Work" about 2 hours. Have been casting up my accounts find that in 20 weeks we have spent 66.18/ & owe about £35 besides, the excess is chiefly in the House money, about £15 or 15/ per week. This is Emma's bad management. In pleasure & all extras we have exceeded £2.10 or 2/6 a week. This is our trip to St Albans I suppose, I allow about 5/ a week for these. How are we to go on Heven only knows (6 hours). Rossetti has been here 6 weeks & Nurse two, besides the children & Woolner & William Rossetti. This must be deducted from Emma.

11th up at ½ past 10. Head still queer, wrote to old Seddon & the Illustrated News about Building Societies, id est Mortgage ones – made up my mind to make up a parcel of Emma's shawl, some papier maché ornaments & two engravings after Claude with the large shipwreck of Turner[7] to send by the carrier to old Williams tomorrow for him to pledge. If we do not have a letter with Ritchies money[8] before the carrier calls – something must be done as there is only 3/3 in hand and Emma about to be confined. Poor Emma, she seems rather worse tonight. I am getting a regular Haydon at pawning – so long as I do not become one at cheating my creditors it matters little. God help us, I see nothing but ruin by progressive stages – no work today.

---

[6] Richard Burchett (1815-75), historical painter and, at this time, headmaster of the South Kensington School of Art.
[7] Turner's *The Shipwreck*, 1805 (Tate), was the first of his paintings to be engraved (1806).
[8] Ritchie & Smith, stone and slate merchants, Ravensbourne Wharf, tenant of Brown.

11th Up at 10 sent off the things by the carrier – started myself about ½ past 12. Walked to Anthony's at Westbourn Grove, saw his pictures, very fine in many respects but all unfinished & in a state that will not admit of their being so, save by his taking them back to where he painted them. He has a habit of late particularly of making the skys so heavy that they quite spoil all the fine qualities other way evinced in his works, the picture of Stratford church[9] however is magnificent in every respect save the sky which, if he can paint it, will be one of his finest works – it is admirable colour but his other works look somewhat opaque. Thence to Dickinsons to see about the large picture for Paris, then called on Lowes at his new gordeous rooms.[10] Afterwards to St Pancrass church at 6 P.M. to meet old Williams, a nice affair, he had just been pawning the "Shipwreck" after Turner, given me by Lowes before he left for Italy. Poor old Williams took them to 6 places in all & could only get 13/6 in all. I gave him one & some copper obtaining. I must reward him better when he gets them out. I walked with my 12/6 to the Britania bus to Hampstead, met a young Lady at North End afraid to encounter the darkness alone. Escorted her some-way past Golders Green then by a cross road regained this Finchley one & got home very tired have only 1 bun.

13th no Letter from the scoundrel Ritchie so its well I pawned the things, no letter from the scoundrel Cole C.B. so its ill I wrote to him, but I derived some satisfaction at reading to day that the Belfast school of designe has under his precious care died a natural death, not getting fat it seems on self support.[11] Read a great part of the morning, begun to paint about 1 at the childs bedgown, dined, & at it again – after for one hour. At Dark walked to Hendon by a forbidden private foot path & bought Cathy a Pr of boots. Walked home again by the same, quite dark, found the gate locked, clambered over at the risk of being Ruskinised[12] but only was cought for a short time by the seat of my trousers – this eveng got my Lay figure in here & painted the ladies collar & the brooch, also the marriage ring. Read. Emma still going (4 hours).

16th Up disgracefully late, down by 11 – worked on the head of the Mama in the little picture, no other work (2½ hours). Talked with Emma about

[9] *Stratford-on-Avon-Evening* was shown at the R.A., 1855.
[10] Langham Chambers, at the bottom of Portland Place, a new building consisting chiefly of studios. "Millais' [new rooms op] posite Langham Church are handsome; Dick [inson] still more so – he having come earliest and got first [choice,] but I would rather have my bridge river view than their indoor magnificence" (*Letters*, partly mutilated, p.242).
[11] Closure of Government Schools in Cork and Limerick followed shortly. They had been set up contingent to their being partly financed by local resources but when these failed they were discontinued.
[12] In Brown's vocabulary "Ruskinise" probably stood for "lacerate". The O.E.D. definition: "To advocate or adopt Ruskinian principles" is obviously inappropriate here.

getting money. A letter from some underling of the scoundrel Cole C.B. enclosing sheets of print again, subterfuge, & insolence – no go in that quarter – A letter from Scott – the poët. Yesterday Seddon came back after more than 20 months of absence, looking thinner & genteeler than ever & in high spirits. I went with him to Kentishtown leaving my work just begun. His pictures are cruelly P.R.B.'d. I was very sorry to see he had made less than no progress. The places are not well selected nor addapted & the high finish is too obtrusive. However they present quantities of drawing & truthfulness seldom surpassed but no beauty, nothing to make the bosom tingle. Could I but have seen them in progress – I will do all I can to make him improve them yet, but it is late. Hunt, he tells me, gave him no advice at all, he has been prepossessed against him I fear, it is a great pity. There is not a better hearted fellow living nor a truer gentleman. He is to be married in June, these pictures all his wealth, how strange.[13] I dont think them worth much as yet, but that is nothing to the point, commission will do it. He makes friends. Sunday I painted at the ribon & divers, eveng the Hair from Emma (5 hours). Hunt used to be in agonies about his joking propensities & lecture him & get mighty sulky if things did not go right – & tell him secrets of great worth for his getting on in the world, & expect him to do all the housekeeping, which he declined after a time, & indulge in many whims incompatible with the locallity & circumstances. But Seddon entertains a high opinion of his worth & gallantry. Hunt knocked an arab down & they afterwards stood with pistols cocked at each other a space of time. Seddon used to camp above the valley of Jehosophat for 3 months alone with his servant, in a place considered unsafe by the consul & others of Jerusalem. They used to sleep each with a revolver at hand but never were disturbed, this was plucky. Hunt since is gone to the dead Sea. I am lazy & low in spirits.

17th up at ½ past 10, shower bath. Out to Hunt up Ritchie for his rent, got none, out from ½ past 11 till 8, walked about 18 miles in snow, ordered liberally of my tailor, who is a brick. Emma still the same, funds 11/3, no work, no adventures.

20th This morning at ½ past 12 a.m. Dearest Emma was delivered of a son, my first. he is very red, a large nose, eyes & shape of face like a calmuck Tartar, shape of head like a Bosjeman,[14] sucks liberally, Emma dearest pretty well, feverish. Thank heaven it is over comfortably. I wrote

---

[13] Seddon was staying with his parents at 27 Grove Terrace, Kentish Town, until his marriage to Emmeline Bulford whom he had known for some time in France. He had irritated Holman Hunt when abroad by his easy-going ways, his willingness to wear arab clothing and his taste for practical jokes.

[14] Oliver Madox Brown (1855-74), with the head of a bushman (Bosjeman), became a youth of great promise and some achievement as writer and painter, but died at an early age.

4 letters & to bed at 4 this morning till 11. The surgeon who is fat & stupied to look at turned out a very pleasant clever fellow, well informed & this was because he is a scotchman – knew all abut my grandfather, says his doctrine is every year coming more into practice.[15] Today I have done nothing but write. Yesterday I painted some hours at the little picture (3½ hours). Left off to go to surgeons. After, a check from Ritchie come for £9 & I went & payed the butcher & baker & got a bottle of Wiskiy. To day sent money to get the cloak & picture back. Iten to Emmas mother in arrears, net result £1.16 in pocket. Shoes leaky. On Thursday I worked at the little picture, the head, face, etc. In the eveng drew at the Designe of "Work". The couple on horse back (6 hours).

21st This day I got up at ¼ to 10. Shower bath, to work about 12 at little picture, scraped out part of the chair & repainted (3 hours). Since then I have written 3 letters one very important. Last night "Work" (1 hour).

25th up at near 11 – got the ballance of £16 from Ritchie last night. Paid away all but £5.10, *my all* till I raise money. Worked at my sons portrait[16] about 3 hours then Hendon (3 hours). Paid Smart the grocer £10. Last night I was at Seddons & there saw Mary Howit she is unaffected & dresses nicely two rare qualities in a Poetess. Seddons sister very beautiful only 15. Tom in full Arabicals. Christina Rossetti put on a Sirian dress.[17] Yesterday only drew at my boys face (3 hours). Up very late having been to Charles Seddons party the night before & very tired, got home by ½ past 3 (3 hours). All sorts of queer looking people. Rossetti is teaching away at the Mechanics Colledge, Red Lion square, makes the fellows draw each other. Fred Warren it seems is a poet.[18] No answer to my enquiries about Building

[15] If the doctor was James Corrie (see p.111, n.94) he would have been familiar from his medical student days in Edinburgh with the famous "Brunonian system of medicine", which was to strengthen with food rather than weaken the patient by fasting and blood-letting. With this reform Dr John Brown (1733-78) attacked the received doctrines of the Edinburgh medical profession and provoked such controversy that he had been obliged to leave Scotland and set up practice in London, where he soon gained a following.

[16] Drawing of a baby's head (Private Collection). Signed with monogram and inscribed along the top: "Oliver Madox Brown Pater su Des Jan 23 1855 Aetas Die [illegible, presumably "3"].

[17] Mary Howitt (1799-1888), wife of William Howitt (see p.133, n.62), wrote verse and was the author of many children's books. Born a Quaker, she showed a leaning towards Unitarianism, then became a dedicated spiritualist, and finally espoused the Roman Catholic religion. Emily Seddon later married Henry Virtue Tebbs, lawyer and art collector, who was responsible in 1869 for the formalities attending the exhumation of Elizabeth Siddal's coffin at Highgate Cemetery. Christina Rossetti (1830-94) had recently applied to go to the Crimea as a nurse but, because of her youth, had been refused. She had been a pupil at the North London Drawing School during Brown's tutelage, but her creative powers were already directed towards poetry and the year 1854 had seen an increase in her work which had included sonnets, love lyrics and devotional poems.

[18] Unidentified, but two artists of the name of Alfred Warren are recorded, one an engraver, the other an etcher. Rossetti taught at the Working Men's College on Mondays and had given his first class on 22 Jan.

societies. Tuesday I drew at the boy without his cap & they said I had given him a cold (3 hours). Monday I began it, worked at it with great care but I fear it is not worth any thing (8 hours). Monday eveng at "Work" (3 hours). Emma well. This eveg designed at "Work" about 2 hours.

28th Sunday Rose at 10 shower bath. In a state of great despondency & nervousness all day. An unsuccessful man is a bore to every one. Took a walk but could not walk it off, came back & penned an advertisement for the "Times" "wanted £300 on mortgage of good freehold property" – so one gradually rides to ruin. This evening I have tried to sleep off my head-ache & low spirits without much success. I have so managed things that at the age of 34 or nearly, after having worked vigorously all my youth, after having repeatedly roused public attention in more than one country & been considered a man of genius, that far from being able to make a lively-hood by my work I have not even one friend to whom I can apply to for advice how to raise money on the property I have. Some people have rich friends who get a poor devil occasionally out of a mess. My friends cannot muster sufficient sympathy to give me advice on such a dellicate subject. I thought I might apply for some information to old Seddon & to get W. Rossetti to ask his uncle Polidor, who is in the law, something about build-ing societies. Old Seddon takes no notice of what I wrote to him & William has asked his Uncle but without success or any very evident pleasure in the matter.[19] An unsuccessful man is a bore. Last night I dined at the Rossettis, Gabriel who invited me never came home of course. Woolner was there in fumes sulfurious about the ministry & aristocracy, says also Carlyle as well as Ruskin consider Patmores book a glorious one, this after having sent an insulting note to W.B. Scott about his poetry[20] – so much for Carlyle's critical powers. Some how or an other there is no where common sence to be met with in this world, neither among ones friends nor among ones enemies nor any known set or sect. Yesterday I went to town to see about my large picture[21] of [for] Paris. A Gallery Dickinson has found, but the picture must not remain should it let, nor in any case after 17 feby next. Much bother to ascertain if the government packers can take it from

---

[19] Henry Polydore, solicitor and brother of Mrs Gabriele Rossetti, was a conscientious and cautious man. The Building Society movement had been established in the first quarter of the nineteenth century.

[20] Thomas Carlyle (1795-1881), misreading the title of W.B. Scott's *Poems of a Painter* for *Poems of a Printer*, "wrote off at once to the imaginary printer to tell him to stick to his types and give up his metaphors" (*Letters*, p.232). Ruskin praised *The Angel in the House*, writing to its author: "You have neither the lusciousness nor the sublimity of Tennyson, but you have clearer and finer habitual expressions and more accurate thought . . . Tennyson is often quite sinfully hazy" (*Ruskin*, 36, p.224). Patmore had received "a most flaming letter of praise from Carlyle who said all he could say of a poem almost" (*Letters to W. Allingham*, ed. H. Allingham and E.B. Williams, 1911, p.289).

[21] *Chaucer.*

thence when required. Secy at Marbro' House not able to say till he has consulted the *board*. Obliged to write a letter. Running backwards & forwards all day & the one before. They evidently belong to the same sort who are starving our unfortunate soldiers in the Crimea. Captain Fowke R.E.[22] They seem to have nice snug births of it & plenty of coals provided. The same bother to obtain my steps from the Clerkenwell school.[23] A certain unyielding pleaseman [policeman] has no idea of acting without a *written order from the treasurer – written in the dark*. I have no hope in me.

30th up at 10, cold in my head, deep & still thickening layers of snow cover every thing all round.[24] With this & a cold in my head I decide not to stir out for the day, although it is anxious time with me now – so I sit in Emmas bedroom & from a cargo of books I sent her yesterday I select the life [of] "Washington"[25] & read all day. A godlike man – a rare example of an unselfish man. If Cromwell was a great man, Washington was a God, spotless, – passionless. The booke is ill written, passing the pen over many superfluous passages might improve it, but the matter is eternal, unchangeable. Yesterday I walked into town through Hampstead and put an advertisement in the "Times"[26] & sought out Building societies – much fatigue – some snow & a cold the result. Dearest Emma looking blooming again in a new cotton wrapper.

4th Feb Up at 10 shower Bath, to work abut 12 till 5, languidly painted at the Babys gown, at its cap, at both its hands at one of the mothers & her face. This evening read, wrote & reflected on tomorrow (4 hours). Wednesday I walked to Archway & took bus to the city to see about Building societies – walked to Pall Mall, entered the Winter Exn. saw my "studies of Head"[27] there but not the other two, viz "Beauty" & "the

---

[22] Captain Francis Fowke (1823-65), "the Secy at Marbro' House", was secretary to the English Commission attached to the Paris Exhibition. Shortly afterwards he was appointed Inspector of the Science and Art Department at Marlborough House. Later still he was the principal designer of the Albert Hall. Wykeham Deverell, younger brother of the late Walter Deverell, was at this time junior clerk in the above Department.
[23] Brown would have needed his painting steps for his large *Chaucer*. The "Clerkenwell school" is unidentified; perhaps either the Finsbury School of Art in William Street, Clerkenwell (later attended by Kate Greenaway), which had some connection with the Department of Science and Art, or Clerkenwell Parochial School, which moved to Kentish Town at some date unknown and in 1858 to Highgate.
[24] This winter, one of the coldest for many years, remained "cold, nipping and miserable beyond record" till the end of June, the wind being "almost uniformly N.E." (*Annual Register*).
[25] Perhaps *The Life of George Washington*, C.W. Upham, 1852, 2 vols.
[26] "To small capitalists. WANTED, to BORROW £300, on mortgage of good freehold property. Address to B.Y.Z., Shaw's Library, Hampstead" (*Times*, 31 Jan. 1855). Mr Shaw was a bookseller in the High Street.
[27] See p.82, n.33.

Beast". I had no catalogue & I asked no questions but I feel pretty certain they were not there. Slap No 1 – then I walked in fast snow to the Br Institution having received an intimation that it was varnishing day which means your picture is hung. I looked every where but could not find it & pretty sure feel it is *not* hung.[28] Slap No 2. No answer about the large picture from Marlborough House, Slap No 3 – altogether I began to feel as though the tide were against me. Told R Dickinson I did not feel in spirits to come & work at the large picture, went home with a determination to work vigorously at the small one. Thursday worked at it about 3 hours, scraped out the table clothe three times & at last made it right with a dash, got very pleased with it, went to Hampstead for the answers to advertisement – found 11. Curious examination. Found I was right in my conception regarding the sort of people who sent them – but that the difficulties are greater than I imagined. Walked that day, friday, at least 20 miles, went into a Coffee shop & wrote 5 letters then walked home. Yesterday I painted about 3 hours but felt intensely languid & inert. It was yesterday that I put the clothe right as said above. Thursday I did the cradle & painted at the cloath but it looked wrong. Dreadfully nervous, anxiety about immediate money wants & the melancholy prospects of future ruin I suppose cause it – but I do not much worry about it neither, only when I wake up in the morning I feel it rather. Emma is very well & the boy getting fat. Funds £3.2/nearly all owing.

5th To town, Dickinson had not sent for the picture.

6th To town. The picture could not be had, after bother got them to promise it. Spent some time with Lowes then with Thomas, dined with William Rossetti – neither satisfactory about money.

7th To town, found my picture placed in the gallery, worked on it till 5. Then to Furnivals Inn to see after my steps,[29] home very late (6 hours).

8th to town, worked at the Chaucer altering bits of the color to make more harmonius, giving more color here & there to the Flesh – make the whole more solid & round till ¼ to 5 (3 hours).

9th have been to the city first after money, about 30 shillings being my all. Worked from 1 to 5 at Chaucer. White called to see it – came home by 7, found Seddon here, consulted him about my affairs. Money I must have –

10th to Town & at the same till 5, the fool, the cardinal & the women giving them color & substance, could not manage the old woman (5½ hours).

[28] *An English Autumn Afternoon* was hung.
[29] There is no explanation why the steps were at Furnival's Inn, Holborn, a building consisting of chambers. (Dickens had lived there in his early years; it is now the site of the red brick Prudential Insurance Offices.)

18th Sunday a day of rest in reality – after a week of most harrassing work. I have done nothing today except settle the pattern of two frames for my Emigrants & my little "turnip Field". Last Sunday I walked to the Swiss tavern[30] & took bus to Maddox St, worked from ½ past 12 till halfpast 4 (4 hours). Monday I went to call on my uncle about the money I wish to raise on mortgage, found it would be attended with great difficulties, consequent discouragement. Worked about 2 hours I think in a state of mental anguish. In despair I called in on old White, he told me to send him my duplicate of "Waiting" & my Saturday Night Virgin (2 hours).

Tuesday 13th I saw him, told him price £20 each, he abused both, but would buy neither that day. I told him about Seddon & his works & promissed to take him there the next day which I did. Old White again abused the works & I promissed to alter *his* little picture of "Waiting" as the fire light is too red. Thence to the City to see if my tailor would lend money which he declined – came back dejected & as a last trial sent to fetch my duplicate of "Waiting" from Old White to see if he would keep it, he let it go – home in despondent state. Thursday to London to see after some money-lender – not knowing where to apply could not get hold of one. At the gallery found Gabriel Rossetti & his sister looking at my picture. Went to Blackfriars with him wasted my time as is inevitable when I get someone to talk to. Friday I called on Seddon & asked him about money-lenders, he told me his father would lend me the £50 I wanted on security. This relieved me, I walked on into town & met a man more to be pittied than myself. Poor Papworth, son in Law & assistant to the old scoundrel Baily whose 5th Bankrupcy leaves for the time destitute[31] & with a family. Worked about 2 hours, went & tea'd with Woolner who seemed desirous I should see his nice comfortable room[32] (2 hours). Got home by one a.m. Saturday read the paper in bed, walked to swiss tavern, at work on the large picture (5 hours).

19th Up at 9 retarded by bowels out of order, started at 11 for city, walked to Archway then bus. Saw old Seddons Lawer, all right, saw my uncle Madox who has got the old lady to send me the 500£ which is an immense relief. I can now go to India or continue my picturs as may seem prudent. So to Maddox St & worked till 5 on the "Chaucer", Gallery full of fog. Kings head, Princess' hair & scharf. Little boy with Jelly. Indescribable touches to all, to improve the solidity & truth of color. Eveg blank (2½ hours).

---

[30] The "Swiss Cottage Tavern" at the junction of Finchley (New) Road and Avenue Road.
[31] His extravagance and negligence had landed him in this critical situation.
[32] Woolner had recently taken a room in the house of a John Tullet Esq., 27 Rutland Street, Hampstead.

20th Up at ½ past 8 out by 10 to Archway, bus to city – Penny news room, read Layards speech who has come out like a brick. Palmerston's reply very tame[33] – walked to the gallery & began work about ½ past 1 – till 5 – Chaucers head & hands more colour – distance iden – item battlements & sundry blue shadows. Ordered frames for "Last of England" & the "Corn field" – home by 9 P.M. (3½ hours).

22nd up at ¼ to 9, at 11 started for the Archway bus to City, got Seddon's 50£, took a pen'orth at a news room, got home by ½ past 4, was to have returned by 2 to take dear Emma to the Mercers to buy things for baby – started with her about 5, back by 8, imprudent after tea, paid butcher, baker etc. Yesterday I called on the Seddons then to town & worked 3 hours, then dined at the Seddons. Heard that Windus[34] had bought four of my pictures from White, the cunning old rogue never told me this. I consider this may save me from going to India, I have felt hopeful again since I heard it. He has the Wickliff & the sketch of do., the Winandermere & the "Cordelia parting with her sisters".[35] We shall see etc (3 hours).

23rd up at 8 to town per bus, fare 1/6, being a snow storm. Began work about 11 at changing the cloak of the female in converse with the page, from grey to reddish brown – did more than half then fell short of colors, went out & bought a tube of Mars yellow & buns for the old womans children & walked far & wide up oxford st to look for a cloak for my son. Went back & found the red brown tint did not suit, so at much cost of rag I wiped it off & hit, I dont know how, on a peculiar kind of blue which seemed to me to improve the picture much – nous verrons demain. This was a change suggested by Robert Dickinson, who however proposed black which would have spoiled the picture. Worked till dark in excellent spirits, the weather being however much against doing any good. Bought a hood & cloak for my son & embroidery for a frock for him – did not get home till 9 in consequence & being tired & dinnerless, I was very sulky & abused every one. The cloak was not to my taste, I had proposed to have one made after my own designe. Smoked, filled up my account wrote letters & business matters & am filling this in at *2 A.M.* (4½ hours).

24th up at 8 missed the Bus through the wind having veered round in the night which caused a thaw & also prevented us from hearing the horn of

[33] In the House of Commons (Sir) A.H. Layard, Liberal M.P. for Aylesbury, had called attention to the inefficient manner in which the Crimean War was being conducted. Lord Palmerston countered this with an explanation of the measures he was prepared to take for the prosecution of the war, and was loudly cheered.
[34] B. Godfrey Windus, a coachmaker by trade and a generous art patron, had made his fortune with a medicine for children, hence Brown's nickname for him, "Godfrey's Cordial". He had now retired and was living at Tottenham Green.
[35] See p.72, n.3 (Private Collection).

the bus,[36] as we have while the wind was in the north – walked to Kentish-town called on Seddon & advised him – to work by 12 at the grey cloak – found the color not so good as I thought it, changed it to a greener hue, then touched the pavement. This took me till ½ past 5, walked home, set my accounpts in order, find the little brute Oliver has cost £7.15 for cloaths, I am an ass (5 hours).

25th Sunday off by the 9 oclock bus, to work before 11 till 5, walked home (6 hours).

26th off by 9 oclock bus with Emma & baby to see "Chaucer", took her to her mothers in a cab, left her at door & went & bought boots & colours & gave my umbrella to be recovered.[37] To work by 2 having been to order frames for "Corn Field" & "Last of England". Repainted the yellow hood of Gower & the courtier's face who is speaking with him. Then dined, called on Rossetti & fetched Emma home (3 hours).

27th Fog – got up & missed bus. Called on Seddon who strongly urged me to call on Windus of Tottenham. To work by 1, found what I had painted in the fog the day before all yellow & bad, repainted it & made it good – William Rossetti called to see it & took me home to dine with him. Bus home (4 hours).

28th Missed the bus, walked to Swiss Tavern & bus. Worked at the pages on each side of Chaucer etc etc & determined to do no more as it must dry, so left the sky all covered with finger marks (4 hours).

1st March Wasted the morning writing letters to Windus & others & then worked on the "Waiting" picter which is now to be "An English Fireside & 1854-5", did not much good (4 hours).

2nd up at 9. I have sold one of the 3 works I sent to the winter Exn, the "Studies of Heads". I think it was £10 I put on it, this pleased me, wrote an order for the other two, walked to the Drapers to buy things for Emma & to see about registering Oliver. Dined & did hardly any work like a most extreme fool, my time being now exquisitely precious having only one month to finish the last of England for the R.A. Put my accoumpts to rights. A letter from Windus that shows favorably. I am to call on him on tuesday. Man came & registered "Oliver Madox Brown" (1 hour).

[36] Leighton's ran an omnibus into London at 8.45 a.m. which stopped at the Queen's Head, the inn just to the north of St Mary's Church and within a quick walk of Grove Villas. The Royal Mail omnibus passed through to London daily at 8 a.m. and a coach from St Albans halted at the Torrington Arms on Finchley Common to pick up passengers.
[37] The umbrella had served as a prop in *The Last of England*.

3rd worked at "English fireside" finished all but head – cough – bad (5 hours).

4th Last night I awoke with excruciating pain in my chest & almost fainted in bed, slept again & in the morning do. so lay in bed – got up towards eveng. Arranged frames for the second "Windermeer" which I will cut down like the other Windus has. Took my first chalk drawing of "Chaucer" out of my book of sketches & settled to send it to be mounted & framed do. with the water-color of the Fresco which Haydon admired.[38] The frame of the "Brent" to be cleaned.

5th Got up early to go to Town with Emma, which I did not expect yesterday I should do to day. Emma & the babe with me to the Gallery, Maddox St. Could not get in, put them in a cab. Met Seddon who is looking for rooms to show his picters in.[39] My Chaucer sent for by Green. Rejoined Emma, bought her a dress & bonnet, then to Gravesend to fetch Lucy & joined Emma again at the Rossettis & cab home. Money spinning.

6th walked to Tottenham to call on Godfrey's Cordial, found him polite but not too empressé – told me his rooms were full, which is surely true & that he did not buy any more pictures, only a sketch now & then of "White" – he thinks old White "of Exquisite taste". He has Millais' Isabella & Lorenzo, which looked much faded but I suppose it is I who have brightened, it is however very fine in Expression. His Huguenot was being engraved. Windus would not let Millais make a sketch of it. Millais threatened "he should never have an other picture of his". If he sold one to a dealer it should be with the proviso that "it should never be sold to Windus". Windus would not let it go to Paris. His collection is a strange medley of good, bad, & indifferent – some noble drawings of Turner however – one good Etty, Robinson Crusoe – a fine Bonnington. A lot of Stothard drawings & some XXX PRB's. Also a noble study of Millais, an ugly girl in black receiving bad news, also a very queer one of a girl all hair with a wedding ring.[40] My Wickliff looks quite faded, but my sketch of Cordelia & her sisters noble. He did not ask to see what I was doing, nor I him. I had better not have gone, it was Seddon made me.

7th at the English fireside again. Finished it. Then took "Emigrants" & looked (4 hours).

---

[38] See p.1, n.2.
[39] Seddon hired rooms at 14 Berners Street where he showed his paintings from 11 Mar. until the beginning of June. A good light and dull green wallpaper showed off his pictures to his satisfaction.
[40] Besides *The Huguenot*, 1852 (Private Collection), pictures by Millais in the Windus collection mentioned by Brown were *Wandering Thoughts* ("ugly girl in black"), *c.*1854 (Manchester), and *The Bridesmaid*, 1851 (Fitzwilliam Museum, Cambridge). Windus owned very nearly two hundred oils and drawings by Turner, also the oil picture *The Indian Maid* by R.P. Bonington.

8th in bed all day ill with fevor or cold, towards eveg perspired & all night do.

9th Up at 9, fire in back room found the little picture still faulty, made Emma sit to me again at which she sulked. Set it right, began the babies hand in the Emigrant picture from Emma & Oliver, painted them in badly. In the eveng drew in the mans hand again from self & Lucy in a glass (7 hours).

10th up at 9 to work by 11. Drew at the mans hand again, then painted in the womans glove from Lucy holding the Nurse's hand – dined, then at 4 P.M. out into back yard & painted the mans hand from my own with Lucy holding it (in a Glass). Snow on the ground & very cold. Tea in Emma's bed room she having a sore throat. Paid nurse £4, she going this even. Found the hand too small & arm to long, the eveng worked towards remedying it – but not energy enough to rub it out. Accoumpts, & this filled up since the 3rd of current (6½ hours). I had a letter from Rossetti, Thursday, saying that Ruskin had bought all Miss Siddal's ("Guggum's") drawings[41] & said they beat Rossettis own. This is like R. the incarnation of exageration, however he is right to admire them. She is a stunner & no mistake. Rossetti once told me that when he first saw her he felt his destiny was defined; why does he not marry her? He once told me that Hannay when he first knew him used to be so hard up, that he used never to be at home in the day time because of the "rent". He used to go out before the people were up & go home when they were in bed.[42] This was constant with him & he never apparantly eat at all – when he had a little money he used to go & get beer or grog with it. Rossetti & he having been all the fore noon together found about sixpence between them on which to refresh themselves. Rossetti proposed to go to some "alamôde beef" place[43] & get as much to eat as it would afford, Hannay quite stared – he expected it was to go for beer, however Rossetti stuck out for food of a solid nature & prevailed. Hannay now does well, only is so precious idle. His satire & satirists is a delightful book & will last. They say his wife & child are very beautiful. I hope Oliver will be better looking than my two other chicks promiss to be. Katty seems if she

---

[41] "Ruskin saw and bought on the spot every scrap of designs hitherto produced by Miss Siddal. He declared that they were far better than mine, or almost than anyone's, and seemed quite wild with delight at getting them. He asked me to name a price for them . . . He is going to have them splendidly mounted and bound together in gold" (*Letters*, pp.244-5). Rossetti was aware of the encouragement this brought her.

[42] James Hannay (1827-73), journalist and novelist, was the author of *Satire and Satirist*, 1854, a collection of lectures given the previous year. Impecunious and dissipated in youth, he changed his lodgings seven times in the space of two years. His wife, Margaret Thompson, whom he had married in February 1853 bore him several children (the second, a daughter, Elizabeth, had been born on 1 Mar.). She sat to Rossetti for Beatrice in *Dante's Dream* (1856).

[43] Eating houses in the commercial quarters of London, where stewed beef was served.

would turn out witty – Funds reduced to £5, not received the money for the picture.

11th Sunday obliged to work. Rain so could not paint in the yard. After sweeping away the snow, altered the drawing of the hand again – painted the skirts of the coat in doors, after tried to get out again but it came on to rain. I hope this will not be a month of bad weather or I am floored, only 28 days left. This eveng put the "English Fireside" in its frame & set my pallet for tomorrow. Read the Specr at intervals (5 hours).

12th out in the yard, 3 hours at the hand – rain, then worked at it 3 hours in. Eveng little boy & nurse as models, he too big so drew in Katty (7 hours).

13th To preparations by 10 & at work by 11 till 2, & ¼ to 3 till ½ past 5 at Trousers outdoors (6½ hours).

14th Head queer, out for a walk, changed cheque £9.9 – for "Studies of head" received. Enquired after models. All the red headed boys in Finchley came here to day. Tried to work from one, could do no good, painted in the hair of the boy in corderoy detestably, sent him off by 5. After tea an other boy with Mary[44] & my Kate for the group behind the principle ones – terrible work, trying to do any things from a woman & two children. However, I did what is the only way in such a case, I did nothing, not even get in a wax and at last I saw some faint glimmer of an opening to begin through. I did a very little & then after they were gone I drew the group from inspiration. Katty sits well (5 hours).

15th up by 9 took a walk & began work by 11, painted the boy's boots & breach, & made one in his cap – intensely cold out of doors all day. Received a note given me over the wall by the next neighbour who is the landlords agent.[45] I owe him 2 quarters & on the 24th 3 do. I must write & explain. This eveng again the servant boy and Katty & muddled, about 7 hours. Seddon wants me to be at his place on Saturday to meet Millais, Rossetti etc. I wont go – £10.5 in hand & I mean to keep it there & not be such a fool as to pay rent, "base is the slave"[46] etc.

16th Up early to work by ½ past 10. After a walk, the cap, one boot, the hand & the jacket – evening worked about 3 hours at the cartoon of this picture (10 hours).

17th to work about 11, rain, worked indoor at females head without nature for about 3 hours – no good – out per bus & rail to Limehouse to get a net & tackell – no success & rain, at last saw a pig-net & an old block

[44] Perhaps a servant girl.
[45] Mr W.J. Joyner, agent to the Householders' and General Life Assurance, lived at 2 Grove Villas.
[46] "Base is the slave that pays" (*Henry V*, I, ii).

at a marine store shop, brought them off in triumph with a coil of roop for 2/10d, to my frame makers, colour man, & hair cutter, & then to Seddons to meet Millais, Rossetti & Collins.[47] Rossetti in joyful state about Miss Siddall who has got lots to do & Mrs Tennisson insists upon her having a share of the illustrations to Tennisson. Sooner than not she writes to Moxon "she will pay for them herself".[48] Conversation between Seddon, Millais & Collings [Collins] highly morale & religious, they of opinion that no really good man is ever unsuccessful in life. If he dies & leaves a wife & 15 children they are sure to be well provided for & he not to bother about, Millais citing as instances 2 examples to the contrary of irreligious men going to the dogs. Rossetti off early. Millais when a hanger at the R.A. *to write to the Times* if they do not put the best picture in the best place? Collins occasionally chuckles hysterically at these grand projects — believes Millais a second revelation, but himself I like.

18th Up at 8, still at Seddons, breakfast & talk, Hunt writes no end of letters it seems, being of opinion that it is more needful than painting to an artist. Home per bus by 1 — before dinner examined the female head found I had injured it scraped it all over with penknife. Eveng cartoon — (good) (4 hours).

19th up at 9½ dressed hurriedly & to work by ½ past 10, fine day, showers at intervals but kept on under large umbrella, painted the womans glove & part of shawl holding boy — his jacket & hair again & quite successful — do. his hand — & comforter — good day till ½ past 6. Tonight pallet, accounts & this (6½ hours).

20th Up at 9, tired & out for a walk with Lucy & Katty to get a green apple — to work by 12 till 2 indoors at arranging the childs hood & womans skirt. After dinner Kattys head & apple & hand — eveng at the cartoon (8 hours).

21st Up at 9 to work by 10, boys comforter — very cold — scraped out the red hood of the child — painted one arm & hand & began the other. This Eveg scraped out the green skirt & laid it in crome yellow for tomorrow, pallet & this. Read King Arthur[49] (7½ hours).

22nd Up at ½ past 9, to work about 11 till dinner at Katty's hands & from ½ past 2 to 6 at Emma's head. Must see tomorrow if it is improved. I scrape it well over with my pen-knife to begin getting thereby the ground

---

[47] Charles Alston Collins (1828-73) was influenced by Millais and ranks as a minor Pre-Raphaelite. He was a brother of Wilkie Collins, the novelist, and married Dickens's daughter, Kate.

[48] Of the fifty-four illustrations to the edition of Tennyson's *Poems* published by Edward Moxon in 1857, thirty were executed by the three leading members of the P.R.B. Rossetti contributed five, Holman Hunt seven, Millais eighteen. There were no illustrations by Miss Siddal.

[49] Probably Tennyson's *Morte d'Arthur.*

partly seen through, for the repainting this head is with *zink white* on zink white ground. I keep it faithfully like Emma. After tea I am ½ hour at the cartoon indoors, the head being under umbrella (7½ hours).

23rd Up at ½ past 9 to work at Emma's head from ½ past 10 till ½ past 6 (7 hours).

24th Up at ½ past 8 out with Emma & children. She gone to see her mother with Oliver, to work by 12 till 5 at the head without Emma. Thought I had improved it & then got disgusted with it just before leaving off – consequently in a state of great despondency, this invariably the case when I work at a female head or any principle one. I cannot believe it is fit to be seen till I have put it away for a week. But to day I have been nervey about the head & irritable (5 hours).

25th Sunday to Church with Lucy, & day of rest – irritable though, and annoyed at Emma to whom I gave 1£ yesterday to go & see her mother and to come back by the bus & she stayed with the baby till 6 this eveng & then came home in a cab, breaking all promisses as usual,[50] & spending more money.

26th Repainted the womans skirt olive green from "feeling" & I forget what. Evening I made a piece of frame work like the bulwark of a ship (7 hours).

27th Katty's hood, face & hands & sundries. Ordered Green paint & painted the bulwark & fitted on the netting, got it all ready to paint from by 12 at night (6½ hours).

28th Began retouching the red shawl & the olive green skirt & actually worked the whole day at them & did not succeed. In the eveng an old washerwoman for the widdow mother of the profligate (9 hours).

29th to work by 10 till 1 at the confounded skirt again. After dinner placed the bulwark out in the yard & began painting it through the window. This eveng drew in the netting, ropes, & the old widow (10 hours).

30th Up at ½ past 9 – stupid feeling, trifled away much time – out to see after cabbages – failure – to work by 12 at the bulwark. After dinner finding that cabbages *must* be had, I out with the boy who is digging the garden. Our greengrocers red cabbages all spoiled, brought back 2 red & 4 white – then begged two more of our next neighbar, trimmed them & hung them round the bulwark & to work till 7. After tea languid, sat &

[50] This may be a reference to Emma's extravagance, but it is more likely to be the first allusion to her drinking propensities which were, intermittently, to bedevil their relationship.

looked at Oliver & his mother, then hung up one more cabbage & brought my picture in & scraped at the sea which must be repainted. Supper, this, & to bed 12 oclock (7 hours).

31st up by 9 to work by 10 painted two cabbages. Rossetti came & bothered me just as I was engaged on the second. Worked till dark and then tea & talk till 2 a.m. he doing water colors for Ruskin & Miss Heaton. The usual jargon about art – brought Crabbe with him[51] (8 hours).

1st April Up by 10, instead of going to Church I stopped at home to work but through talk did not begin till near one. Talking about King Arthur, in prais of, & how it would illustrate.[52] Seddon it appears has not yet sold any thing nor had many people come. Rossetti abusing Mrs Ruskin & praising Mr.[53] I the reverse. Only one half cabbage to day (5 hours).

2nd up at ½ past 9 to work by ½ past 10, finished the four cabbages in the eveng, read Crabbe then the Spectator, ment to work but did little (8 hours).

3rd up before 9 to work about ½ past 10. All day at the rope & netting cordes and umbrella. As it rained dreary work & I feel as though I had done none, so mechanicel was the work & so mechanically worked I. I now see that I cannot have done for the R.A., is it for good or for evil? I know not, yet it is vexing – had I not painted the two little landscapes in the autumn I would have had time. I have foolishly trifled away my time, & am punished (7 hours).

4th Up at ½ past 7 to go into city to see after my mortgage having made our Landlord a promiss to pay him by the 15th. Bad news, little hope of being able to keep my word. Tom Seddon.

---

[51] Rossetti had been reading the poems of George Crabbe (1754-1832) that winter. 'I fancy one might read him much oftener and much later than Wordsworth – than almost anyone', and was lending the volume to Brown (*Letters*, p. 241). The eccentric and wealthy Ellen Heaton, from Leeds, was influenced by Ruskin in her patronage of Rossetti of whose work she was to acquire a fair number, though nothing of Brown's work, equally through Ruskin's influence. Rossetti had received the following commissions from Ruskin and Miss Heaton: *The Nativity, Dante's Vision of Matilda Gathering Flowers* (both untraced), *Paolo and Francesca da Rimini, Dante's Vision of Rachel and Leah, Dante's Dream at the Time of the Death of Beatrice* (all at the Tate), *Arthur's Tomb, La Belle Dame Sans Merci,* probably *Ruth and Boaz* (Private Collections).

[52] One of Rossetti's contributions to Tennyson's *Poems* was an illustration of *King Arthur and the Weeping Queens.*

[53] Effie Ruskin had left her husband the previous April and was living in Perth. Rossetti was grateful to Ruskin for his patronage and his encouragement both to himself and Miss Siddal. In the full flush of gratitude Rossetti wrote to his aunt: 'he is the best friend I ever had *out of my own family*; or, at any rate, I never had a better, not to do injustice to one or two more' (*Letters*, p.250).

5th Thursday up before 9 to work by 10. The rope, netting & drops of water all painted – a lot of drops & half the netting till 7 P.M. (8 hours).

6th Good Friday church, Seddon in the eveng. Received a disagreable intelligence, John P. Seddon is Building a Chathedral in Whales, he has persuaded the Bishop to have a painting in the Alter & his brother asks me if I think *Rossetti would undertake it*, when he has bought my King Lear at an auction for £15 and knows I am on the point of being driven out of England through general neglect. It is to toady Ruskin – I do not grudge Rossetti the work, but in truth Seddon need not ask me my opinion about it.[54] However let it pass like others.

7th up by 9 to work at "Carrying Corn" for the R.A. A letter from Windus to say my Cordelia is at my service for the R.A. One from White to say I may send for my Ladye of Saturday night, not having the slightest chance of disposing of it. Worked about 3 hours, out with Emma & children, wrote letter about money. To night accompts. White was so hot about buying the drawing 6 months ago & after getting me to alter it & send it to him now says he has not the slighest chance of disposing of it. Old Ass.

8th Got my Ultramarine by post from Seddon, painted the sky & finished it. William Rossetti dined with us, a walk at Dusk & talk with him, says Gabriel pitched into Wornum about Waagen at Lucy's supper, Wornum having presumed to quote him. Miss Siddal going to Ruskin[55] (3 hours).

9th to work about 11 at the bulwark and netting in the "Last of England". Pumistoned the water in the "Brent" sketch & worked at it one hour as a délassement. Out in the yard from 5 to 7 P.M. Wind high (5 hours).

10th Sending in day at the R.A. Emma & children gone to Hampstead to buy some things for Lucy & for donkeys. I obliged to stop in waiting for my frames, then off per bus to framemakers, sent in the Turnip Field – at least if they found the frame – also Cordelia – idest if they found White at home. Called on Seddon, tried to find Woolners new studio in vain.[56] Back

---

[54] J.P. Seddon had undertaken the restoration of Llandaff Cathedral. There is no evidence (if this was Brown's meaning) that Ruskin was in any way influential in determining Rossetti's contribution of an altar triptych, *The Seed of David*.

[55] R.N. Wornum (1812-77), critic for the *Art Journal*, was Keeper of the National Gallery and had recently been appointed secretary to the Trustees. Dr G.F. Waagen, whose *Treasures of Art in Britain* (translated by Lady Eastlake in 1854) had had a large circulation, had annoyed Rossetti by writing a letter to the *Athenaeum* in July of the previous year "on the Pre-Raphaelite heresy...the efforts however well meant...are totally mistaken". Elizabeth Siddal, accompanied by Rossetti, had visited the Ruskins at Denmark Hill on 11 Apr: "All the Rs were most delighted with Guggum. J.R. said she was a noble, glorious creature" (*Letters*, p. 249).

[56] Woolner's studio room was in the house of William Walker, "historical engraver", at 64 Margaret Street, which runs across the southern ends of Great Portland and Great Titchfield Streets.

to Hampstead per bus & walked home very dejected – & so all eveng (1 hour).

11th up at 8. Very absent & dejected no prospect but going to India. With difficulty roused myself to work about 11 at my pallet & preparations till 12, then till 3 at work & from ½ past 4 till 7 out in yard. Cold north wind yesterday & today has given me a cold on my chest. This eveng cleaned pallet & worked at Emmas head, the drawing I made at Hampstead when I began the picture. Emma would not sit so I worked from feeling. Yesterday she had a sad fall from off a stile & in bed, was fainting last night – poor dear. This morning accompts before wash (7 hours). Millais it seems has finished his "fireman" picture although 3 weeks ago he had more than half uncovered they say. How he does I cant tell. Glass has sold an other picter for Seddon to Mr Ardem.[57]

12th Took Lucy back to school – bad cold on my chest – took her to Mrs Rossettis & met Millais who was waiting for Collins to [go] cock-horsing on hire.[58] Told me he had terribly scamped his picture of the fireman but thought he must send in this year. Very amiably disposed & humble in manner so I promised to call on him. So we missed our train. Took Loo to the Pantheon & there stopped so long looking at Anthonys picture put there by the old scoundrel Thomas the sergeant[59] that we miss our train again. Anthonys things there, every one of them wellnigh look glorious, color Like Constable only better by far. Oh the perverseness of men in general & picture buyers especially. A story of Johnny Millais: William Rossetti, he & Collins dined at Campbel's[60] a short time since. Millais summoned the waiters & with utmost noise ordered every thing that was good in the place, kept up such a noise that very soon every thing was brought & Millais ate as he can. A modest man in the next box had first asked for a chop & continued asking till Millais being well stuffed & ready to leave, suddenly takes to pitting the ill used one. Sir, sais he, these

---

[57] Millais' R.A. exhibit *The Rescue* (*The Fireman*: National Gallery of Victoria, Melbourne) was executed in haste. It earned praise from Ruskin and Rossetti and was bought by Mr Joseph Arden of Rickmansworth Park, who already owned four works by Millais and had commissioned *The Order of Release*.

[58] A nursery term used for "riding astride", and in this instance indicating the hire of horses for riding.

[59] The Pantheon was the third building of that name on the same site, on the south side of Oxford Street, facing the Princess's Theatre. Reconstructed in 1834 as a bazaar and picture gallery and fitted up in a most splendid manner, its front incorporated part of James Wyatt's original building, though the portico had been remodelled by Sydney Smirke. Ralph Thomas (1803-62), who had begun life as a shoemaker's apprentice, and bookseller in Oxford Street, was called to the Bar in 1831 and in 1852 was admitted a serjeant-at-law. He was an early patron of Millais, who soon found his terms too illiberal.

[60] Campbell's Scotch Stores was a popular eating place in Beak Street where the walls were hung with works by Theodore von Holst, a painter of supernatural subjects, whom as a young man Rossetti had admired (see Rossetti's letter to Brown, Appendix I).

waiters behave very badly to you, were I in your place I would bully them frightfully, why sir we've actually got our dinner & eaten while youve been waiting for your chop. Were I you sir when it came I would send it back, leave it on their hands. The poor man got incensed & did so, which having witnessed, out stalked Millais triumphantly. William suggested that the poor man would have to go else-where & begin waiting again for his chop (6 hours).

13th bad cold breakfast in bed – to work about 12 at the sketch of "Last of England", cuttlefished it, scraped out spaces for the cabbages & coppied them in from the picture & divers till 7 P.M. This eveng a letter from Gabriel saying Ruskin the rogue had made two propositions to Miss Siddall, *not* proposals although he would be capable of that – one to buy all she does one by one – the other to give her £150 a year for all she does & if he sold them for more the difference to be hers, if not to keep them. D.G.R. in glee.

14th out to the city to get £20 from the lawer to pay the rent. Made him give it me. To Rosetti where came Miss Siddall whom I accompanied to sundry colormen, to the pantheon to meet Gabriel who of course was not to be found, then to dine, having after much trouble found him – then to his mothers – where I slept. Miss S's first intervue with do.[61] Late talk while Gabriel saw her home.

15th Sunday with Gabriel & William called to see Mary Howit – she not up, her daughter away & we *forgot to ask for the father* William Howit, who by the buy, they hate.[62] Home by 2, Emma at dinner pretending to be sulky. Lucy had called the day before.

16th out to pay Rent – about 3 pound left in pocket. Tax-man called I think for the 4th time for poor rate; sent him about his business – worked at the sketch of "Last of England". To day I am 34, a dull thing to consider. How little done Oh Lord, & how much gone through? How many changes, how many failures? Is it fate, is it fault? Will it end or must it end me? A bad cold on my chest with pain therein these 3 days (6 hours).

17th up at ½ past 9 to work at the sketch as before. From 11 till 6, unsatisfactory. To night accoumps, also unsatisfactory. I find two things

---

[61] Writing to Brown the previous day, Rossetti had asked if he would "go some day with Guggum to Roberson's [Charles Roberson & Co., of Long Acre], and superintend the purchase of oil colours . . . Lizzy will take tea, perhaps dinner, at my mother's tomorrow" (*Letters*, p. 249). Now that the Ruskins had shown their approval, Rossetti was resolved to introduce Miss Siddal to his family.

[62] William Howitt (1792-1879), journalist, and one-time Quaker turned spiritualist, was connected with the *People's Journal* and *Household Words*. The reason for the Rossetti brothers' dislike of him is not known.

quite impossible, the one to live under £300 a year & the other to do a reasonable amount of work. Try as I will it cannot be (6 hours).

18th up at 9 shower bath resumed, cold better somewhat, a little digging & to work about 11 at the Picture Last of England, female head from Emma till 7 P.M. Cuttlefished it & very light repainting, scraping at times. Tonight a little of Crabbe & a letter & nervous (7 hours).

19th worked at the head again till 4 P.M. without Emma & then from her. When satisfied with it got ready & went with Emma, Katty, Oliver & the maid, to Mill Hill & had tea there at some gardens (lost 3/6) (5 hours).

20th woke up very unhappy. Shower bath. Frames came home last night, ·& wrong. I tried the picture in it once & then the head of Emma struck me as very bad & made me miserable all night. This morning I scraped at it with my penknife & so widened the cheeks some, & improved it, the color is good but the chin & jowls look heavey. After this I trifled away much time, took the stretcher of Windermeer to be cut smaller. The Frame man has mistaken the size of the oval, I am at a loss if to use it or not. After dinner worked at the rope & netting & then after 7 dug (5 hours).

21st up at 9 shower bath, still expectorating, trifled away my time. I find as usual I have got lazy now the screw (R.A.) is off. Worked after dinner at the rope & netting. Oliver vaccinated, did not wince, dug a good piece to day. Rossetti & Miss Sid came per bus to night (5 hours).

22nd R. & Miss Sid here all day, one of perfect repose – talk till 2 a.m.

23rd do. & do. here still, walked off to Hampstead this morning. I lazy after, but in the eveng did a little to the designe of "Work", altered the pot-boy (2 hours).

24th to the city about the mortgage, much in want of tin, made divers calls & went to Lowes Dickinsons, where Seddon & Woolner – he preaching phrenology & the Greatness of the deceased Emperor Nick. I suppose Carlyle has by this time reached this conclusion.[63]

25th Up at 9 shower bath, went out after powder for Oliver & trifled away the morning. After dinner out in the yard & painted a lot of drops of water on the netting, very cold, & I not in cue (3 hours).

26th began work, out of sorts, pumisstoned the mans hand & oild it to repaint it out of doors, but enlarged the fingers from feeling & although

---

[63] Perhaps a reference to Carlyle's *Latter Day Pamphlets* in which he advocated the rule of strength. The Emperor Nicholas I (the 'Iron Tsar') who had died on 2 Mar. was a harsh disciplinarian.

the day was propitious, no sun, yet I felt loth to do the bother of going out in the yard & so unconciously what Bacon calls our "affections" prevailed & I began altering the females head from "feeling", id est without nature & so spent the day till 6 when I gardened. The jaw & mouth had displeased me for some days. I certainly improved both but somewhat at the expence of the colour (2 hours). In the eveng worked at "Work" as I did last night also, the pot boy calling out "beeawe", & the *navy* [navvy] tossing it off (8 hours).

27th Up at ½ past 10, bath, garden all day, eveng "Work" (the children) (2 hours).

28th up at ½ past 10, bath, garden all day, eveng children again (3 hours).

29th Sunday up at ½ past 11 disgraceful! breakfast & "Spectator" in bed, shower bath, dinner, all day at the designe of "Work". This is now to me a species of intoxication. When I drew in the poor little vixen girl pulling her brothers hair, I quite growled with delight. A Bon mot of Woolners was, "that it should be a point of honour with women to *stand "smoke"* as with men to stand fire." (5 hours).

30th at the garden all day I reckon it will be somewhat spicy.

1st May worked all day at the mans hand & injured it considerably (6 hours).

2nd To town to finish the mortgage. Called on Marshall & heard that the scoundrel Louis Napoleon had been shot at. Called on Dickinson & heard that every one had been ill used at the R.A., Millais "talking about giving up his diploma".[64] To the city & got £460 remainder of the mortgage money. Lawyers bill 20! Made up my mind going along not to lend my uncle any of it should he ask. After his partner had given me the cheque I walked out with him to the bank & I verily believe the stern looks I wore deterred him from asking me. Went & lodged it in the London & Westr Bank & then paid my frame maker a "cheque" for £10. There is a certain feeling, common to the species I suppose, about drawing a cheque which were superfluous to analize. Called on Thomas, in state of fidget.

3rd Made up my mind to do much work & did nil, but go to Highgate & Hampstead shopping with dear Emma & home in a donkey chaise in a biting easterly wind which gave the dear a cold.

[64] Amongst their circle, the attempt on the life of Napleon III on 28 Apr. in the Champs Elysées, was as nothing compared with the commotion occasioned by the skying of Millais' *Rescue*. Commenting on the rumpus, Lear wrote to Holman Hunt: "...the row and hullabaloo he made was stupendous...threatening to resign instantly...No such scene ever was known" (Angus Davidson, *Edward Lear*, 1968, p.91).

4th Meant to do much work, but only drew at Nolly & in the eveng accompts (much shocked) (2 hours).

5th to Hendon, paid grocer & bought flowers & watering pot. After dinner tried to work but could not get up the steam so drew at the designe of work. This I have ever found is the way – when every thing one can desire favours one, the spirit fails. At other moments one thinks if this that & the other were so & so, how I should get on (5 hours).

6th sunday Worked at trying & arranging the boat, scoundrel etc. Tried the boat green but it was not encouraging. Frames maker. Yesterday a a letter from Seddon to ask if I would give lessons to Sir John Slades daughter & to say his Pyramids were kicked out.[65] What a sell to art! *I* feel Haydonish & old & down in the mouth (4 hours).

7th To town to see Seddon about Lessons to be given to Lady Slades daughters. Got too late there. To my Bankers & drew. Called on Seddon again after buying a hat. Am to give the lessons.

8th Drew at the Blaguard & boat & after went & got my watch & other things out of pawn (6 hours).

9th Gave my first lesson for a guinea & am no longer a gentleman. Pottered about to the color man & after casts for them. Saw L. Dickinson & called on Woolner who seemed in a rancoross condition.

10th Wasted the morning. Came home wet last night on foot. Answered Millais who has kindly offered to patronize me but shant. Told me he had revolutionized the Acady, or nearly so. Worked a little at Blaguards & their mother (3 hours).

11th Worked all day at designing the boy, getting cabbages & repainting sea (7 hours).

12th Up at 7 shower bath, out by 8, bought a folio & a cast for the girls, gave the Lesson. Saw William Rossetti. The academicians are setting up Leightons picture[66] against Millais it seems – saw Millais – & he described

---

[65] Seddon's *Pyramids of Gizeh* (Private Collection) had been rejected at the R.A. General Sir John Slade, Bt (1762-1859), had distinguished himself in the Penninsular Wars. The family, consisting of eleven sons and four daughters by his second wife, lived in Lowndes Square and had, according to F.G. Stephens, 'red-breeched flunkies and swells hanging about'. A few months later Brown tried unsuccessfully to induce Annie Miller (see p.181, n.51) to sit to the Slade daughters (D. Holman-Hunt, *My Grandfather, His Wives & Loves*, 1969, pp.153-4).

[66] *Cimabue's Madonna Carried in Procession Through the Streets of Florence* by Frederic Leighton (1830-96) caused a sensation among the public and gained the approval of Ruskin. It was bought by Queen Victoria and no doubt the Academicians saw in Leighton a challenge to Millais.

to us with gesture his fight with the academicians. Shook his fist in their faces, etc etc. talked for an hour.

13th Cave Thomas here till monday morning, in disgust with the R.A.

14th Emma into London with Oliver. I worked greater part of the day I dont know how & did little good. After, Thomas, Woolner, here in the eveng. Much politics, ending in gloomy aprehension for the British Empire (3 hours).

15th Began work after Woolner had left. Thought I would again alter the place of the boat. Did do an improvement but meanwhile all seems in a in a disgusting mess. Emma came back at 6 & displeased me so we sulk (4 hours).

16th Shower bath, up at ¼ to 8, to town & give my lesson. Met Emma in Camden Town, bought her a parasol & called on Mr Charles Seddon.

17th Walked to Watford & back to see Miss Green.[67]

18th Up at ½ past 9 bath, out after the old washerwoman for a model. To work by ½ past 12 till ½ past 1 & from 3 till ½ past 5 & from 6½ to 7½ in the yard from the old woman. Painted in the mother of the reprobate (4½ hours).

19th Up at ½ past 7 bath, bus to Town to give the lesson, met Emma at Seddons, Hunts father there perorating curiously, a comical brave old cock. Called on Cave Thomas saw the sketch of his picture & did not like it, thence to Maria Rossetti.[68]

20th to Town to see if Rossetti would join in a newly projected exhibition,[69] being of the opinion that unless he & Anthony would that it could have no chance. Of course he would not, being the incarnation of perverseness. Miss Siddall there looking better. Rossetti after much desultory conversation began abusing Cave Thomas's picture, but so spitefully & unfeelingly that at last I lost my temper & accused him of venom & spite & delighting to set friends against each other. This of course he did not agree to & it ended in my telling him to keep to *his* friends, as to me his ways were disagreeable. So I went off, for the first time parting in dudgeon. He has left off abusing his enemies, that apparently having lost

---

[67] Unidentified.

[68] Maria Rossetti (1827-76) was a devout Anglican. She had pupils to whom she taught Italian. Perhaps Thomas's sketch was a study for *Rivalry*, his R.A. exhibit. Holman Hunt's father was in straitened circumstances, having been defrauded of money at the time of his retirement as manager of a city warehouse, but continued to litigate about it until his death.

[69] According to W.M. Rossetti this was a plan to exhibit work apart from the R.A.

its zest from over use & now vituperates his friends, or those of the person addressed as more provoking.

21st To town to prevent Seddon from committing himself in any way. Stopped all day, in the eveng the meeting. Halliday a synecurist & gent — swell & hunchback & artist combined, known chiefly as a friend of Millais & Hunts. Not at all bashful. Martinaux common looking & silent. Arthur Hughes, young Hamson & silent, Monroe goodmannered & tritely talkative. William Rossetti Placid as wont. Cave Thomas Red in the face as lobster boiled and cheery. Woolner fierce as ever. Burcham, a new artist & quondan apothicary[70] — 40. Nervous & modest. Gabriel held out his hand as though nothing were, so I said I had been too crusy & it passed off. Slept in Albany St.

22nd to home to fetch Emma, bus to R.A., met William R. by appointment, Millais' picture more admirable than ever, Fireman perfect — Children wonderful, but the mother ill conceived — still as a whole wonderful. Leighton picture a mere daub as to execution, but finely conceived & composed & the chiaroscuro good — very difficult to judge how he will go on. So much discrepancy twixt execution & conception I have not yet seen. It is strange. Miss Boyce the best Head in the rooms. Martinauxs picture good — as far as can be seen. Dyce pretty & mannered; McClise as usual manered. His best bad. The Cordelia beautiful however, but wrong in action. A lovely little picture by Inchbold high in the Architectural Room. No good scupture.[71]

23rd Gave my lesson. Back to the Rossettis being too lazy to go to French Exhin.[72] Yawned all the rest of the day, home here by myself leaving Emma still at Albany St.

24th up at 9 shower Bath. Out to get the old woman's shawl, saw a poor

---

[70] Among those who gathered at Berners Street were Michael Halliday (1822-69), a clerk in the House of Lords, and amateur artist (W.M. Rossetti comments that he was not "a gent, but a gentleman"). Robert B. Martineau (1826-69), genre painter and pupil of Holman Hunt. Arthur Hughes (1832-1915) was an artist closely associated with the P.R.B. who had two works rejected by the R.A; he shared a studio in Pimlico with the sculptor Alexander Munro (1825-71). R.P. Burcham was a pharmaceutical chemist and amateur still-life artist.

[71] Joanna Boyce (1831-61), soon to marry H.T. Wells, was the gifted sister of G.P. Boyce (1826-97), water-colour painter, diarist, and intimate friend of Rossetti. Her exhibit *Elgiva* was highly regarded by Ruskin who thought that she might eventually number among the first rank of painters. Martineau exhibited a scene from *The Taming of the Shrew*; Dyce, *Christabel*; Maclise, the wrestling scene from *As You Like It*; J.R. Herbert (1810-90), *Lear Recovering his Reason at the sight of Cordelia*. John Inchbold (1830-88), who sought with outstanding success to apply Pre-Raphaelite principles to landscape, had three works in the exhibition, 'The Moorland': Tennyson was the one admired by Brown. Munro showed two marble groups, and medallions, in the Sculpture Room.

[72] The exhibition of the French School of Fine Arts opened on 5 May for its second season at Gambart's Gallery, 121 Pall Mall.

wretch with a nose I thought would do for my scoundrel, worked at him the rest of the day till rain. Painted the fist (5 hours).

25th up at 9 shower Bath. Wretch again all day, painted in the face & coat of scoundrel & quarreled with Emma all day about her extravagance. But the weather was heavy and head bad so perhaps it was my fault. I have quite forgotten how to paint moreover, it would seem. So ends this Boke.

[Book 4 of the Diary ends here and is continued in Book 5.]

24th June I have not written at this now for one month I find, so one omission breads many & each is self impregnated. To the best of my remembrance I have spent the time as –

26th May Up late & off to Lady Slades without breakfast in rage.

27th Sunday rest.

28th The old womans bonnet & shawl on the lay figure & painted in the hand (6 hours).

29th Finished them & off to Seddons in the eve to see him the last time before his marriage. Slept there (5 hours).

30th From Seddons to Lady Slades & then to Gravesend.

31st I forget.

1st June painted at the boat & sundries, alterations & cogitations (5 hours).

2nd Lady Slades.

3rd Sunday Painted all day at the sky, sea, steamer etc, good day. Changed the horizon, made it Lower & level instead of tilted up (8 hours).

4th Placed the veil on the umbrella, a tough job. Afterwards painted at it till 6 when William & Maria Rossetti came (6 hours).

5th Miss Rossetti still with us, walked out afternoon. Veil. Heard of the death of my poor niece Helen, only 17[73] (3 hours).

6th to Lady Slades – to buy mourning & to Helen Bromleys & made a sketch of her child in her coffin – home by 12 night (1 hour).

7th Thursday veil again, I do it indoors, it would be impossible out (6 hours).

[73] The daughter of Mrs (Helen) Bromley who ran the school at Gravesend. Brown had noted the girl's illness in his diary (19 Oct. 1854, p.103). Four days later he heard of the death of another relation, Anna (Madox) Jones.

8th Friday do. & then off to Gravesend (4 hours).

9th While there heard of the death of Anna Jones, my cousin, two days after that of Helen, same hour – shocked. Brought Lucy back after the Funeral.

10th Sunday Letter to Aunt Jones about Poor Anna. Veil (6 hours).

11th Lady Slade, Home by 4 & Idle.

12th Painted in the blue ribbon on the Brown bonnet (execrably) (6 hours).

13th Lady Slades. Called on Woolner, then to dine at William Rossettis with Burchem, Chemist & artist. Saw his very clever drawings of Flowers, mosses etc. With him to hear Monti's Lecture, very interesting with frightfully bad diagrams, poor man. Then back again & met Cayley the translator of Danté & a young parson named Anderson, an Inductive Phylosophy man.[74]

14th home about noon. Gardened.

15th do.

16th bought cabbages & placed them & painted all day at the netting & then behind the female (could not paint) (7 hours).

17th Rehung my pictures & then at yesterdays work, made it good (6 hours).

18th Placed a green Cabbage in doors with reflected light. Could not be bothered to go out & it rained – painted (8 hours).

19th finished it out in the yard (very good). This is a green one in lieu of another red. Scraped out, then daubed away at the childs hand inside the shawl (8 hours).

20th Painted at the child from Nolly & Emma, & I spoiled it – then she went out (7 hours).

21st Called on the Seddons with Lucy.

22nd To the Christal Pallace with whole Family & one servant. Saw the glorious statue of the Florentine Captain & much else.[75]

---

[74] The third lecture of a series on "Ancient and Modern Sculpture", delivered at the premises of Messrs. Colnaghi, Pall Mall, by Raffaelo Monti, a Milanese who worked mostly in England. Charles Cayley (1823-83), scholar and translator of Dante, had at an earlier date been taught Italian by Gabriele Rossetti. Later he was to propose marriage to Christina Rossetti. Mr Charles Anderson was a friend of W.M. Rossetti.

[75] The visit was probably partly prompted by Brown's wish to see Monti's work at the Crystal Palace. This consisted, in addition to a replica of the sculpture in the pediment of

23rd Childs hand scraped out & painted again all day (I cant do it) (7 hours).

24th Today I went to Church with Lucy & then painted at trying to better the brats paw (4 hours).
25th Garden all day. Ment to garden till 11 only, but alas!

26th Up at ½ past 9, garden & idle till 1, then an old man to sit for the hand smoking a pipe, after which scraped out & repainted the fist of the scoundrel (6 hours).

27th Up latish to work about 12 after gardening a little when in popped old White & carried off the "Brent" for £10, the "Carrying Corn" for 12, the Drawing or designe for the "British Poets" which I made in Rome in 45 & which I gave to Millais 3 years ago, & he forgetting it I have now sold for £8 – & the sketch for the Last of England at £10, this last remains to be finished. In all, £40 today – Gloria in Excelsis – I take a 3 months bill for them.

28th Up at 9 shower bath, out in the garden for a few minutes & came in with an apoplectic feeling, heat being intense. After, worked all day hard at the sketch of Last of England – then in the garden about 8 P.M. & came in with the same sensation as this morning. Lay on the sofa with shirt unbuttoned & vinegar compresses for about 1 hour, felt numb at the left extremities (7 hours).

29th Woke up still queer with apoplectic numbness about the left arm. Had Breakfast in bed then an enormous shower bath & up. Worked, a little dinner, well, then John P. Seddon called in & so the eveng passed (1 hour).

30th Up at ½ past 9, bath, felt better worked all day at the sketch for White. Seddon was married to Emiline Bulford to day at Paris (6 hours).

1st July Breakfast in bed, read the Examiner & up at ½ past 12. After dinner scraped out the womans face in the sketch & repainted it, made the picture look quite dull & faded & I consequently unhappy (4 hours).

2nd New servant *nurse*. Emma began the day with quarreling so I determined to give her a dose of it as otherwise she becomes unbearable. Painted all day at the sketch – did not speake to Emma nor she to me (8 hours).

3rd Emma took Lucy to sleep with her & locked me out. This morning up

the Parthenon, of two fountains in the north nave and colossal figures typifying the "four great families of the human race, white, copper, red, black". The bronze equestrian statue of Colleoni was a copy of the fifteenth-century original in Venice by Verrocchio.

early & retouched old Whites sketch & sent it off. All day after at the hand of the scoundrel in the picture trying to make him with a glass of Brandy & water in it. Lucy sitting for it with a glass of beer spilt the whole in her lap being asleep. Divers touches (8 hours)

4th Emma started off to London this morning without letting me know, before I was up, borrowing two shillings of Lucy & more of the servant. To day I painted out the brandy & water which in such a small hole did not do & the coulor of it would not harmonize – put in a black bottl which every [one] knows is the name of scoundrelism.[76] Painted or tried to paint at the head & hand of the healthy ruffian drunk & grinning. Emma has just returned & gone up to bed with Lucy without seeing me (7 hours).

5th Up at 9. worked at sticking the peas till 11. After worked all day at the fellow getting vegetables for the cook. Tea at 6 & as Emma had gone out with Nolly & Katty I walked out with Lucy to Mill-Hill. Afterwards pea sticking, then as Emma was still not returned I wrote a letter to her, the answer to which our fate seems now to hinge on. I am writting I don't no what scarce, because the moment is heavy with dread thoughts & I must occupy myself. When I was young a disappointment in painting used to give me a dreadful pain in my throat, now other miseries take the place of these & the nervous system feels most acutely about the heart & chest – no pain is like this. What would become of my children if I were to finish my wretched Existance & what is to become of me if I do not. O God! have mercy on me & save me (6 hours).

6th Woke up on the sofa in the Parlour at 4 A.M. Dreamt I had been dining with Rusking who boasted that he had got *one* child out of his late spouse at least, whatever the slanderous world might say. Got up being all dressed & went & looked at Emma & Oliver asleep. Saw him trying to get the breast in his sleep. Poked it into his mouth & slipped out of the room again. About 6 went & washed in Lucys room & then out into the garden undecided what to do. Presently Lucy brought an answer to Last nights note, Emma gives in so we are all happy again thanks to God if he did it. Went out with Emma & the Children to buy things at the drapers. Worked at the man in the boat & vegetables (4 hours).

7th Dreamt all night about Seddon & his wife, how that a weeks Marriage had well nigh killed him, but with a gastly whisper, having lost his voice, he

[76] "Black Bottle" had a special significance owing to the introduction on the dining table of an undecanted bottle of Moselle at a large mess dinner of the 11th, Prince Albert's Own, Hussars, given in May, 1840, by the Lieutenant-Colonel of the regiment, the seventh Earl of Cardigan (later of Balaclava fame). Thinking it to be a bottle of porter, the sight of so vulgar an ornament to the table drove Lord Cardigan to such a frenzy of rage that the culprit who had ordered the bottle was put under arrest the following day. "Black Bottle" became not only a catchword, but a term of abuse, and the affair a nine days' wonder.

was telling me that he liked being married exceedingly & would marry again every week if women would have him, but they must be penny weddings as he could not afford any more of the sort he has just had. He told me moreover that his wife had jolly pretty legs, but did not show them as readily as Lina used – I dont know if this is funny but it seemed exceedingly so in the dream & I woke up laughing & could think of nothing else. Got up at 9, gardened a little then gave Lucy her music Lesson, set to work about 7 at the ropes about the boat's davits. Till 8 at this (7 hours).

8th Sunday Lucy was not able to go to church so I set to work at the ropes all day (5 hours).

9th The boat, ropes, & davit – also divers touches (7 hours).

10th worked all day at the drunken scoundrel (feeling) (7 hours).

11th Ment to go to London but it rained all day & I was out of order in the region of the bowels. Worked at the infants hand & Katty's hand & face from feeling – then placed the drapery for the morcel of the Ladyes purple dress & painted it, then began the end of the infants Cloak. Heard from Gabriel that Scott is in town (7 hours).

12th Began painting the infants foot – & out with Emma to buy the dear some jewelery with the money I got for the sketch I gave to J. Millais & sold to White. Went to call on old White to get his promissary. He kept me so long that it was too late to take it to the bank & I had scarce any money with me, however we went & selected the things & among others a bracelet in mosaic gold, so beautiful that I could not resist it. Took Emma & Lucy to see old Mrs Thomas – & home per bus (2 hours).

13th after dinner into London per bus the heat being intense & I feeling apoplectic. To the bank & paid for Emmas things, then Rossetti's for the night, never spent a pleasanter evening – Scott, Hannay, Pawl Leifchild[77] brother of the sculptor, Monroe, Hughes, Martineaux & William Rossetti. All in charming humor till 1 A.M. Heat intense & lots of strawberries I forgot Caley, the translator of Danté, who looks mad & is always in a rumpled shirt without collar & old tail coat. Stopped up talking with Gabriel till 3 then talked in bed with him till 5. After breakfast concocted a letter with him for the Marchioness of Waterford, declining to give her Lessons "à domicile" *by my advice*, then took it to Mivarts[78] & back to the

---

[77] Paul Leifchild is unidentified. His brother, Henry (1823-84), exhibited at the R.A. Another brother, Franklin, was said to have literary ambitions. There were two further Leifchilds in Moorgate, merchants in land and timber.

[78] Lady Waterford (1818-91), wife of the third Marquess, was a dedicated and accomplished amateur painter. Rossetti, who thought her "such a stunner" and "great on design", had been suggested by Ruskin as her teacher. It may have been partly the fact of Ruskin's interest that made Brown persuade Rossetti to send a refusal to Mivarts (later

studio, then while I was smoking a pipe in shirt sleeves "Enter to us" *Ruskin*. I smoke, he talkes divers nonsense about art, hurriedly in shrill flippant tones – I answer him civilly – then resume my coat & prepare to leave. Suddenly, upon this he sais "Mr Brown will you tell me why you chose such a very ugly subject for your last picture".[79] I dumbfounded at such a beginning from a stranger look in his face expectant of some *qualifiycation* & ask "what picture", to which he, looking defyingly, answers Your picture at the British Exn. What made you take such a very ugly subject, it was a pitty for there was some *nice* painting in it. I, from his manner coupled with the knowledge of his having *praised* the subject to Gabriel a few days before, being satisfied that he intended impertinence replied contemptuously "Because it lay out of a back window" & turning on my heel took my hat & wished Gabriel goodbuy. Ruskin seemed by this time in high dudgeon & would not look at me as I left the room. So much for my first intervue with the "stoneless" expostor [of] stones.[80] It would appear that his vanity was hurt at my not hanging longer on his skirts & vented itself in impertinence. According to his accoumpt, he is not *stoneless*, far from it. On the contrary, during his years of marriage "he proposed *three or four* times to his wife" that they should "live as man & wife" but she declined – what an impassioned husband!

15th Gabriel & Scott dined here, Emma enchanted with Scott as all women are – a truly nice fellow & an honour to know. Took him to the Brent & he chaffed Gabriel about his religion which I, knowing he does not relish, gently averted.[81]

16th Glazed & worked at the shepards plaid shawl (5 hours).

17th Up by 10 bath. The same to day. In deep dejection at not getting on faster (6 hours).

18th do. First the shawl & all day at the mans coat, glazing etc. (8 hours).

Claridge's Hotel), but he had previously expressed the view that it was degrading to give lessons (diary, 9 May 1855, p.136).

[79] *An English Autumn Afternoon.*

[80] A reference to Ruskin's book *The Stones of Venice*. Brown's animosity towards Ruskin had increased since the break-up of the Ruskins's marriage. He uses the words "stones" and "stoneless" in a mildly obscene *double entendre* as also in an earlier letter to Thomas Seddon: "Ruskin has been kicking up a great row about Rossetti till his wife drowned it with still greater row she has raised by bolting & publishing that the vilain has lived with her seven years long and never yet shown any performance, the stones of venice being the only ones as yet of which poor Mrs R has had the advantage" (Morgan Library). Ruskin, on his side, aware of Emma's mischievous influence upon Elizabeth Siddal, viewed Brown's friendship with Rossetti with disfavour.

[81] The influence of a deeply religious home had made some indefinable impression on Rossetti's imaginative mind, whereas W.B. Scott was a thorough sceptic.

19th up by 9. Bath, to work by 11 till ½ past 7. Coat, tarpauling & sundries (7½ hours).

20th do. Out to Highgate with Lucy & Katty, dinner at ½ past 3, to work about 6 till 8. Finishing Windermeer for Manchester Exh.

21st Up at 9, to work by 10 till 5 at Windermeer 6 till 7 at the Last of England. Out for a walk with Katty, Emma and Lucy & nolly being gone to town to see Maria Rossetti. This eveng lettered Windermeer & pasted it in the frame by the time Emma returned. She is a silly pus & I am very wretched tonight. Looked out for landscapes this eveng, but although all around one is lovely how little of it will work up in to a picture – that is without great additions & alterations which is a work of too much time to suit my purpose just now. I want little subjects that will paint off at once. How despairing it is to view the loveliness of nature towards sunset & know the impossibility of imitating it, at least in a satisfactory manner as one could do would it only remain so long enough. Then one feels the want of a life study such as Turner devoted to landskape & even then what a botch is any attempt to render it. What wonderful effects I have seen this eveng in the hay fields, the warmth of the uncut grass, the greeny greyness of the unmade hay in furrows or tufts, with lovely violet shadows & long shades of the trees thrown athwart all & melting away one tint into another imperceptibly, & one moment more & cloud passes & all the magic is gone. Begin tomorrow morning all is changed, the hay & the reepers are gone most likely, the sun too, or if not it is in quite the opposite quarter & all that was lovelyest is all that is tamest now, alas! it is better to be a poet – still better a mere lover of nature, one who never dreams of possession.

22nd Sunday Up at ½ past 9 to work. Shawl, green paint of ship (7 hours).

23rd Lucy back to school, took her to Spring gardens terrace to see her aunt Clara first.[82] Fetched Emma from Rossettis.

24th to work by 11 at the green paint, no go, so gardened (2 hours).

25th Garden all day & then to Highgate for Emma.

26th Garden & then to pay the visit to Seddon & his new wife.[83] She is very sweet & beautiful & he a lucky dog, but looked uncomfortable. Afterwards called on Lowes Dickinson & stayed there till 9.

27th Garden all the morning them worked at the sea & shawl, improved both & took a walk with Emma. Saw in twilight what appeared a very

[82] Clara Bromley and her husband (see p.24, n.4) were now living at 1 Spring Gardens Terrace.
[83] Rossetti, who had also been bidden, hoped they might go together, "these introductions being solemn goes" (University of British Columbia, Vancouver).

lovely bit of scenery with the full moon behind it just risen. Determined to paint it (2 hours).

28th Garden all the morning then prepared my traps to go & do the Landskape. Got there by 5 & found it looking dreadfully prosaic. However began it & worked till 8½ [84] (3½ hours).

29th Sunday at work by 12 at the boat & turnips, did little. After dinner a long walk with Emma & the children (3 hours).

30th July up at ½ past 9 to work about 11. Painted the sky of my little Moon piece, then the boat & boy. After 4 dined & to the field by 6, found my sky rubbed (till ½ 8) (7 hours).

31st do. as above. Painted the turnips, finished sailor & childs shoe (7 hours).

1st August do. − painted piece of a hand & colored kerchief to the woman crying behind the Male figure. Would not do so rubbed it out − from two to 4 at the principal head from feeling. Dined & from 5 till 8 out in the fields at my moon piece (7 hours).

2nd Up at ½ past 8 to work by 10 at the head again till 2, then at the woman behind him & again at him till 4 − dined & after dinner it rained so I must needs touch it again & spoiled it partially − before which it looked good (head apoplectic till 8½) (8 hours).

3rd Up at 8 to work by 10 at the mans hand till 4, dinner, moon piece till 8½ (8 hours).

4th Up at 8½ muddled away the morning. To work about 12 at the hand from my own in a glass out in back yard, quite spoilt. Too disgusted to go out to Moon Piece, came to bed to poultice a boil, feel very queer either from laziness, illness or dejection. I don't know which but certain it is I have apoplectic symptoms, imaginary or real. Had a mushroom for tea & thoughts about death − which after all seems to me a very natural consumation. A young farmer here cut his throat last week after being married just one week to a very pretty girl because he failed to loose the marriage knot. That, as it would seem, too often gardian knot to these Ruskins. This poor fellow however behaved like a gentleman (4 hours).

5th Sunday Cave Thomas & Lowes Dickinson here, saw the picture liked the heads very much. Thought the frame cut it off to close & injured it. Thomas is severe upon all frames which his father does not make.

6th went to the haberdashers with Emma. Afterwards determined to send the frame to have its sight made larger & went to a carpenter & got him to

[84] *The Hayfield* (Tate, Plate 17).

16. *Carrying Corn*, Tate Gallery, London

17. *The Hayfield*, Tate Gallery, London

cut two pieces off a pannel. Came back & carefully glued & screwed them on to the side & top of the picture where the sea & sky is. Puttied them & then dressed & off to the frame maker & then to Rossetti to see & make part of a collection of Fossils which he had dug up, namely Cross, Lucy, Anthony, Woolner, Munro, Sedden [Seddon] & William R, & the young inductive parson. These "ancient Pistols" fired away in the stile common to the species with loud report & much smoke till at last they all went off together about 12 & I remained talking to Rossetti till 3 a.m. he showed me a drawer full of "Guggums", God knows how many, but not bad work I should say for the six years he has known her. It is like a monomania with him. Many of them are matchless in beauty however & one day will be worth large sums.

7th Slept at Blackfriars, out with D.G.R. to Stafford house to meet Munroe & the Parson. Found Seddon & his wife there. The magnificence of the place, such as I had never witnessed but in Pallaces, gave food for much reflection & made the visit a very pleasant one & full of new emotions. Oh how strange a place is this world, only those seem to possess power who dont know how to use it. What an accumulation of wealth & impotence is this which is gained by stability & old institutions. Is it for this that a people toils & weared out its miriad lives, for such heaping up of bad taste, for such gilding of hidiousness, for such exposure of embicility as this sort of thing is. Oh how much more beautiful would 6 model labourers cottages be, built by a man of skill for £100 each. As Carlyle sais "enough to make not only the angels but the very jackasses weep"! Saw Miss Siddal Beautifully dressed for about £3, altogether Looking like a queen. The Duchess & her daughters look I'm told like W's — [85]

8th up at 10 to work about 12, scraped & cuttled away at the sky & sea, then repainted at them with not much success. Tomorrow I must hope for more. Painted the sow'ester. Saw Glass yesterday in state of subdued cockyness talking about his grey hairs (6 hours).

9th to work by 12 at the sky. It was all wrong and is now worse (6 hours).

10th do. from 10 till ½ past 7 at the sky with scarcely any result (7½ hours).

11th do. from 10 till 4, improved it. After dinner at the moon piece (8 hours).

---

[85] Stafford (now Lancaster) House, St James's, was the home of the second Duke of Sutherland and his wife, Harriet, Mistress of the Robes to Queen Victoria. Of the four surviving daughters of the marriage, three became Duchesses: of Argyll, Leinster, and Westminster. Built by B.D. Wyatt for the Duke of York, second son of George III, the house was occasionally opened to the public. It was richly decorated and famous for its picture gallery which included works by Titian, Tintoretto, Poussin, Velasquez, and Van Dyck, none of which Brown mentions.

12th Sunday Worked till Woolner came at the sea & sky, then after dinner a walk with him & talk about Australia & how certain convicts took a great liking to him & wished him success heartily, adding that "as for all you other b------rs I dont care whether you find gold or no..". As I was accompanying him back part of the way he narrated to me how, being at Marloe [Marlow] on the Thames one day when he was about 20, a clownish looking fellow offered to show him some fine scenery and when in the midst of a wood took out a pistol & told him he did a little in that line. I takes out writs, said he, & if they wont surrender I shows 'em this & that does it. Woolner was quite cool & he put it up again, his intentions remaining a mystery to this day (2 hours).

13th Rossetti & Miss Siddall here behaving (Rossetti) very badly.

14th Went out with them in a phaeton to see Totteridge & with Rossettis assitance got through much money.

15th Rossetti here still painting at his drawing of Rachel & Lea.[86] I suggested his putting in Danté in the distance & sundry great improvements & now he is in spirits with it & will ask 5£ more for it. I crossed out the glove in my picture the one holding the baby's I mean, & put in a hand instead. It is not good enough yet (4 hours).

16th Emma went into town with Miss Siddal before Rossetti was come in from his rooms at the Queen's Head,[87] so that when he did come his rage knew no bounds at being done out of the society of Guggam & vented itself in abuse on Emma who "was always trying to persuade Miss Sid that he was plaguing her etc etc, whereas that of course Miss Sid liked it as much as he did etc etc." Then it was to poor Katty "O! go and be damned" in tones of a most impassioned despair. I did not know whether to laugh most or to be angry so did both, laughed at him and d----d him & at length thought it best to tell him where he could find them as Betsy was to follow them as soon as she could dress Nolly & join them in Kentish Town. This appeased him & presently off he started. I took a shower bath not having had one since Miss Sid came, she having my room. After this, much pleased to be at peace once again. I set to work at the portion of ships netting that covers the piece added to the side of the pannel, went & cut a cabbage in the garden, placed it & worked *well* from about ½ past 11 till ½ past 4, when back comes Betsy with a note from Rossetti to say I must be at Chatham place by 5 as they were all going to the play. This, just as I was getting in cue for work. Well, in much dudgeon I dined & dressed & off to Hampstead, getting to Blackfriars in time to find a note saying was to follow them to Astley,[88] of all places in the world. So I went to my frame

[86] *Dante's Vision of Rachel and Leah* (Tate).
[87] For the Queen's Head see p.124, n.36. Brown's house was filled to capacity and Rossetti was sleeping at the inn. Betsy was the servant girl.
[88] Astley's was on the Surrey side of Westminster Bridge. With a stage, and a central space

maker & settled about cutting the frame larger, then to my colorman then to a coffee shop, then to Astleys to enquire when the performance ended & finding I had just one houre & a half to wait & not choosing to go & witness the conduct such as it might be of these three, at the pit of Astleys, I entered a coffee shop opposite, & with a glass of negus spent the time, then walked over as the crowd came out but they were gone. So in a cheerful temper I off to Blackfriars & there found Gabriel gone & Miss Siddall in bed, so backed out of it and past 12 went & got a bed, Emma being gone to sleep at her mothers (5 hours).

17th Up at ½ past 7 not having closed my eyes. Walked up to Hampstead, got the newcomes & home in a violent sun. Breakfasted, dressed & to work at a bit of cabbage stork, dined & out at the moon piece (4 hours).

18th Up at 9, to work about 12 at the females face from feeling. Glass called with a man called Ingram, told me of the suicide of an American named Woodville I think, who was becoming a Pre Raphaelite & married a German Lady unbeknown to his father, the fear of which being discovered is supposed to have affected his mind & he got 20 grains of acetate of Morphia & so hooked it amen.[89] The Newcomes is done, the end though a disappointment to me as construction, is for pathos & deliniation of the human 'art beyond any thing he has yet done. No end of kerchiefs might be wetted over it but I read it dry being used to misery in its actual state but the denoument disappointed me I own, Thackeray seems to have got them into a mess & either to lack the skill or the courage to get them out of it. In my humble opinion Ethel should have died just as Clive would have been enabled to marry her, after which he should have taken to art seriatim & have achieved a position & so have learned the value of suffering. Clive should have wept her & then turned serious & virtuous & married some one just to take care of boy. Or his wife should not have died & they should at length have loved each other & been happy. In the end this would have been far more moral, more probable & more satisfactory to me. But he is the great word artist of now. I long to hear about Sveaborg, but Oh how hard is the fate of these poor Russians & what a

which was covered with earth and sawdust and ringed on three sides by the pit, it was celebrated for pantomimes and equestrian performances, sensational spectacles and military cavalcades. The programme on that evening consisted of "Scenes in the circle" and *Mazeppa* or *The Wild Horse* (a performance in which thirteen years later Ada Mencken, a friend of Rossetti, made her spectacular appearance in tights and leopard skin, strapped to a circus horse, with Swinburne among the enthusiastic audience).

[89] R.C. Woodville (1825-55) from Baltimore, was working in London at the time. A posthumous son was born in Jan. 1856. The Bostonian, Herbert Ingram (1811-60), had founded the *Illustrated London News* in 1842, mainly, it was said, to advertise an aperient, Parr's Life Pill, the receipt of which he had purchased from a druggist in Manchester.

horrid thing it is for fleets at a distance to destroy a town without the loss of a man, how cowardly one might say[90] (6 hours).

19th To work about 12 at the man's head till 7. The woman is now quite right (6 hours).

20th Breakfast in bed, lazy – to work about 1 till ½ past 7 at the womans hand from Emma & baby, & my own hand, Emma holding it in the back yard. Nothing but rain, wind & sun alternately, in despair brought it into front parlor, no good done to day at all. (5½ hours).

21st The same as yesterday only from feeling. No good at all (6 hours).

22nd The same again today out in the yard, Emma holding my hand, & my mouth & moustach in glass. No good (6 hours).

23rd out by 10 to call on Seddon not wishing entirely to cut him. Back by 1, to work by 2 till 7 at filling up places where the oval of the frame has been enlarged, then at the sea again & if any thing spoiled it. The picture looks worth half as much money again now that the sight of the frame is made larger (4 hours).

24th Up at 9 to work from 11 till 7 at the green paint of the vessel & filling up blank spaces round the cabbates (7 hours).

25th To work at 10 till 7, cabbages filled up, ships paint, no go sky (6½ hours).

26th Sunday to work from 11 till 7, painted the sea & sky again (7 hours).

27th Monday to work by 10. Worked at the Mans hand, made it disgustingly bad, left off about 4, quite ill. Shall not work tomorrow, have been at it too close (bad head) (4 hours).

31st began work again today, intensely thick about the upper regions, but felt that I must begin again. Worked till dusk from ½ past 1, scraped out the hand but felt too stupid to venture to touch it again. Did a lot of promiscuous touches. All the week I have been ill with a tired brain & relaxed bowels. I think anxiety as well as work affects my head. Indeed to see how things are going on with me is enough to drive any one mad. This is the last day of August & the picture which was to have been finished & "exploité" by this time is still on the easel. At quarter day we leave here & till I know whether I go to India or not it is no use seeking a fresh abode & till the picture is shown to some people I can not decide upon going & now that the picture is nearly done all the people will be out of town. I have as yet had no time to do Whites landscape in – this confounded picture takes

---

[90] The arsenal and fortress of Sveaborg in the Gulf of Finland had been successfully bombarded by an allied squadron on 9 Aug.

up all the time that I might apply to more saleable works & looks worth nothing now that it is done. I sometimes think it looks most execrable, but this week I am ill & in such a state of nerves that every thing looks distorted. What a miserable sad thing it is to be fit for painting *only* & nothing else — no [? outlet] no hope! I have touched the sky & cliffs again however, to advantage (5 hours).

1st [Sep] worked at the scoundrels clenched fist from my own in the glass indoors, but it is not better, also the fantail & sundries (6 hours).

2nd Sunday to day fortune seemed to favour me. It has been intensely cold, no sun, no rain — high wind, but this seemed the sweetest weather possible, for it was the weather for my picture & made my hand look blue with the cold as I require it in the work, so I painted all day out in the garden & made the mans hand more what I want than it has looked yet. Afterwards tried to mend the scoundrels fist but was not so successful at it however. After work took a four miles walk to warm myself in the dark — came back & set to work, drew in the mothers hand holding the babys in the drawing which has never been done yet — then wrote my name on the picture (9 hours).

3rd Up latish, bath, to work about 11 till 1 at sundries. In to London with Emma, looked at several houses not knowing if we should want one or I have to seek my fortunes in a far countrie. To a room at 33 Percy St, for one week 10/ to show the picture in[91] (2 hours).

4th My last day at the picture Thank God — finished the mans head, scoundrels hand & sundries. At 4 took my moon piece, the sky of which had cracked all over through being painted on zinc white, scraped it & repainted after 5, foolish for night caught me. After tea Pasted the drawing of Last of England into its frame & nailed the picture into its do., took down the Baa Lambs, the sketch of Justice & Drawing of Beauty & by 12 got them ready for tomorrow (7 hours).

5th packed my five pictures in a cart & at 10 a.m. started on my way to London down the new Finchley Rd — I *driving* because it was too heavy to sit both of us in front & perched up behind was any thing but comfort. However, the pony being a mettlesome beast had no idea of going unless his own master thrashed him & seemed to dispise my attempts in that line, so we had to change seats. It is Barnet fair & we were taken for return show men on the road. As I got to the door in Percy St Old White was knocking there. He looked at it the picture for about one hour & was most warm in

[91] A Mrs Cranmer lived there and let out rooms.

his eulogium. I said last figgure was £200 with copy right or £150 without. I think he did not intend to buy when he came, but he seemed loth to leave it, at last he said I want you to give me copy right in & will give you a bill at 6 months for £150, so I said as it was *him* I would take it, indeed I would not have done so otherwise. Then he took the pencil drawing for £7. He promisses speedy fortune & that in two years more I shall no longer sell my pictures to him but command the highest prices in the art market & only give him a picture for remembrance of old times. Amen! say I.

9th Sunday On Thursday I guv a party to which Munro, Rossetti, Cayley, & Seddon came, so we are reviving slightly towards each other[92] — time of breaking up ½ past 1 a.m. Friday I worked a little at altering the seat on which they are, too green — at the suggestion of old White. People all speak in high terms of the product. Last night I had the mulligrubs & went for the first time to Munnros & saw Hughes picture of the Lovers quarrel[93] — it is very beautiful indeed. The girl is lovely, draperies & all, but the greens of his foliage were so acid that made my mulligrubs worse I do think. I break-fasted with Lowes Dickinson to day & he says that there is a fortune to be made in India, but he does not think me the man to do it. I shall not go at present at any rate. Came home by 2 P.M. Am quite undecided what to do next. There is "Work" begun, then Cromwell, then subject of the "commission" in Hide Park.[94]

15th All this week I have only worked one day, Tuesday, when I finished the green bench, bought a rope & painted it, put some rust on the boat & boats davit to please old White, touched & finished the veil do. the sky & put a string to the man's hat (7 hours) Called on Seddon & on Lucy this week, calotyte of his Cromwel[95] looks very well & full of individuality. Sebastopol gone at last, all the south of it, but the French did it not our soldiers. Since last winter when all our real soldiers were destroyed by the raskally government, it seems to me we have done nothing of note — our army I imagine is disgusted & disorganised morally if not physicly. Wednesday I packed up the picture carefully in a sheet & took it to old Whites in a cab at his request & there got a 6 months bill for £157, I paying for the stamps. Then to the bank & drew £15.10.10 sent me by good Madame Casey in payment for my plate, which being in their hands at the

---

[92] Brown appears to have had some unspecified grievance against Seddon (diary 23 Aug. 1855). [93] *April Love* (Tate). Exhibited at the R.A., 1856.
[94] The Cromwell subject, *Cromwell on his Farm* (Port Sunlight), was begun in 1856 and completed in 1872. The second subject is obscure unless an incident during the Civil Wars dealing with the Commissioners of Parliament and the Army in early 1660 and enacted in Hyde Park.
[95] The calotype was probably of Charles Lucy's *Cromwell Resolving to Refuse the Crown*.

time of the revolution in /48 owing to its having been left at the *Mons de Piété*[96] when bringing poor Lizs bodey to this country, I found myself without the requisite money in Paris, I requested them to have melted down if in need of money. Then to Rossettis where Emma was to meet me to *dine* & go with him & Miss Sid to Drury lane by orders. When we got there he had forgotten that after a certain hour we could not get in, so Emma & I paid 5/ & he & Guggum went home. We were late & ill placed, discomfort & heat fierce & intollerable acting (english operatics) do.[97] Altoghether before it was over I felt ill, & by next morning, Thursday, was quite so, being still at Rossetti. Stopped in bed all day in a raging fever in the midst all manners of squalls & discomfort, Emma having to nurse Nolly who did not seem to relish the change. Ruskin came meanwhile & Rossetti ignored us, the babby giving an occasional squall from the next room. Rather better towards night, Dear Emma doing all she could for me. Passed a second sleepless night there with an intense feeling of nausea. Next day, yesterday, felt somewhat better & got up to breakfast. Poor stevens [Stephens] came in & Rossetti not liking him of late, I believe owing to his speaking irreverentially on the subject of Guggum, told him *Mrs* Brown was in the next room ill & that *I* therefore would not come in. I did come however but Stevens seemed at a loss & soon left.[98] Altoghether it was a sceen of the strangest phisical & moral confusion, discomfort, & untruth mixed with dirt & feeling of reckless extravagance, for all toghether this going to the play, *by orders*, cost me £2.10. Gabriel being scant of tin we had to pay for all we had & his Laun Dress charges Hôtel prices I do believe. However, except that I was ill we were merry enough although, as Gabriel says, Ruskin had been sticking pins into him as was his wont for a couple of hours every 3 days. Got back here by 6, ill but rejoicing, quite determined never again to go to the play by Rossetti *orders*. This morning I am still in bed at 2 P.M. but feeling well again & I hope am so, as there is but 2 weeks now to get a house in. In bed till 3 then dressed & walked into the neighborhood of the Swiss Tavern to look for houses. Emma was done up having walked full five miles so I put her in a cab & sent her [to] see a family reported to be in great distress & as we had met Thomas Woolner I

[96] Mont-de-Piété, rue des Blancs Manteaux, Paris, the famous state pawnshop, founded in 1777.
[97] The programme consisted of Acts II and III of Bellini's *La Sonnambula* (which they probably missed), followed by *Rob Roy*, an operatic drama.
[98] F.G. Stephens (1828-1907), one of the original P.R.B., painted a few pictures in accordance with Pre Raphaelite principles (all in the Tate), and contributed to *The Germ*, but from 1861 onwards was an art critic of the *Athenaeum*. He was an intimate friend of Holman Hunt, who was still in the Near East and who had asked him to keep an eye on Annie Miller (see p.181, n.51); Holman Hunt was in love with her and feared Rossetti as a rival. Stephens's visit to Blackfriars may well have been to inform Rossetti that Holman Hunt had proposed marriage to Annie by letter, and finding such confusion he "seemed at a loss and soon left", not liking to speak.

I walked with him. He can get nothing to do whatever. Met Emma at the Rossettis, Bill just back from Paris, now thinks the French the only Art nation in the world,[99] so men change. Back per bus with bad cold.

15th [?16th] in bed all day till 5 P.M. Languidly up now at this.

23rd I was in bed Monday & Tuesday with a cold. Christina Rossetti came here from Tuesday eveng till Saturday. There is coldness between her & Gabriel because she & Guggum do not agree. She works at worsted ever & talks sparingly. Bill was here thursday till Friday morng. Wednesday till yesterday I was after houses & took one opposite Fortess terrace, 10 rooms £45 quite new. 50£ if I have a glass studio put up in garden. Yesterday I had occasion to speak to very rich man, the owner of half Fortess Terrace & God know how much more property, I am quite sure he had been a shop keeper, but so bumptious quite a carricature of the class. This eveng an old Gentleman warned us not to go down a certain path cross fiels, it was all bog said he, pointing to his boots. I said to Emma that man sure is either a nobleman or a very distinguished officer. I don't know who he was but we since met him afterward going into the house Garrick had at Hendon, & three minutes after we had turned the corner we met him coming out of that property, & he crossed the road to Lord Annersley's — I suppose it is he. N.B. it was not but Mr Weire[100]

22nd October This month has passed without entries. After taking the last mentioned house I fell out with the builder, so took this one in Fortess Terrace at £52.10 a year.[101] I intended to let the first floor but as poor dear Emma had had a sad fit again since we have been here it makes me doubt the feasability of this plan so I think I must make it my painting rooms. On the 8th I began work again at the Hendon moon piece on Lord Tenterden's property, by the by it was he I ment when I said Lord Annersley. The weather has been most trying, however I have stuck at it, sometimes walking 14 miles & only getting 2 hours work in all, with to day 9 days or 36 hours — in two more I think I shall finish what I can do to it there. Thursday I went to Finchley & slept two nights at the Queens Head & to

---

[99] W.M. Rossetti deprecated this suggestion having meant to imply (after his visit to the Paris Exhibition) that the French were in the forefront of European art.

[100] For "Mr Weire" read Samuel Ware, of Hendon Hall, close to Hardiman's farm (see p.xiii), a house once owned by David Garrick but in which he never lived. The original structure of the house is barely distinguishable in its present transformation into the Hendon Hall Hotel, Parson Street, Hendon. For "Lord Annersley" read Lord Tenterden (Diary, 22 Oct. 1855, above) who lived at Hendon Place.

[101] 13 (now No. 56) Fortess Terrace, Kentish Town, which was to be the Browns' house until 1862, faced on to Junction Road (now Fortess Road), a few hundred yards north of the junction with Highgate Road, and on the east side.

day I took a cab, vigorous proceedings this. During this month for notobilia I have been to Sadlers Wells & seen Miss Atkinson a new actrice whom I pronounce to be admirable & better than Miss Glyn. Then I called one night at the Howits & saw William do. & Mrs do. & Anna Mary do.[102] all professing to believe much in dreams. Lastly I have lent £15 to Gabriel, he having spent 20 of Guggums with which she was to have gone to France so that otherwise she would have been impeded. She is gone & I hope Gabriel will work all the better for it. He has finished the Rachel & Lea for which Ruskin gave him 30 Guineas instead of 20 asked, & since has finished an other of Launcelot offering to kiss Queen Guenever at the tomb of K. Arthur, for which he had 20 having asked 15 — also Ruskin — [103]

2nd December   I have delayed all this time filling in because I had made a breach which to fill up was a trouble & so I continued day by day making it worse putting off the trouble — the old story. I think I finished at Hendon on the 24th after which I did not paint again till 9th November when I began a small king Lear from the drawing I had formerly made for the etching[104] which I have never finished of the picture in John Seddons possetion. This work at till last thursday, just three weeks, when I got tired of it & as the purple ran & would not let me go on with it except in the horizontal position with the dust descending on it, I gave up & began working up the fore ground of my Hendon Landscape. Yesterday I went to Cumberland Maket[105] & sketched a hay cart. Afterwards put it in (120 hours). During the time I did not work, that is paint, I did much in the upholstery line & saved thereby (in two weeks) about 10/ — It must be said in my excuse however that two men severally saw the sofa & chairs to cover, & the last was pale & thin by being out of work declared that the things were in such a state that he would *rather not undertake them*. I have made them look splendid in the drawing room, all equally so although the things would not perhaps pass muster at Seddons or Gillows. Nolly has been christened since last entry,[106] also the prizing at the Paris exhibition have

[102] Anna Mary, the Howitts' daughter, aged thirty-one, was an amateur painter, an upholder of women's rights and a believer in the supernatural. Miss Atkinson was playing Gertrude to Phelps's Hamlet.
[103] *Arthur's Tomb* (Private Collection). Miss Siddal had gone to France for her health.
[104] Untraced.
[105] At the bottom end of the Regent's Canal basin and to the west of Euston Station. Established for the sale of hay and straw when these were removed in 1830 from the Haymarket.
[106] Baptized Oliver Madox on 25 Nov. 1855 at Kentish Town Parish Church (St John the Baptist) by the Rev. W. Milner. No names of godparents are given and it is probable that none were appointed. Six other children were baptized at the same time. No dues were paid. Gillow & Co., prominent merchants and upholsterers on the north side of Oxford Street, between Duke and Orchard Streets.

been disposed of. But the most important fact apertaining to this history is that White has at my instigation bought Chaucer while at Paris from Robert Dickinson for £50. This I consider a grand stroke achieved. Miss Siddal has gone to Nice with a cousin of Rossettis, Mrs Kingcain [Kincaid]. After she had been gone 6 weeks or so, letter came to Gariel saying she had spent all her money – at Paris. Gabriel who saw that none of the drawings on his easel could be completed, before long began a fresh one *Franchesca di Rimini*[107] in *three compartments*, worked day & night, finished it in a week, got 35 guineas for it from Ruskin & started off to releave them – saw her off by rail for Nice & came back in an other week. This is how Gabriel can work in a pinch. I must say however that as yet my 15£ are in abeyance but I live in hope. Ruskin sold his Rachel to Miss Heaton for 40 Guinnees, I suppose he had the difference. He will grow rich at this rate, perhaps pay his debts. He says there was nothing at all comparable to Ingres & Delacroix at the Beaux Arts, Delacroix specially he now thinks the greatest painter of modern times.[108] I have always stuck up for Delacroix although seeing but few of his works.

4th Yesterday all day at the empty Hay cart & foreground in the Moon piece. After dinner called on the Thomas's. Lucy has just returned from Paris to fetch over his children & other impediments, Mrs L being there now. He has taken an appartment at £120 year & a studio at £30, altogether 150, how is he to make it pay? Today the same as yesterday (8 hours).

5th today Idem, began work at 2 P.M. Lazy & up late. At Julien's last night[109] where met old White in a half boozy state, glad to find that the prizes giving away at Paris had not damped his ardour, but he talkes of doing great things with it – find Windus has my "Last of England" (2 hours).

6th Same as yesterday. Evening to Rossetti's about Callowtipes for the "Crayon"[110] (5 hours).

7th Put in the figure in the Forground. After dinner to Whites to see after the permission about Callowtip of Last of England. He objects. The Copy right is now half his & half Windus' of Tottenham. Perhaps they may engrave it. Evening little K. Lear (6 hours).

[107] *Paolo and Francesca da Rimini* (Tate).
[108] Delacroix had thirty-five works at the Paris Exhibition, and Ingres over forty. "Delacroix is of the mighty ones of the earth", Rossetti wrote (*Letters*, p.284).
[109] Monsieur Jullien's successful Promenade concerts were held at Covent Garden Opera House. A Mendelssohn Festival was being presented.
[110] A new weekly journal devoted to the arts, published in New York by W.J. Stillman (1828-1901), who later married Marie Spartali, Brown's most dedicated pupil (see p.202, n.4).

8th Set the lay figure in the concervatory for the Hortis with umbrella etc. Very cold painting on the stairs. In the eveng I worked at setting it all right from feeling (6 hours).

9th Sunday obliged to work as my great coat is impressed into the service of the group in the concervatory. Bitter cold evening, rest (4 hours).

10th Last night I found it would not do, so to day I have planned how to break the dark line of trees which painfully cuts the Picture in two. Worked at the figure also, this evening painted in the farmer & men (good work) (7 hours).

11th Placed & painted in the Paint box & canvas & easel etc. After lunch found they would not do, rubbed them in and did them again, no end to even such small jobs as this (5 hours). This even I have written letters, cast up accompt & must write more & then if time's left paint (Changed color of the horses) (2 hours).

12th Painted in the Easel, Paint Box & [?wife]. Went to Juliens, could get no seats after dressing & waiting ¾ in a biting cold, so to the Olimpic[111] – English Theatricals, dooced slow however, Place felt headachey. Robson tremendous but getting spoiled.

14th Up at ½ past 10, Bath, painted Lears head & arms (7 hours).

15th up at 9½. Bath, Worked over Lears head & arms, Painted Cor's face, rubbed it out. Worked in the eveng at her face in the drawing of it which I made for the etching & am now about to finish, having got a frame for it. Intensely sleepy & stupid after Dinner, think it is indigestion – always remark that after a good day or two I become stupid all at once (7 hours). Read the 3 vol of Carlyles Misscellany. The glorious kind hearted old chap. Boswel, Diderot, Cagliostro & the necklace are the best in the book, & among what he has ever done best. The Johnson, Goethe, Edward Irving, among, to me, the unsatisfactory ones, overdone, too many immensities, eternities, or such like superfluities, sometimes whole pages of mere gilded wind bladders looking something like real nuggets but not so. Seek to grasp them & they bob off in most tantallizing fashion. (This is Carlylian I hope.) On the other hand we must allow the great man his occasional weaknesses & caprices & flatulencies. Real gold & solid weight & close packed wisdom is not wanting in the general run of it, more indeed than is attainable in any other writing now published, I opine. As he sais

---

[111] The Olympic Theatre, which stood in the notoriously disreputable Wych Street (on the site of what is now the Aldwych), was a popular theatre for light comedy where Frederick Robson played farce and burlesque with outstanding success. The bill consisted of the farce *Still Waters Run Deep* and concluded with *Catching a Mermaid*.

himself Roland of Ronceval must himself have been constipated at times.[112]

17th Painted Codelias Cloak. Evening stretched & washed Mary Stuart[113] (4 hours).

18th Painted Cordelias face & arm, Mrs Rossetti & Maria called; eveg to ye Seddons (3 hours).

19th worked at the sketch of Hampstead[114] for Woolner (it is jolly) (7 hours).

20th Cuttle-fished the little landscape & painted ye moon (from nature). Called on Woolner who declares we are more devil worshiper than Christian. His reason for the great popularity of Lord Palmerston is that he is treacherous & pugnatious which are the two chief characteristics of us english & that therefor being the most so of any, he by natural force or gravitation is the king of England. However Prince Albert is *our King* worse luck. John Cross told him that Mons. Picot who was president of the Royal Commission of Fine arts at Paris affirmed that it was entirely owing to the pressing solicitude of Lord Elcho that the prizes were given as they were – that the French jurors had awarded the chief medal to Mulready. McDowal voted for himself 19 times so they gave no medal to the sculptor.[115] A lot of other stuff too base to deserve transcribing (5 hours).

21st Morning at the landscape. Went carefully over all the part I painted in at Hendon from nature (5 hours). This even, King Lear, Pencil (8 hours).

22nd To Gravesend to fetch Lucy, left Emma in bed with a bad cold, came home by 7, found her in a fit raving & did not know me. Very sad – these fits –

23rd worked at the foreground of the landskape, Emma better, dull day (3 hours).

24th Emma up again, spent the morning putting up Holly & evergreen instead of working. I fear I have much to repent on the score of idleness. Read Carlyles Miscellanies. This eveng worked at Pencil K. Lear (3 hours).

---

[112] Brown is referring to "The Diamond Necklace" in Carlyle's *Critical and Miscellaneous Essays*. "Roland of Roncesvalles too . . . found rainy weather as well as sunny . . . was saddle-sick, calumniated, constipated."

[113] *The Execution of Mary Queen of Scots* (Untraced) had been painted in 1841.

[114] *Heath Street, Hampstead* (Manchester), a study for the background for *Work*.

[115] Ill-feeling was provoked by Sir Edwin Landseer being the only British artist awarded the gold *médaille d'honneur*. The sculptor Patrick McDowall (1799-1870) earned an "honorable mention".

26th to work at 11 till 4 at landskape. In the eveg at the Pencil K.L. (9 hours).

27th out with Emma & the Children. To work at 2 till 4, eveng King Lear Pencil (5 hours).

28th To work by 11 till 4 at the cart horses, children etc. Lowes D. came in the Eveg (5 hours).

29th Up late, to work from 12 till 4 darkening all the hayfield which Lowes D. thought spoild the background. Am disgusted. Accoupts & Carlyle.

31st worked at the same. In the eveng to see Albert smith[116] with Emma & Lucy (4 hours). Last night our chimney took fire. Emma saw *one spark* fall, lazyness itself could make nothing out of it but "the chimney on fire", so we looked & it was so. Water & wet blacket seemed ineffectual. In the street passers talked of "smell of soot", Sparks seen from chimney. So I had to put down my cigar & go right at it. Up the trap on to the slates & stuff a blanket down the aperture, then waiting one quarter – complete success resulted from these bold & vigorous measures. In the mean time Gabriel had also made himself useful. Emma found him raking the live coals out *all over the room*, large holes in our new kiderminster of Claret powdered with chockolate fleurs de lis.[117] Described to him my new subject of Christmas, he approves. Gabriel was such a swell as I never saw before but looking really splendid. Every thing about him perfect in taste except his *shoes*, it will be some time before he goes that length. Otherwise his brown suit was most in the fashion & he looked handsome & a gentleman – talking of buying a "ticker" but not of paying me back my £15 Alas! However he has sent Miss Sid in all £55 since her departure.

---

[116] Albert Smith had originally joined his father in a medical career. Later, as a lecturer and author of extravaganzas, he held his public entertainments at the Egyptian Hall, Piccadilly. "Mont Blanc", his most popular attraction and which the Browns were witnessing on New Year's Eve, was a lecture comprising sketches and painted illustrations descriptive of his ascent of the Alps.

[117] By the middle of the century four thousand looms were working at Kidderminster, an old weaving centre in Worcestershire. A reversible, hard-wearing carpet, it fulfilled a growing demand for elegant furnishing. It is also an indication of Brown's improved finances.

1856

1st January/56 a dull foggy day, disgusted with my landskape, stuck it up against the wall & worked at it from a distance. Painted out all the easel box etc in front that took me such a time to paint from nature. Made the whole right again. Seddon came in & saw it before I was aware or he should not have. Liked it much. Eveng K Lear (8 hours).

2nd At the field, hay, cart etc. doing well. Even. as yesterday (9 hours).

3rd the artist, & as yesterday. K Lear Pencil. Seddon again called with a letter he had just from Hunt who is on his return. I am glad to hear, but ill I fear a nature that works beyond its strength. To night after work I am up hear in bed room to *ween* Nolly. Emma gone upstairs, so I begin by Carlyle & this stuff, & now proceed to accompts 1 A.M. (9 hours).

4th up at 11 to work by 12 till 4 at landscape, not done yet. After dinner slept on the rug for an hour & a half not having had more than 3 or four hours last night – very stupid this eveg. (4 hours).

5th Worked from 2 till 4 at the King Lear, stupid through master Nolly keeping me awake at night, feeding him with milk (Cow's)[1] & cakes. In the eveng took a short walk in the rain & worked at the pencil King Lear & finished it, my destiny being as Novalis said of Goëthe "to finish whatever I may have begun"[2] (7 hours).

6th Sunday up at 12 through the like cause of the previous night. Emma & Lucy at Church. Spent the morning in a sort of luxury of idleness tidying up the painting rooms & hanging up two fresh pictures in them, Vid. the pencil King Lear & a study of Major Freulich's horse,[3] painted at Ghent

---

[1] G. Parker, cowkeeper, who lived close at hand in Clarence Road. Kentish Town had been one of the best milk-producing localities for London and still had grazing-ground, though much reduced.

[2] The opening passage of Carlyle's "Goethe's Helena", 1828, in *Critical and Miscellaneous Essays*, refers to Novalis, the German Romantic poet and novelist, as having "rather tauntingly asserted of Goethe, that the grand law of his being is to conclude whatsoever he undertakes".

[3] This drawing remained with Brown throughout his life (Untraced).

when I was 15 or Sixteen at the time I painted my fathers pourtrait & the head of the old woman I still value. At this time when I first began art seriatiom & before I fell into any kind of manerism, many of my studies are better than I was able to do for many years afterwards. This same horse which is the facsimile of the one it portraid was the most unmilitary looking bruit I think I ever beheld, or at any rate ever saw major mounted on. It fell under me one day as I was trotting it over one of the flemish wooden draw bridges & peeled the skin off my chin. However with the loss of a saddle girdle we were none the worse for it much, either of us.

[Book 5 of the diary ends here and is continued in Book 6]

27th Jany For want of a book I have omitted entries since the 6th inst. During this blank I worked two whole weeks (sundays included) at the reduction of King Lear, besides one even, also one eve at the present drawing of do. – also one good day at the "Hay Field" (100 hours). On Monday last White called but did not like the latter, said the hay was pink & he had never seen such. He seemed doubtful about the "Lear", said he would call again in a few days if I would make Kent's head & one of the officers & cordelia's hands *less red*. He did not seem to have his wonted *élan* but ended by taking the pencil K Lear for £6.6/ minus 25 per cent discount which I now always allow him on the price. I succeeded in taking him to see Tom Seddons pictures which he seemed to like very much but did not buy. After this he had not time to go to Woolners as he promised me, moreover he did not pay for the Chaucer picture, £45 of which still owing. He was to have paid on receiving it from Paris. Tuesday I did what he wished to the King Lear & after called on the Rossettis having a mind to try if Maria would undertake Lucy's Education inlieu of sending her to school. The room was too full to talk however & Bill with a man named Clayton[4] jawed to nasiously about Ruskin & Art that I felt quite disgusted & said nothing.

On Wednesday as I was debating what to begin, Robert Dickinson came in & proposed that I should help at his portrait manufactory from Callow-types enlarged,[5] three days per week at one guinea a day to be done at Lowes D's studio. I said I would think it over & in the eveg called on Lowes

---

[4] Owing to Emma Brown's intemperance Brown wished Lucy to live away from home (Private Information). John Clayton (1827-1913) helped to found Clayton and Bell, glass painters, and was himself a painter on glass.
[5] It is difficult to come to any clear understanding of Brown's work for the Dickinsons. He regarded it as hackwork while his grandson referred to it as being "not actually degrading. Brown's part was to 'pull the pictures together', another artist doing the actual enlarging" (Hueffer, p.106). In the portrait of Lord John Russell (National Portrait Gallery) painted later that year, signed by Lowes Dickinson and dated "1855", Brown did more than pull it together, he appears to have designed and painted the composition.

and am to begin on Monday, tomorrow. Thursday White came again & after much moaning over my brickdusty color took off King Lear for £20 also the study for the head of the black Prince which I painted in /48 from Maitland in sun light (in doors). The face was done in half an hour, the hair & cap from the wig of the lay figure took I think two days. I afterwards worked on it about one hour at Hampstead in /52 after it had been kicking about for 4 years. I gave it more sollidity through altering the back ground & made it altoghether one of the best heads I have painted. For this He gave me also £6.6 minus one fourth discount. Then he would have Rossetti's drawing of the Lovers on the battlement which he painted in two evenings at W.B. Scotts at newcastle & I took it in lieu of debt of £5.8. At first I demurred at parting with it but White offered £10 & insisted, so I took it off to Gabriels & told him if he had no objection I would part with it, paying him over £5 & keeping the 5 for which I took it. He agreed nothing loath to the 5 pun but generously insisted that I should keep it in part payment of the £15, which I rejoined that I certainly would. So I took it to Old White who requested me to call again in 10 minutes which I did but then found Barlow the engraver there, so after an hours jaw I left to dine with Gabriel off a lobster.[6] He is at work on two drawings in water,[7] as usual both threaten to be admirable. One is a monkish missel painter at work on his knees in his cell. A boy behind him is teasing a cat which has nestled itself among the folds of his habit, he having been so long motion-less at his work. The other is a Ladye & a Knight praying before an altar. He offers his sword, she fixes her sleeve on the basnet. Over head in the distance seem a "blacke tower" & beside it a "blacke" knight mounted, waiting with his lance in rest for the combat. These two together form an admirable picture of the world of our fathers with its 4 chief charackter-isticts, Religion, Art, Chivalry & love. His forte, & he seems now to have found it out, is to be a lirical painter & poet & certainly a glorious one. Friday I called on White by appointment but he was out so I came home & set to work to think over my christmas subject which along with "Cromwell on the farm" I have decided are to be my works for the next 13 months. I forget whether I have mentioned as yet about this subject. It occurred to me on Christmas eve as we were putting up the holly in the parlour (our drawing Rooms) for

[At this point (the bottom of a recto page) an unknown number of pages are missing, probably one double leaf of four pages. Brown's practice in

---

6 Rossetti's *Carlisle Wall* (*The Lovers*; Ashmolean) was executed in June 1853 after a day's expedition with W.B. Scott from Newcastle to Carlisle. T.O. Barlow (1824-89), mezzotint engraver, made plates after Turner, Landseer, Millais.
7 *Fra Pace* (Private Collection). The second water-colour was probably *Chapel Before the Lists* (Tate) in its original form which Rossetti may have intended to call *The Seven Towers* (*Letters*, p.325).

this later copybook (Book 6) was to write across two facing pages. See Appendix II for the adjoining recto and verso.]

14th [February] To Dickinsons again. Painted at the Chair, Bonnet & shawls till ½ past 4. Came home & went with Emma to the Rossettis to dine. After dinner we deffinitly agreed about Lucy. Mrs R consented to take £40 Per annum.[8] A Blessed thing for Lucy (6 hours).

15th To Lowes D's before 10. The shawl & "part of the trenches before Sevastopol" in the portrait of Colonel de Bath.[9] Eveng wasted (6 hours).

16th The same. Took up Gabriel on my way there. Painted lot of sand bags, 2 Men & a great gun. Gabriel off with Lowes to divers exhibitions (7 hours).

17th Last night too tired to work. This morning went to see Seddon's picture then Seddon called on me. At Dinner Gabriel called in & stoped till 2 a.m.

18th Somehow the day wasted, perhaps I worked a little at Cromwell. After play tickets but was too late. In the eveng Seddon & Fred Warren came to Discuss the affairs of the North London School. As I would be glad to hit Cole the scoundrel C.B. I agreed to be on the committee again if it be remodelled & the school rescued from the throttling graps of government.

19th All day after the tickets for the Princess' Theatre. In the evening went there to the Dress Circle with Emma & the 2 children & William Rossetti. Gabriel who had chiefly made up the party having decided that he could not go because he must go again that night to the strand Theatre to see a certain stunner.[10] Katty after the play told William who was alluding to the Angels in Henry VIII "that she once saw some real angels up in the sky".

20th Worked all day uninterruptedly at the designe of Cromwell (8 hours).

21st The same, only in the eveng the Rossettis brought Cayley here who was as monosilabic & ornithological in the way of wispering out his gasping sentences as ever. I drew at a portrait of Bill[11] (8 hours).

---

[8] The £40 fee was for Lucy's board and lodging. Nothing was to be paid for tuition.

[9] Colonel (later General) Sir Henry de Bathe, 4th Bart., Scots Fusiliers (Untraced).

[10] The Princess's Theatre was giving Shakespeare's *Henry VIII* with Mr and Mrs Charles Kean in the rôles of Cardinal Wolsey and Queen Katherine. Meanwhile Rossetti had gone to admire his "Stunner No 1", Louisa Ruth Herbert, who was playing that evening in a "Favourite Commedietta", *Time Tries all*, and a farce, *Never Despair*.

[11] Perhaps an (untraced) study for the portrait by gaslight of William Michael Rossetti (see diary, 16 Mar. 1857, p.194).

22nd Did not work much to day but the designe again.

23rd The same as yesterday, lazily. No news. Seddon painted these 2 days here (10 hours).

24th Sunday Went & fetched Lucy. Worked but little at the designe.

25th From 10 to ½ past 4 at Lowes D's. Made it a snow storm (9 hours).

26th Last night at Cromwell, 3 hours. To day at Colonel De Bath from 10 to ½ past 5. This eveng read Lewes' Goëthe[12] & accompts (10 hours).

27th This morning by 10 at Colonel De Bath. Called on R Dickinson who has not yet heard from White, but gave me £10. This eve from 9 to 12 Cromwell, then Goëthe (9 hours).

28th All this day long read and breakfasted in bed. Not up till 12, tried to work but it would not do. Slept nearly all day & to bed early (2 hours).

29th Worked hard all day at the gun-carriage & gun in Lowes D's portrait of Colonel de Bath, this even. very little at the designe of Cromwell (8 hours).

1st March At Lowes D's from 10 to 6, gun carriage, road, snow etc. In the evening drew in the two men cleaning the hedge row in the Croml. Design ('½ hours).

2nd Sunday To work at copying Houses etc out of Knights Pictorial Hisy[13] for the Cromwell. This evening drew in the cattle in it (6½ hours).

3rd At Dickinsons from 10 till 6. In the eveg went with Emma to the strand Theatre & see Miss Herbert,[14] a discovery of D.G. Rossettis. She is lovely (7 hours).

4th At Lowes D's from 10 to 6. Came home & found Dalziel here with a note from Rossetti, wants me to do him a Prisoner of Chilon on Wood[15] (7 hours). I will this even (2 hours).

---

[12] G.H. Lewes, *Life of Goethe*, 1855.

[13] A search through its pages reveals no particular example for the Elizabethan manor house represented in the painting.

[14] A double bill presented Miss Herbert as Portia in *The Merchant of Venice*, and as Lady Teazle in Sheridan's *The School for Scandal*. Her golden hair and magnificent looks were such as to appeal to Rossetti and his friends and during her climb to theatrical success her beauty was recorded by Watts, Sandys and Prinsep, and above all by Rossetti, who made many drawings and paintings of her.

[15] This was for *Poets of the Nineteenth Century*, an anthology edited by the Rev. R.A. Wilmott, published by Routledge, 1857. On 6 Mar. (but dating it "6 Feb." in error) Brown wrote to Edward Dalziel (one of the Dalziel brothers, the leading reproductive wood engravers of the time) agreeing to undertake the woodcut from Byron's poem *The Prisoner of Chillon* for the price of "8£ treating it in the way I spoke of to you" (Huntington).

5th Called on Dalziel & saw Millais' wood cuts of Tennison.[16] They seemed to me admirable. At Dickinsons from ½ past 10 till 6. Eveng the Prisoner of C. (9½ hours).

6th Took a holliday, called on Gabriel with Emma. Saw a lot of his works gathered there from Ruskin & others as a bait to induce old White to come & buy his monk. We started Emma back, & off to Whites where the plan (which I had devised) took perfectly. Rossetti told him that there were some drawings of his which he had finished for Rusking. So White said he should very much wish to see them before they went, so he is to go I believe. Seddon wished me to dine with him to meet Hunt & Rossetti. I half promised but wont. He has taken the member for Cardif to see Rossetti & the altar piece turns out a fine thing for them. In the eveng I designed but could absolutely do nothing. I kept thinking of Gilbert & his great facility[17] (3 hours).

7th At Lowes again, he very ill with ear ache. I repainted his head of Colonel de Bath again for him but made it very bad & I am quite ashamed of it. This is the worst of painting in public as it were, no errors escape people. In the eveg at home. I began to make something of the Prisoner though, which partly revived my spirits again. I designed the three nearest [figures] (10 hours).

8th At Lowes D's again, repainting divers things Thomas had done to fit them for the snow effect. The worst of it is people cannot be kept out of the studio & so every one soon will know I have been daubing for them which is horrid. Oh! Money! (7 hours).

9th Sunday all day at accompts, in the eveng I drew at the design of Prisoner of Chillon (4 hours).

10th At Lowes D's painted in a hand of ye Colonel & his pipe & retouched his sword & part of dress. This eveng at the prisoner of Chilon, 3 hours. Saw Hunt again who has taken a house at Vauxhall bridge, being a cheerful situation.[18] Lowes is to come here on Thursday, Mark Anthony do. (8½ hours).

---

[16] Millais' work was for Moxon's edition of Tennyson's *Poems*.

[17] (Sir) John Gilbert (1817-97), successful artist and prolific book illustrator. For the Llandaff altar triptych see diary entry 6 Apr. 1855. H.A. Bruce (later Lord Aberdare), who had negotiated the Llandaff commission, was Liberal M.P. for Merthyr Tydfil, not Cardiff. Rossetti asked £400 for the commission: £200 for the central panel and £100 each for the side wings.

[18] Rossetti, on the contrary, thought this house in Pimlico was "a very nice one except for its dismal situation & the almost impossibility of finding it, since Claverton Terrace consists of 3 houses, and his is No. 49" (*Letters*, p.294). The house was shared by Martineau and Halliday, with F.G. Stephens close at hand in Lupus Street.

11th & 12th Again at Dickinsons finished the portrait of the Colonel. In the evening at the Prisoner as before (20 hours).

13th Out shopping, then to University hospital to ask John Marshall about a dead boddy. He got the one that will just do. It was in the vaults under the disecting room. When I saw it first, what with the dim light, the brown & parchment like appearance of it & the shaven head, I took it for a wooden imulation of the thing. Often as I have seen horrors I really did not remember how hideous the shell of a poor creature may remain when the substance contained is fled. Yet we both in our joy at the obtainment of what we sought declared it to be lovely & a splendid corps. Marshall evidently loves a thing of the kind. Home again by 5; in the eveng Anthony, Bill Rossetti & Stevens. Also Seddon. All conversation seems used up, no more the genial flow of soul as in youth. How inferior middle aged people seem.

14th to the University by ½ past 10. Draw the corps till ½ past 2. Got on quite merrily & finished it 2 hours sooner than was obligate on me. As I was going met Marshall who could not keep away from the sweets of the charnel house. I went home with him, he talking away as ever. He has lots of work on hand. I saw his little girl, very nice.[19] Then to the bank & sundries. Eveng Prisoner (3½ hours).

15th Up late, to work about 1 till ½ past 3 then to see Stevens & Hunt & Holliday. Stevens picture a progress evidently. Hunts are without doubt the finest he had done yet. The Christ & Mary in the temple is one of the grandest works of modern times & the lantern maker[20] also is a lovely little work, but ill drawn. Hunt has at last decided against private exhibiting again so that is all knocked at head after so much jaw on his part about it. I don't know what to do (3½ hours).

16th Sunday to church with Emma; after to walk with her to poor Liz's grave in Highgate. Worked a little in the eveng (3 hours).

17th Drew in the dead body in the corrected sketch in Pen & Ink. It is rather dreary. Worked at sundries from self in the looking glass (8 hours).

18th worked all day from self in looking glass in shirts & draws. In the eveng had a model & so finished the figure of the jeering grave digger (8 hours).

19th accompts. Did not begin till 2 when a lean man sent by Rossetti came

[19] John Marshall, now married, was living at 10 Savile Row. This was his first child, Ellen Henriette, not many weeks old.
[20] Holman Hunt's paintings (Birmingham) were *The Finding of the Saviour in the Temple* which was still in progress, and *The Lantern Maker's Courtship*, not completed till 1860. Stephen's picture was perhaps *Mort d'Arthur* (Tate) which remained unfinished.

& so I used him & drew in the hands of the corps & the legs of the old grinning grave digger & one hand of his till 6. After dinner, accounts a tough unravlement, & this. Now to work again (4 hours).

20th To works. Drawing the clothes of the old grave digger, made up a kind of sleeve & had it Pinned on to my waistcoat. Eveng Willm R, Woolner, etc (5 hours).

21st The head of the corps altered also its shoulder raised & the hand of the old grave digger. To Monroe's, met Patmore but did not speak to him much (6 hours).

22nd Out to see Rossetti deffinitivily about sending to the R.A. or not. He advises not. I don't know what to do – really & truly. I must to work. Prisoner of Chillon (3 hours).

23rd Sunday To work but Emma induced me to go out after she came home from church so that I have not done much (5 hours).

24th To work at the designe again all day & night.

25th To Lowes to finish Colonel de Bath for them. In the eveg Prisoner again (18 hours).

26th to work by 11. Drew in the figure of the Prisoner pen & ink (8 hours).

11th [April] Since last entry I have worked at the design on paper & the drawing on the block 12 days & four halves. The block is nearly done. During this time I had an interview with Windus at White's where it was decided not to send the Emigrants to the R.A. I have seen Rossetti's last drawing of Love showing Dante Beatrice dead in a vision,[21] the finest he has done yet. I have seen Millais' picture of this year the Autumn leave, the finest in painting & color he has yet done – but the subject somewhat without purpose & looking like pourtraits. He in a very excited state, bullied Inchbold in ernest for looking at them disrespectfully – he, a *young* man. Inchbold it seems *was* very cheeky. Leward [Luard] in a state of awe.[22] Millais abusing every one, Hunt because he has wasted his time (this was to

---

[21] *Dante's Dream at the Time of the Death of Beatrice*. Shortly before this entry Rossetti had urged Brown to inspect the completed water-colour. "I want you to see it in the frame which is spiffy" (*Letters*, p.297).

[22] Millais was showing his pictures at his studio in Langham Place before sending them to the R.A. *Autumn Leaves* (Manchester) had been painted the previous autumn in Perthshire where he and his wife were living. The models for the two girls in the picture were Mrs Millais' sisters. Millais' *Blind Girl* (Birmingham) was also exhibited this year. Inchbold was only a year younger than Millais. He had two pictures at the R.A. J.D. Luard (1830-60), whom Millais had taken under his wing, exhibited little at the R.A. though his pictures were hung in 1855 and 1857.

Lowes), Rossetti for getting an immense reputation & *having done nothing to deserve it*, I for not sending to the R.A. What could any one find to say against the justice of the R.A. (this was to Seddon) his large picture is I believe sold to Miller for a *thousand guineas*. I dont like it much, the subject is stupidish & the color bad but some of the expression beautiful & lovely parts. He sais (to William Rossetti) that it was painted in five weeks this is a palpable lie. I hear from Lowes that it was originally intended to be called "Absent on urgent private affairs" this accounts for the made up look of the thing.[23] The blind girl is altoghether the finest subject a glorious one a religious picture, a pity he has so scamped the execution. Woolners bust of Tennisson[24] is fine but hard & disagreeable. Somehow there is a hitch in Woolner as a scuptor, the capabilities for execution do not go with his intellect (115 hours).

20th wednesday last I finished the drawing on wood of the P. of Chillon having worked at it pretty regularly except monday the 14th when through going to work at Lowes D's I did not do much & when I got there nothing to do (28 hours). Robert D. wished me to go & see the picture of De Bath at Bond St where he had some alterations to suggest & what should I see but the picture daubed all over with water color & pieces of newspaper stuck over it to get up the proper effect with gradations & Focus etc. etc. He wished me to alter it all according to his plan, this I politely but emphatically declined, since I have heard nothing more from them. Millais is off to his wife again. I saw him at Lewards on Monday, showed me proofs of a Dozen wood cuts he had done, most of them very beautifully drawn & full of beauties but scarcely illustrations from Tennisson, however he proposed that he should get Moxon to give me some to do, which might considerably modifie any opinion adverse to the merits of his, but this proposition was forgotten unfortunately.[25] I found he was adverse to going to Rossetti's, he first said R had never shown him any thing for 3 years & he thought did not wish him to go. Then it came out that Rossetti was always speaking of Ruskin as though he was a saint of the callender & not showing one word of simpathy for his wife. I excupated Rossetti as well

[23] *Peace Concluded* (Minneapolis Institute of Fine Arts), the "large picture" (45 x 35½ inches), rumoured to have been bought by John Miller, a Liverpool patron, for £900. As its earlier title, a catch-word at the time, shows, Millais at first intended to represent an officer luxuriating in an unearned home-leave from the Crimea. With the coming of peace he hastily changed the subject and the composition was adapted to show the officer convalescing from the ardours of war in the loving care of his wife. His children are grouped around his knee and in his hand he holds the *Times* newspaper displaying the peace terms.
[24] Woolner's cast of the original clay model of the bust was completed this month; in the following year it was carried out in marble (Trinity College, Cambridge). In 1856 Woolner also made a second medallion of the poet in plaster.
[25] So far as is known Brown was never approached by Moxon for any designs, though see diary entry for 8 May 1856.

as I could although as I had some months before lectured Gabriel on this same head I could not altoghether think the charge was without foundation. However I got him to go to Chathem Place with me & Lowes & certainly I never witnessed a mortal more delighted than he was with these admirable drawings the last one particularly, also the "Francesca" one & the two "Lovers" set to 2 notes of Music regardless of ryme or reason.[26] He kept returning to one after the other & bursting into such raptures as only Millais can. After he went I told Rossetti of Millais' soreness & he seemed penitent & agreed that on Millais coming up to Town again he would call on him & his wife & be cordial – so I have done the charitable deed, and also in the case of Thomas & him, for last Sunday I asked Thomas too [and] William R. & of course Gabriel must come in to dinner as he was not asked. If he had been it might have been otherwise. William had told me that Gabriel was coming for the pleasure of having a pitch into Thomas & I feared between them any thing but a pleasant afternoon, however they were both very amiable & so a kind of reconciliation takes place. I met Cave Thomas at Chatham place last night & on Thursday next they all go to the "Cristiall" toghether. All went off very smooth last night. I have been pottering over my Cromwell designe since thursday & Seddon has been here 3 days at his Pyramid picture which I found on going to see him as he asked me, was becoming so infernally bad that I took compassion on him & made up my mind to make him improve it as much as possible for I am tired of being cool to him seeing that he will not notice it so if I can make him improve his picture I will. A third invitation from his mother to Emma which we will nowise notice however – nothing *from* them ever again.[27] Millais when I saw him on Monday, although for 3 years I have scarcely seen him twice, began holding forth at such a rate about Ruskin & Mrs Millais as quite surprised me. R. is a fiend whose true charackter will one day burst forth to the world in spite his pious disguise. Among lots of other things I most noted these three. J.R. on going off with his wife in the carriage she being a girl of sixteen (on his wedding day) told her that henceforth they were to live toghether like *two blessed catholic saints*, she being a girl of sixteen & not at all understanding what the devil he could mean. Afterwards J.R. made her take a great oath on the bible not to *divulge* his secret for *10 years*. Finally since she left him he has written to mutual friends stating that before she cut away she was *impure*. J.M. further states that in order to have her divorce she was forced to undergo

---

[26] *La Belle Dame Sans Merci* (Private Collection) is inscribed with the musical notes "G.D."

[27] Seddon's painting of *Pyramids of Gizeh* had been begun in Egypt in 1854. Its reworking and completion was consuming a disproportionate amount of Brown's time. A year previously he had received a loan from old Mr Seddon (see February 1855, p.122) and perhaps some false pride lay at the root of the Browns' refusal of the invitation.

an examination which perfectly substantiated the fact of her purity. Furthermore that he, J.M., has most complete certainty of innocent & virtue in every respect.[28] All that I can add to that any one who could have witnessed Millais excitement & uncontrolable loquatiousness on the subject could not but be satisfied that he was speaking the truth. He seems pasionately fond of her & only indignant at the way she has been treated. I though somewhat of a weathercock must do myself the justice to say that I have ever taken *her* side in the matter (12 hours).

Monday 21st directed Seddon nearly all the morning then out with Emma. Called on Dalziel who had sent me a check for the 8£ found that he wished me to put a slashed sleeve on the arm of the Prisoner to give him a more mediavel look.

tuesday 22nd I worked a little at the block in consequence, but think harmed it (7 hours).

Wednesday 23rd wrote to Dalziel & then painted all day at Seddons sky in his pyramids: a rash thing but I believe I did it some good if in drying it does not spoil itself. Altoghether I have made him improve the general color of the picture (8 hours).

Thursday 24th to the Cristal Palace with Emma. Met by appointment Tom Seddon & Gabriel & well looked at the tracings from Giotto – which as I had seen the the works in Italy seemed to me very bad. However they are glorious works, the kiss of Juday, the virgin Mary's return home, the dead Christ, strike one as the most complete in expression but they are wretched tracings.[29] To day Friday I have tried to work at the Cromwell but am utterly unhinged & stupid (2 hours).

Saturday 25th [26th] Lowes D. came in before I was down I am to go there again monday. Query am I right in going there for one guinea seeing that my expenses are more? I must think it over. To day I have bought 10 penny cakes of water color & have been all day & this eveng coloring the pencil designe of Cromwell. It does *not* look well in its Present state. We shall see (8 hours).

Sunday half a day at the Cromwell (6 hours).

[28] Effie Millais was four weeks short of her twentieth birthday (not sixteen years old) at the time of her marriage to John Ruskin. This was annulled in 1854 on grounds of non-consumation and a year later she married Millais.

[29] These tracings after the frescoes in the Arena Chapel at Padua were commissioned by the Arundel Society from W.O. Williams. The woodcuts of the frescoes by the Dalziels were published at intervals between 1853 to 1860 with an explanatory text by Ruskin. The Arundel Society was founded for the purpose of making reproductions of early Italian works of art. To Rossetti the sight of these tracings was "a most glorious treat... The woodcuts published give no idea" (*Letters*, p.299).

Monday to Lowes D's. Millais there. I proposed that they should send my work home here then walked with J.M. to the R.A. he conversing much about babies & the advantages of marriage, the disgustingness of stale virginities etc in allusion to Hunt. He said he supposed the reason of Hunt's being able to be so long virtous was that before doing any thing whatever he always held a sort of little council with himself in accordance with which he acted. This is very true I believe. Millais is on the contrary the creature of impulse. Came home & worked a half day again at the Cromwell & Tuesday all day (14 hours).

Wednesday a half day or 7 hours at the lord John Russell[30] for R. Dickinson, the back ground (7 hours).

May 1st Thursday the chair & part of coat.

Friday the Coat.

Sunday designed the Gallery (18 hours).

Monday 5th About to set to work when I was attacked with a peculiar kind of dizziness which I have not felt for many years. It commences with a sort of dimn spot to the left of the point I am looking at & increases something like a dull Catharine wheel till it covers up the thing I look at but all to the right of it is clear enough − that is clear [as] the objects usually are next to the point one looks at − when it goes off, & it lasts about an hour, a violent head ache comes on & it did not fail to day. I went out with Emma & about 4 PM being well again began work till dinner 7 then tea then work from 9 till 12 at the Gallery & Lord John (6 hours).

Tuesday 6th At Lord J for 6 hours.

Wed 7th 7 do.

Thursday Out after Lucy's Music. Met Millais (6 hours Lord J.) N.B. Millais told me that he had got Moxon to give me the designs for Tennisson which were for Rossetti as he would never do them. Ergo Briccum est. Of course I will not take Gabriels work without his concent[31] (19 hours).

Friday Today Lord J (9 hours).

Saturday Worked from 12 to 6.

[30] Lord John Russell is seated beside a table with a view of a picture gallery beyond. He leans his head on his left hand; in his right he holds a paper. Signed and dated "L D 1855" and inscribed "Retouched from Life 1867".
[31] Rossetti, whose five designs for the Tennyson *Poems* drove Moxon near to distraction, was dilatory in their execution, troublesome to Dalziel the engraver; and finally extorted £5 more for each design than was given to the other contributors.

Sunday Rest.

Monday from 12 to 5 & from 9 to 1.

Tuesday 6 hours Lord J (21 hours).

Wednesday thursday & friday 6 hours each.

Today, Saturday only 3 having to go out. My eyes being bad (pain & weakness) I have left off night work (21 hours).

Wednesday Miss Siddall came here & stayed the night & next day to Miss Siddalls Lodgings.[32] Were going to meet them along with Gabriel who came thinking to find her here, it appears (from some freak or notion in his head) that Emma sets Miss S. against him. He did not speak one word to Emma either how d'y do or good bye. I did not notice this but on Emma's telling about it next day I thought it would not do to put up with this so wrote to him asking explanation which is yet not come to hand. I put down these things not from any wish to be always giving the unpleasant side of him, but because I think him (as I hope it sufficiently appears in this diary) so great an artist, that any thing tending to give a correct insight into his character is as it were public property & should not be withheld but I will give some of the bright side, here on this page to ballance with. No one perhaps ever showed such vehement disposition to proclaim any real merit, if he thinks he discovers it in an unknown or rising artist. A picture in the suffolk street of a butcher boy by I forget whom, struck him as good & he not only tried to get Ruskin & Boys [Boyce] to purchase it but got Dallas to give it a good notice in the "times" — & would have done the Lord knows what for the man had it been in his power. The picture sold, most likely owing to his disinterrested praise of it to Dallas, who does the Times.[33]. Again the picture by Windus,[34] now in the R.A. He forced Ruskin to go with him in a cab instanter because he had not noticed it in his pamphlet & extorted the promise of a postscrip on its behalf from the man of "Stones". He would have made Boys purchase it but it proved to be

[32] In Weymouth Street. Many domestic rows were occasioned by Emma supposedly inciting Miss Siddal to disobey Rossetti.
[33] The annual exhibition at the Suffolk Street Galleries had opened at the end of March. In the *Times* of 27 Mar. E.S. Dallas, editor and leader-writer, reviewed the pictures, giving some prominence to No. 110 *Eavesdroppers — the Asking*, by James Campbell, a Liverpool artist. The subject of the picture was an old man and a youth listening to a butcher's boy, who unaware of their presence, is making a proposal of marriage to a milkmaid.
[34] *Burd Helen* (Liverpool) by W.L. Windus (1822-1907). Influenced by the P.R.B., he was instrumental in getting their work accepted for exhibition at the Liverpool Academy of which he was a member. The subject of the picture for which Ruskin wrote close on five hundred words in the Postscript to his *Academy Notes* (1855) was based on a ballad from *Percy's Reliques*, 1765. Ruskin classed it as the "second picture of the year; its aim being higher, and its reserved strength greater than those of any other work except *Autumn Leaves*" (*Ruskin*, 14, p.86). Rossetti echoed this praise in a letter to Allingham.

sold. I could narrate a hundred instances of the most disinterrested & noble minded conduct towards his art rivals which places him far above Hunt or Millais for greatness of soul & yet he will on the most trivial occasion hate & backbite any one who gives him offence & spunge on any one & rather hate them than otherwise for it. The dislike he has taken to Emma is most absurd & all on the grounds that she possibly puts Miss Siddall up to being discontented with him, which she does not, for poor Miss Sid complains enough of his absurd goings on not to require that sort of thing. In short Emma was his very good friend till this sort of brutish conduct the other night which is difficult to overlook. Woolner was here tonight & has brought me one of the two side groops of his Wordsworth sketch, The father curbing the passions of the boy.[35] It is admirable as a design for sculpture, beyond comparison with most modern works.

Sunday 5 hours work for Dickinson's Lord John. Gabriel sent a letter of appology & in the eveg came with Miss Sid (5 hours).

Monday Worked two hours at Lord J. then took it home in a cab. Left Emma at the Sid's & off solus to the R.A. (2 hours). Went over it all, catalogue in hand from No. 1 to the End. Very little good, only 3 historical works & they not good, Leighton, Cross, & Thomas. Hunt & Millais unrivalled, except by Hook[36] how for color, indescribable charm, is preeminent even to hugging him in ones arms. A perfect poem is each of his little pictures. Millais' look ten times better than in his room owing to contrast with the surrounding badness. Hunts Scape goat requires to be seen to be believed in & only then can it be understood how by the might of genius out of an old goat & some saline incrustations can be made one of the most tragic & impressive works in the annals of art. In Pictorial composition the work sins however, the goat being right in the middle of the canvas & the two sides repeating each other two much which is always painful & gives a studied appearance to a defect arrising from the lack of it. The background also is at present hard in color & eats up the foreground. I do not remember being much struck with any other works. Millais blind girl looks splendid, there is & a little landscape by Davis[37] of

[35] A work of 1852 forming part of Woolner's design for the competition for the Wordsworth monument to be erected in Westminster Abbey. After his failure to win the competition, Woolner emigrated to Australia.
[36] The R.A. exhibition had opened at the beginning of May. Frederic Leighton exhibited *The Triumph of Music*; John Cross, *Lucy Preston's Petition A.D. 1690*; Cave Thomas, *The Heir Cast Out of the Vineyard*. Holman Hunt was showing *The Scapegoat* (Manchester) and three other canvases. J.C. Hook was exhibiting *The Brambles in the Way*, *A Passing Cloud*, *Welcome, Bonny Boat*, and *The Fisherman's "Goodnight"*.
[37] William Davis (1812-73), painter and Professor of Drawing at the Liverpool Academy, his "leefless tree" noticed by Brown in the picture of *Wallasley Mill, Cheshire*, took three days to paint out of doors in winter weather. He made more than one painting of the Mill. (H.C. Marillier, *Liverpool School of Painters*, 1904, p.112).

Liverpool of leefless trees & some ducks which is perfection. I do not remember ever seeing such an english landscape, it is far too good to be understood — & on the floor. Supped at Guggum's, Gabriel has given three guineas for a superb indian opera cloke & they are for the Princess's[38] Saturday to sport her & it — they had better marry.

Tuesday worked at Cromwell (6 hours).

Wednesday all day at the Designe of Cromwell. I cannot make any thing as yet of the figure itself, it is aucward & beastly. All the rest goes on favorably (7 hours).

Today Thursday worked as before. I forgot to say that Wards Marie Antoinette[39] is coarse & disagreeable though not defficient in a certain rude pathos but quite smothered up in accessories, none but a vulgar mind could have addopted such a style. The picture Gabriel raves so about by Windus I do not think much of (7 hours).

Friday as before, only improved the figure of Cromwell (7 hours).

Saturday Out with Emma shopping spent lots of tin. Met Robert Dickinson — in a way about Lord John because I had made him sitting in a room. Every one askes why & where is he sitting, it ought to be a generalized place. I told him I could not paint such, I never could, he is an ass but this does not make it more pleasant. Came home & felt ill. Read Macawlay. I love Dutch William.[40]

To day Sunday 25th Emma went to church with Lucy looking like an angel in her new bonnet — I worked at Croml till dark, but ill all day, aguish and as it turned out very irritable for it ended in my getting in a terrible rage with Emma after which I took a short walk & better again (5 hours).

22nd June Since last entry I worked at the Cromwell till 29th, firework day,[41] when I settled it as finished (28 hours). However, Gabriel came to fetch Miss Siddall the morrow & gave me more work to do. Emma was to go

---

[38] The Princess's Theatre was showing *The Winter's Tale* with Charles Kean and his wife in the leading parts. It had had its first performance at the end of April, ran for one hundred consecutive nights and was considered a "masterpiece of stage production". Ellen Terry, at the age of eight, was playing her first engagement as the boy Mamilius.
[39] E.M. Ward's *The Last Parting of Marie Antoinette and Her Son*
[40] Brown must have been reading vol. iv of Macaulay's *History of England*, 1855, of which William III was the hero.
[41] The Crimean War peace celebrations were conducted on a massive scale. The *Times* of 30 May carried twenty-six columns of approving descriptions of the fireworks in Hyde Park and of the illuminations in the streets, on clubs, the houses of the aristocracy, and shops.

on saturday with Miss Sid to Ramsgate but Gabriel stopped her & was very bearish again, so friday & saturday were spent getting her off there. Sunday I worked again at the Cromwell & in the eveg to Woolners where met Patmore & Allingham (intellect *thin* & cutting). Poor Emma got on very badly at Ramsgate, landing in pouring rain, bad passage (6 hours).

Monday worked somewhat at Cromwell (5 hours).

Tuesday Old White called in I promised he should see it same week. Heard from Emma she had lost all her tin out of her pocket.

Wednesday Got up at 5 & reached the Brighton rail by ¼ to 7, fetched her home again leaving Katty with Mrs Banger, the potted shrimp woman.

Thursday 5th Started for Huntingdon at 2 to see the Cromwell locallities. Saw the Entry of his Baptism[42] when he was a small squalling babby & helpless. Lunched on bread & chees & ale & a pleasant walk to St Ives through the fields near the Ouse or as *they* call it "the Oose" — on a lovely afternoon. At St Ives met a man lounging near the "Oose" who was intelligent & obliging & took me to the diverse locallities in the place. Sleep hall has been pulled down alass! but the farm where his men used to reside most likely exists, at least a house or rather two stand there of modern build with a noble *butt*ressed barn of the period. There is also an other Cromwell barn still larger but not so likely to have been his. This Gentleman told me his farmer partner was the farmer who boasted he still used Cromwell's branding Iron to brand his sheep. He made me a drawing of it, it is thus

this being used with hot pitch. It is possible that the iron might have lasted 200 years? Carlyle is evidently mistaken about the Cromwell fields which he places to the south east of the Town between it & the Ouse. This Gent who was well versed in the topography of the place said that this part never belonged to Sleep Mannor at all but before Cromwells time & even to the present moment were & are belonging to an other family. Sleep Mannor, the fields which O.C. had went round from Sleep Hall, whis was on the north east extremity of the town, to the farm which is to the north west & so right round to the north bank of the river to the south west of the town Vid: [sketch map].

I slept at the commercial Inn & next morning went to the farm & explored the land but found the Huntingdon church could scarcely by any

---

[42] This visit was connected with his *Cromwell* picture. The baptismal entry, 29 Apr. 1599, was in the Church of St John the Baptist (now removed to the neighbouring Church of All Saints). Slepe Hall, unlikely ever to have been Cromwell's house, had been demolished in 1848.

possibillity have been seen from St Ives & now certainly not on account of the growth of trees. As to these Carlyle speaks much of the Willow & alder but in reallity, but for a good many of the first, the scenery is much like any other although more level than usual in England. However, to destroy this *levelling*[43] tendency there is right between Cromwells farm & Huntingdon a good sized slope & hillock which they term the "hough" which tends much to destroy the impression of flatness which but for that were correct. The view of St Ives from this hillock or "Hough" is very sweet & pictorial. The river with the picturesk old bridge (with house a mid way on it) combine with the church & a large factory shaft to form a sceen such as Turner has oft pourtraid with satisfaction to himself & others, having all the characteristics as Turner well knew to depict of old England & new England combined. Behind all is the Fen Country stretching away into blue mist with Dutch like souavity & breadth.

I went to the farm but the gent was away & the stupid servant knew nothing but sent me to a woman in the next house who took [me] through the dung yard to find her husband & after bawling for him in vain left me to wait for him. As nothing of him appeard except some inarticulate human grunting from an outhouse outside of which two old sows were running about in a terribly purturbed state uttering fearful squalls, responded to by unutterable squeaking from within, I made bold to ope the door, when out rushed furious as an old boar my man, a most hidious looking fellow all boils like Job & very bloody with a knife in his mouth, he was it would seem gelding young pigs & I had disturbed him at his art for which he would appear to be an enthusiast. I left him & strolled over the grounds & secured a slight sketch of the "Barn" & then off to the rail & reached Cambridge by 2. There wandered much about but finding money running short & the sight of so much wealth & comfort made me sulkey by comparison so I took no guide nor asked any questions but came home.

Saturday 7th Out to my frame makers & divers.

Sunday put the work in its frame.

Monday sallied forth to Old White's. Called on Cave Thomas who seemed very low spirited asked him to dinner on the morrow.

Tuesday 10th A portrait came from Lowes to be finished worked 2 hours (2 hours). Then Thomas came to dine, walked with him, Thomas poor fellow said on seeing the pourtrait I had to put back ground to, "Mrs Brown you see what 'high Art' brings one too". He also having the same sort of work for the Dickinsons. Went out with him when on coming home

[43] Brown is here using a play upon words; the "Levellers" were a political party during the Civil War. For the "willow and alder" see Carlyle's *Oliver Cromwell's Letters and Speeches*, 1845, iii, Chap. III.

whom should we find but Rossetti & Miss Sid up stairs. I was very cool to them for I am sick of them coming here & his rudeness to Emma — besides she borrowed more money to go to ramsgate. Painted at that portrait. 54 hours till Wednesday eve the 18th. Woolner called on monday the 9th & said he had the reccommending of a 300 guinea portrait for Australia — would try & get it for me — this is kind & honest.[44]

Thursday 19th out to Old Whites who had sent for the sketch to see it & show it to Windus. The resuslt was that instead of buying it he strongly recommended me not to paint it, nothing that I do pleases him now. I came home & debated what I should do & by friday night I settled upon two fresh subjects, one in the garden a young lady seated on the wall working under a lilac tree & a youths head just visible on the far side, to be called "Stolen pleasures are Sweet". The other in my conservatory with the beautiful vine in it. Three figures, to be called "How it was", a youth quite a boy home from the Crimea *with one arm*, narrating to a poor young widdow "how it was", a young girl his sister hugging him.[45]

Saturday 21st after some bothers & delays began by 3 & worked till 8 at the garden one. Painted 8 bricks & some leaves (5 hours).

Today Sunday dies non. To church with Lucy afterwards quarreled with Emma. Worked over & above 6 hours at 3 Photographs of my prisoner of Chillon. To day & previously, (6 hours).

Monday 23rd up at 9 to work by 11 having fitted up my tent in the garden for I find one thing very necessary when painting out of doors & that is to shade off the too great light that falls on ones work, otherwise when brought in doors it looks flat & colorless, the colors showing more bright in the open air. Painted lilac leaves till dinner, then tooth ache on the sofa till 6 then at work till seven but tooth ache drove me in (5 hours).

24th Began the leaves at ½ past 10. Mrs Seddon & Tom do. came at half past, worked till 2 at it, made it very bad, scraped out, painted at the hayfield from a field near here after dinner (7 hours).

25th Seddons again. Very hot, worked till 2 at Mrs. After finished the hayfield, then with Emma & Lucy to Panoptican[46] (7 hours).

[44] The sitter, Sir Charles Nicholson, Speaker of the Legislative Council, eventually chose another artist.

[45] The first subject became *Stages of Cruelty* (Manchester, Plate 18). The title shows that Brown must have had in mind the series of four prints of that name by Hogarth, an artist whom he greatly admired. Thomas Seddon and his wife were the original models for the lovers. They were superseded by Brown himself and his daughter Lucy, while the young Cathy posed for the figure of the child. The second subject was never carried out, though Brown made studies relating to the war and family life.

[46] Working in the confines of a tent in his back garden Brown would have found the heat of seventy-eight degrees oppressive. *The Hayfield* was retouched twice this year. In August it

18. *Stages of Cruelty*, City Art Gallery, Liverpool

26th Mrs Seddon missed & so wasted my morning. After I worked at the leaves. Woke at 1 am by a terrible accident, man run over (6 hours).

27th Mrs Seddon came because I did not expect her, drew at her head in pencil – leaves after – then called on the Rossettis (6 hours).

28th W.B. Scott called talked about the heat making one feel like in Paradise then about the changes that had come over him in twenty years, since the time when he believed in the power & efficacy of reason, the perfectibility of woman & Mary Woolstonecraft.[47] Worked at the leaves. Eveng Woolner called, told me about poor Howe[48] reduced to beggary litterally – its seems a man may be a beggar & respectable. This gives rise to a new train of thought, is beggary more honoroble than suicide? (7 hours).

29th Sunday all day cogitated over my christ & peter,[49] decided on nothing!

30th Mrs Seddon missed again. I made a list of what days then remained till the liverpool accay on a piece of paper & allowing time to finish the leaves which *must* be done, I decided I had time to clothe the Christ, then that his legs were of no use, then that it was a pity to scrape them out as they are good, so I cut them out the picture being already lined, & glued in a fresh piece of canvas – & puttied it up.

1st [July] found the seam causening up because I had puttied it before the glue was dry. Did it again then Mrs Seddon then leaves (5 hours).

2nd to Peg well bay to fetch Catty who thank God is all right. I started at 5, got there at 1, drank beer with Mr Banger the fisherman, eat soles he

was bought by William Morris. The Royal Panopticon of Science and Art was on the east side of Leicester Square (it later became the Alhambra Theatre and now the Odeon Cinema stands on the site). Built in 1853 in the Moorish style with minarets at the corners of the façade and the lofty interior domed in the centre, it contained three tiers of galleries provided with equipment for popular instruction. On the day of the Brown family visit there was a diorama showing of Central America at 4.30 p.m., followed by the playing of the "luminous and chromatic fountain" and a grand organ recital at 8.30 (the organ later found a home at St Paul's Cathedral). The evening ended with "Glimpses of Italy". Entrance fee was one shilling but Lucy would have been admitted for sixpence.

[47] As a young man (he was now forty-five) Scott had taken the three watchwords of the French Revolution for his own, Godwin's *Political Justice* for his guide, and the sacredness of woman as "an absolute power of moral defence" (*Autobiographical Notes*, ed. W. Minto, 1892, i, p.101). Mary Wollstonecraft (1759-97) had been a leading radical and feminist.

[48] Perhaps William Hough, still-life painter, who was unsuccessful in exhibiting at the R.A. until 1857.

[49] Brown was preparing to exhibit the picture at the Liverpool Academy which opened on 15 Sep.

had just caught & which he assured me had been *hopping in the pan*. Went & saw Canterbury which is glorious indeed & home by 8, found Lowes D here.

3rd Lowes eveng drew at the pourtrait of William Rossetti (9 hours).

4th friday leaves.

5th Saturday do. (16 hours).

6th Sunday to church with Lucy then worked at Peters green mantle improving the colour for since 51/52 I have improved at that − but Hunt & then Woolner & William came in & stopped me. They 2 went off to Browning's & Hunt stayed & told me about the Bishop of Jerusalem who seems to be one of the meanest scoundrels not yet in hell,[50] then about his sale of the scape goat to White for 450 guineas at 8 months date − then about Annie Millars love for him & his liking for her, & perplexities, & how Gabriel like a mad man increased them taking Annie to all sorts of places of amusement which he had implied if not stated should not be. Annie sat to him for that picture of the swell & his mistress & since that Hunt has promised to be like her gardian & she should never sit to any [but] him or those he would name lest poor annie should get into trouble, & having allowed her to sit to Gabriel while he was away Gabriel has let her sit to others not in the list & taken her to dine at Bertolini's & to Cremorn where she danced with Boyce, & William takes her out boating forgetful it seems of Miss R., as Gabriel, sad dog, is of Guggum. They all seem mad about Annie Millar & poor Hunt has had a fever about it.[51] I told him I could not speak to Gabriel about it as I did not see him, there being a coolness between us (5 hours).

7th Monday Seddon brought his wife to sit without notice again. I asked them to let me know positively if she would sit till it was finished, before

---

[50] The Brownings were in England for the summer and had been lent 39 Devonshire Place, the home of their old friend John Kenyon. The Rt. Rev. Samuel Gobart, consecrated Bishop in Jerusalem in 1846, held the seat for over thirty years. Holman Hunt's intensive study of Eastern religions made him violently opposed to the Bishop's views (the Bishopric itself had come in for criticism by the High Church party for the arrangement by which a Bishop of the Church of England alternated with a German Lutheran). Seddon appears to have enjoyed the Bishop's company.

[51] Annie Miller, a golden-haired prostitute from a Chelsea slum, had posed for the girl in Holman Hunt's picture of "the swell and his mistress", *The Awakening Conscience* (Tate). He had hoped to marry her after her lack of education had been remedied during his absence in the Holy Land. Rossetti had made many studies of her and, disregarding Holman Hunt's prohibition, had taken her to Bertolini's, the dining-rooms and hotel of doubtful repute behind Leicester Square. He had danced with her on the "Chinese platform" at the Royal Gardens, Cremorne, sharing her company with G.P. Boyce. Since January this year W.M. Rossetti had been engaged to Henrietta Rintoul, daughter of the founder and editor of the *Spectator*.

she went, as the time approaches & out of two weeks she has only sat 4 times having missed twice without notice, once with, & twice taken me by surprise, this as Seddon asked me to do it before she went, & I am so engaged I thought it my duty to myself to ask. She would not promiss five more sittings so the others all go for nothing. Really, Tom & Mrs Seddon, this is not right to a friend, what one does for nothing goes for as much[52] – painted at Peters green cloak till diner then leaves (9 hours).

8th last night I set to work on the proof of Dalziels prisoner of Chillon at ten & worked till 3 at it. The heads were all execrable. This morning I took it to him & saw Millais' Birons dream,[53] it is quaint, by the work of a great man, full of suppressed feeling. Began work at 1 till 4 at Peters cloak, then after diner at the leaves (9 hours).

9th finished Peters Cloack then scraped the leaves with razor & set them to right from *feeling* in doors, then out at them again (8 hours).

10th Set the lay figure among the trees to paint those which touch the figure & went on with it. Quarrel with Emma (7 hours).

11th bad tooth ache all night. Began work, found the lay figure would wet as it rained and if required for many days might be much deteriorated so made a substitute for it out [of] a childs chair & some old cushions with the head of the lay figure. This does quite as well & remains on the wall. Painted till dark (8 hours).

12th Up at 6 through Emma's having slept locked in the parlours [illegible]. Painted from 7 am. till ½ past 8 p.m. then William Rossetti came for his sitting so I had to work at him till 11. After Gabriel came too (12 hours).

Sunday Made it up with Emma whom I had offended yesterday. Brought her home & did nothing.

Monday All day at the leaves. Find a great Difficulty in making them deep enough in tone (6 hours).

Tuesday 15th all day as before. Emma dined with the Rossettis & I there after work (6 hours).

Wedy 16th same as yesterday, but more rain. Driven in more than once by it coming down on my sheets in torrents. Been going over my accounts, find I have £225 & that is all including what Dickinson owes me. I must write for it. I shall soon begin to quake again, I fear. Emma called on Miss

---

[52] Mrs Seddon had given birth to a daughter in April and was probably occupied in nursing her child.
[53] Illustration to *The Dream* by Byron, for *Poets of the Nineteenth Century*.

Sid yesterday who is very ill & complaining much of Gabriel. He seems to have transferred his affections to Annie Millar & does nothing to [but] talk of her to Miss Sid. He is mad past care (6 hours).

Thursday 17th All day at the leaves (8 hours).

18th Friday The leaves again (7 hours).

Saturday A great deel of trouble arranging the leaves at the side of the head, pinning on fresh ones where they are blighted & placing the branches were they are pressed to one side by the heat. In the eveng plastered at the joins [in] the Christ & Peter (10 hours).

Sunday church with Lucy. Worked at Designing the two lovers from self & Lucy in a Glass, Lucy being atop of the piano. William Rossetti after diner (2 hours).

Monday Last night worked 2 hours or more at the piece joined on to the Christ. Today 11 till 8 at the leaves. Tonight touched & photo, 6 for Lowes (11 hours).

Tuesday 22nd all day at the leaves. After tea Seddon Called & borrowed £10, full of sickness & getting introduced to every one, but no tin (8 hours).

Wedy the leaves again, all with Robersons medium, but the ground absorbs. I had it prepared by Reeves over the side pieces of the chaucer never gone on with − it is Roman ticker[54] & I had it filled clean up with flake white & copal. Why it absorbs is to me a mystery. The scoundrel may have put Zink white but it is too hard for that (8 hours).

Thursday 24th The leaves again, a bad days work. I dont know why but I could not work felt Restless & unhappy. Cristina Rossetti called, is reading Carlyle with her mother. Tom Seddon called with his little picture to show me. This eveg wrote Hunt who has been sent away to Hastings with Sirian fever poor fellow.[55] He works too hard (7 hours).

Friday 25th Leaves (9 hours).

Saturday at the leaves from 11 till 2. Called on Mrs Seddon with Emma & Lucy. At the leaves again from 5 till ½ past 8. With great effort finished

---

[54] The "Roman ticker" may have been a type of stout linen (tick; 15th century: tikke) which Brown used as painting canvas.

[55] An undated letter to Holman Hunt written from Fortess Terrace in which Brown is replying to an enquiry of Holman Hunt's, probably belongs to this time. The enquiry seems to have concerned Annie Miller's education and Holman Hunt may have regarded knowledge of the French language as an essential refinement. "The address of the master I spoke of is . . . *Monsieur Le Mire Highgate Grammar School*. He teaches there so a letter would be sure to find him. The other school to which the Miss Seddons went at Dinan is broken up" (Huntington).

them by working till it was quite dark having moved my easel quite close to them (6 hours).

Sunday worked at the leaves again in the garden one hour. After at the dress of Peter which had faded owing to Browns Rose Madder (7 hours).

Monday all day at Peter — face acke — Seddon took me away to Hunts at Pinlico to go boating by agreement but dinner was laid & Hunt made no mention of the boat & Seddon was afraid to remind him. Saw Hunts Lantern Maker which is lovely color & one of the best he has painted but like much he has done of late very quaint in drawing & compo[sitio]n, but admirably painted. Anny Millar there looking most siren-like. Hunt went off & put her on board the boat to go home to Chelsea & I with them, not understanding the dinner was served. When we came back Halliday & Seddon had begun as it appears Hunt makes a rule of running out for something just as dinner has been waiting 10 minutes, to Hallidays disgust (6 hours).

Tuesday Peter as before. Lowes D called & as I found his Brother is not away I must call on him (7 hours).

Wednesday Called on the scoundrel Robert who, after keeping me waiting, came & was surprised his brother Gilbert had not answered me. Would I wait till saturday or monday till he came back as he did this part of the business & wished to ask me summat — of course I could, but it is evident that between them they are meditating some black infamy with regard to what they owe me — £44. Came back & finished Peter — in the eveg fetched a model for to morrow (5 hours).

Thursday the brute of a model, a hugh accadimician with a beard & muscles all over like all accadimy models, to stiff to take any pose except the Apollo Belvidere. Sent him off after seeing how Seddons Arab shirt looked on him as christ kneeling, & then placed the lay figure which took up the remainder of the day (6 hours).

Friday [Aug 1st] painted Christ's shirt, eveg Seddon called.

Saturday the shirt again (15 hours).

3rd Sunday painted from 11 till 8 at the shirt as before. I now find I have made the legs under it too long from the knee downward, this will give bother tomorrow — having begun it without drawing in the legs from nature first. It has been so precious hot to day that I was been forced to take off all my clothes & paint sans cullote in flannel waistcoat.[56] I have only got in all 220£ now, that is if Robert D does not cheat me out of part of the 44 owing to me and including 10 owing me from Gabriel Rossetti, 6

---

[56] The thermometer at the Royal Humane Society's Receiving House, Hyde Park, registered eighty-seven degrees at noon.

from Miss S. & ten from Seddon. I trust fortune will favour me in the affair of the Liverpool prize or I fear it will go hard with me Emma & the chicks (7 hours).

Monday painted at the shirt again, finished the bottom part then painted in the Gulla[57] blue, did not like it (7 hours).

Tuesday Spent the whole day thinking of the general color of the pictur & trying it with patches of ribbon etc. Very much disgusted, painted the Goolla green & scraped out the part of Christ body where the body of the dress comes. Seddon brought me his little picture finished, it is really very beautiful. Then Tommy Woolner enterd & so we spent the eveg smoking teaing, chatting & supping − it seems that all hope of the 300 guinea portrait is not used up yet but it wanes. The man it appears dislikes Preraphaelites & smells a rat. Tommy Woolner entertained us with many highly wrought annecdotes, one of which as I had witnessed it myself although he did not seem to remember, I had an opportunity of testing the quantity of coloring matter superadded which seems to be considerable. To another I declare He superadded comments which I remember myself having made at a former hearing of the naration, as part of the tale as it was told him (4 hours).

Wednesday painted part of one sleeve, very depressed all day & could hardly get to work at first (6 hours).

24th Yesterday Rossetti brought his ardent admirer Morris[58] of Oxford who bought my little hay field for 40 gnas, this was kind of Gaggy. He has also brought Browning here lately who is, it turns out, a great admirer of me. I have been all this time hard at the Christ & peter. It must be done by next saturday as I have promised. I have sent Liverl. 5. Vid, Last of England, Mother & child, small King L, Sketch of Cordelia, & the Brent. I have painted every day at the picture except one day I think (140 hours).

1st Sepr This morning finished sending off the "Christ & Peter" to liverpool, finished it saturday. Packed it sunday night, it being wet covered it with calicoe which I *bought* for it, "bought my dear Sir", as old White says, nailed it up tight & pasted paper over the edges to keep out the dust, so careful am I. Since the 24th I have been hard at the Christ & Peter day & night too, quite exhausted & obliged to take wine to keep me up. Two days I was interrupted by going to see Woolner's statue of Bacon which was very fine in design but looked too short & every one affraid to tell him. The first

---

[57] Perhaps Brown's rendering of the arabic word 'galabieh', the long underdress with which he had by then clothed the Christ.

[58] Earlier this year William Morris (1834-96) had been articled to G.E. Street the architect, but by the summer Rossetti had persuaded him to become a painter. Relatively well-to-do, he was able to buy the paintings of his friends. Later he was to found the firm of Morris, Marshall, Faulkner & Co.

time I hinted to him pretty plainly what I thought & got him to alter it slightly, but fearing he would not sufficiently I proposed to Gabriel that we should go toghether & insist upon his head being made smaller or his body longer. Rossetti said he would come but I must be spokesman as he funked it,[59] however while I was looking at the statue & thinking how to begin, Rossetti, who bye the bye had before all along swore the statue was perfect, blurts out I say that chap's too short I certainly think. In this dellicate way he broke the ice & we began in earnest – at last Woolner was convinced & agreed that it was better to loose some of the individuality & truth than to risk offending the prejudices of the multitude who certainly never consider Bacon in the light of a dwarf. To day I have been to see it again & it is all right. Then we went toghether to the national gallery & saw the new pictures, two virgins & children are there which are delicious, the Perugino is fine in tone & truthful as out of doors effect but absurdly drawn as usual[60] (60 hours).

8th September all this week I have been gloriously idle scarcely doing any thing except touch up one or two photographs & make calls etc. Gabriel got Elliott, a parson who writes on the Daily news & the editor, to come & see my pictures & has been at the trouble of writing a long article on them for that journal which is to be in tomorrow.[61] Saturday I called on him & found him at it & was so ungrateful as to make fun of his self inflicted labours so that he could not go on with it for fooling & came home & dined with us, after which no writing was possible for repletion. Yesterday, Sunday 7th, I went to foots cray to see my uncle who has lost his wife. Had a walk from Abbey-wood to the Crays. On coming home at 10, here were Hunt, the 2 Rossettis. They all strongly recommended me to buy back the English Autumn afternoon of Seddon, saying I was sure to sell it again before

---

[59] The statue of Francis Bacon in Caen stone was executed for the new Oxford Museum and stands in the central court. "Some siege ought to be laid to Tommaso . . . but I shall be merely your supporter, as I rather funk the job" (*Letters*, p.305). Later Rossetti considered that it had turned out "a very first-rate thing", though opinion varied. "Woolner's Bacon – a repulsive but clearly truthful rendering of him – but only quà man of the world", wrote A.J. Munby (*Man of Two Worlds*, ed. D. Hudson, 1972, p.65). Dr Acland, of Oxford, one of the most influential promoters of the Museum, thought it "the best statue – and it shall have on every account the best place" (A. Woolner, *Thomas Woolner* 1917, p.123).

[60] Three paintings of the Virgin and Child acquired in 1855 were on view. *The Virgin and Child enthroned among Angels and Saints* by Benozzo Gozzoli; *The Virgin and Child with the Magdalen and St John the Baptist*, Mantegna; *Virgin and Child*, Giovanni Bellini. The Perugino triptych of *Virgin and Child with SS. Raphael and Michael* was bought in 1856.

[61] William Weir, editor of the *Daily News* from 1854 to 1858. The Rev. William Elliott was a friend of Patmore and Woolner. The *Daily News* issue of 9 Sep. carried a review occupying the best part of a column relating to five of Brown's paintings. These included *Christ Washing Peter's Feet* with the comment that since its first exhibition in 1852 the artist had "bestowed further thought and labour upon it", namely that of nudity in the Christ. But attention was drawn in particular to the effect of open-air daylight in *The Last of England*: "the 'everlasting wash of air' as Browning calls it", which could not have been obtained without "a strong mind nor skillful hand."

long.[62] This I went & did this morning, giving Chauls Seddon £50 for it having sold it for 9 gnas by auction at Philips [Phillips]. He after got it from Dickinson for £20 so that I loose £40.11 by it — however I hope to make it up again soon. While I was away Gabriel came here with his admirer & client, Miss Heaton of Leeds. But they were gone before I came back. Really, Gabriello seems bent upon making my fortune at one blow.[63] Never did fellow, I think, so bestir himself for a rival before, it is very good & very great to act so. Ever since he felt he had hurt me some little time ago he has done nothing but heep amends on me one after the other — as Carlyle sais of Mirabeau, how much more easy it is to note the flaws in a circle than to compare them with the whole grasp of its circumference. The pock-marked face may be noble in its proportions. Hunt & he seem all right again. Gabriel has forsworn flirting with Annie Millar it seems, Guggum having rebelled against it. He & Guggum seem on the best of terms now, she is painting at her picture.[64] I must get to work. Hunt says he has heard that I will get the prize at Liverpool. I suppose I shall.

9th & 10th Touched some photographs up & caught a cold working too near the gas & going to the door without my hat (14 hours).

11th Before getting up, a letter saying I had the prize.[65] Out with a bad cold to tell Old White & the Rossettis.

12th White called to see my "English Autumn afternoon". Rossetti here, I in bed swetting but get up at the call of duty & Old White. Asked him 180 guineas, nearly bought it for 150 but not quite. We showed him some unfinished sketches of poor Deverel which he bought for 9 gnas the 10.

13th Out of bed again with bad cold to meet White at Woolners studio. He was very pleased (Woolner away with Scott), wants to have the 3 medalions, Tennisson Carlyle, & Browning.[66] Wrote off to Woolner, Emma in pain.

[62] Five years after buying the picture back from Charles Seddon, Brown sold it to George Rae, of Birkenhead.

[63] With Ruskin abroad and unable to influence Ellen Heaton, Rossetti was eager to ensure a commission for Brown. No purchase was made but Rossetti followed up the studio visit with a letter: "I can assure you as certainly as if it were in the past instead of the future, that anything by Madox Brown will be sure to increase yearly in value now, and that no one's works, except Hunt & Millais, will ultimately be so highly esteemed or stand so high in the market as this" (*Sublime & Instructive*, ed. V. Surtees, 1972, p.195 n.4).

[64] Probably *Sir Patrick Spens*, 1856 (Tate).

[65] The prize of £50 to a non-resident artist was awarded this year by the Liverpool Academy of Arts for *Christ Washing Peter's Feet*.

[66] While Woolner, introduced by W.B. Scott, was on his way to Wallington Hall, Northumberland (to stay with Sir Walter and Lady Trevelyan) D.T. White visited his studio. The Tennyson medallion, 1856 (National Portrait Gallery) was reproduced as the frontispiece to Moxon's edition of *Poems*; the bronze medallion of Browning (an example at Birmingham) was also executed in 1856; and that of Carlyle (an example at the Scottish National Portrait Gallery) in 1855.

187

14th Emma still in pain but nothing immediate.[67] Rossetti called with the blue devils so went with him by rail to Rainham & dined, walked by Guy Fawks' house to Barking & home by 9. Emma dear still in pain.

15th Emma still suffering. Took Katty with me to change a book at Mudies[68] & to the British Musm. There she enquired the first thing if she might eat her sweet stuff. Went after a little girl I had in my eye for a model for my pictur of "Stolen pleasure". Home by 6, Emma worse & gradually more till near one when, thank God, she was releaved & we have a boy. I to bed in my clothes.

16th Emma doing well. The little girl came & sat to me for 2 hours but I was too sleepy to do any good (2 hours).

17th 18th & 19th painted at the head in the picture from the little girl but it is very bad – worked also at times at a drawing of the new boy Arthur,[69] 20 hours, & on Sunday 21st Rossetti & Miss Sid. (6 hours).

Monday 22nd went to see if Hunt would go to Liverl with me as there seems no chance of Gabriel. Found Hunt just started for Manchester & Liverl. It rained & I staid & dined with Martineau who plaid to me (self taught), does not know the notes by name.

23rd made up my mind to go & try my luck at Liverpool, went & bought a ready made coat & trousers for 3 guineas, & all arrangements being complete for swelling it, I kissed Emma & started to go by 9 oclock train – found it was 8 oclock one so slept at a coffee shop & then the next morning 23rd [24th] missed the fast train & did not get to Liverl till 3. Read Emersons English traits all the way, a most surprizing trait of Americanism certainly & a delightful book.[70] Went to the Exhibition then to Millers office & got Hunt's address, met him at his hotel, the Stork, & to the Exhibition again. Left him going to dine with Miller.[71] Went across the Mersey & wiled away the time till dusk. On returning found a note from

---

[67] On 16 Sep. Emma gave birth to a son, Arthur Gabriel Madox, who survived ten months.
[68] Mudie's Circulating Library stood for a number of years at the corner of New Oxford Street and Museum Street.
[69] Private Collection. Signed with monogram and inscribed along the top: "Sep 20/56 Arthur Gabriel Madox Brown Aetas Die [illegible but presumably '4']".
[70] Having missed the fast train Brown was obliged to take the 6.30 a.m., North Western Railway, from Euston Square Station, reaching Liverpool at 3 p.m. Emerson's volume of essays was based on a series of lectures that had been published that year.
[71] John Miller, a Liverpool merchant of Scottish descent was liberal in his business dealings and an enthusiastic picture collector. He was sixty years old, lived at 9 Everton Brow (with a rented house on the Isle of Bute) where he liked to entertain artists to whom he was a generous friend. He was known to smoke cavendish, a type of tobacco sweetened, softened and pressed into a solid cake, favoured by army men and artists. Holman Hunt was lodging at the Stork Inn, Queen Square.

some person unknown asking me to Miller, went there & was more than cordially received. Hunt spoke up well for Woolner. Millar insisted that I should take up with him. Went off with Hunt & supped at his Hotel & talked so long about Dreams & other things that the boots put out the gas & locked us in so I was obliged to take the first empty room. Hunt dillated much on the R.A.s want of virtue & principle. M — y at 70 has seduced a young model who sits for the head & has a child by her, or rather she by him, & old Pickersgill in his own house is found on the rug *en flagrant délit* by the maid who fell over him with the coal scuttle, his own son frequently catching him.[72] Hunt still undecided about exhibiting there again.

25th Saw Hunt off with a Party of Miller's family for Bute. Called on the secretary Pelham who will not show his works. Dined at Miller & to see the pictures of a certain Pemberton, a Lawyer & money Lender, who buyes largely. Found him a regular brute & his pictures daubs.[73] Went there with Windus & Pelham, home to Millar's & talked & smoked with him till 12. This Millas a jolly kind old man with streaming white hair, fine features & a beautiful keen eye like Mulready's & something like John Cross too. A rich brogue, a pipe of cavendish & smart rejoinder with a pleasant word for every man, woman, or child he meets, is characteristic of him. His house is full of Pictures even to the kitchen, many pictures he has at all his friends houses in Liverl & his house in Bute also filled with inferior ones. Many splendid Linnels [Linnell], a fine Constable & good Turners, Anthony's, & works by a French man Delessard are among the most marked of his collection plus a hoste of good pictures by Liverpool artists, Davies [Davis], Tonge,[74] & Windus chiefly.

26th Very ill with vomitting all night, curious — believe it is through having fed all the time since I have left home on salt meat, ham & pork pye — & last night to crown it Miller gave us for dinner a huge round of salt beef. Now on the subject of M's dinners I may notice that his hospitality is somewhat peculiar in its kind. His dinner which is at 6 is of one joint & vegetable *without* pudding, bottled beer for drink. I never saw any wine. His wife dines at an other table with I suppose his daughters when at home. After dinner he instantly hurries you off to tea & then back again to smoke. He calles it a meat tea & boasts that few people who have ever dined with him

---

[72] Mulready was a remarkably handsome man. The fashionable portrait painter, H.W. Pickersgill, was then seventy-four years old; he lived in Stratford Place, Oxford Street.

[73] James Pelham, portrait painter, son and father of artists, lived at Marston Street, Low Hill. Probably Charles Pemberton, Attorney, who lived in Brook Street and had an office in Cable Street.

[74] Robert Tonge, landscape painter, had worked in Liverpool. He had died of consumption at the beginning of the year at Luxor, where he had been sent, largely through Miller's assistance, in hope of recovery. A.J. Delessard (fl.1844-90), French painter of genre and landscape subjects.

come back again. All day I was going here & there with Miller, dodging back to his office to smoke & then off again after something fresh. The chief things I saw were Chain cables forged, & Hilton Crucifiction which quite surprised me & is jolly fine especially the lower half of it.[75]

27th out with Millar & windus to see Robertson's[76] studio, some portraits in a reallistic spirit that promiss well & reminded me of Ingre [Ingres], then to a Mr Robinson where some decent pictures by different artistes, the best a D. Cox – then to a parson who was to get us an introduction to the owner of Speke Hall[77] who has rather the character of an Orson, but after some parley & sidelong glances at us in the car let us in. It rained pitiously & we did not see half the place inside or out, but enough to give us the idea of what a glorious old place it is. The interior of the quadrangle which is completely filled up with two fine ewe trees is one of the most beautiful places in the world I believe, the whole is built of cement & timber in a sort of small diapre pattern. Altoghether it is quite true that the first batch of Elizabethan Architects where eminently artists. In the eveng a party of Artists at Millers where I met Davis who brought in a little sketch from nature, very beautiful. Miller asked me as a favour to buy it of him, which I could not refuse him although it puts me in the aucward position of patronising a man whom I think far too well of to attempt the like with – however it is done. This Davis, who has been one of the most unlucky artists in England (now about 40 with a wife & family) is a man with a fine shaped head & well cut features & his manners not without a certain modest dignity, but, as it were, all crushed by disappointment & conscious dependency of Millar who has entirely kept him for years – & the only man in the world who buys his pictures. Very sad – we must hope his turn will come.[78] Millar bought my little picture of Emma & boy for 84£ & a commission looms in the distance from a Mr Langdale who collects water colours.[79] This is the net result of my labors here.

28th home by rail by 7 oclock. The Rossettis called.

[75] The triptych of *The Crucifixion* by William Hilton (Liverpool) was designed for the east window of St George's Church, Liverpool.
[76] J.E. Robertson, member and treasurer of the Liverpool Academy and highly thought of by Miller, was a keen supporter of the P.R.B. His studio was in Slater Street.
[77] Speke Hall (National Trust) belonged to the Watt family and was owned by Richard Watt who was living there in Sep. 1856. The sixteenth-century house is half-timbered and has fine panelling and plaster-work. The yew trees still dominate the courtyard. David Cox (1783-1859), distinguished painter in water-colours.
[78] Davis's work is now appreciated and sought-after, but at his death from heart disease in 1873 he left a widow and about a dozen children unprovided for. Miller offered immediate assistance and Brown used his influence to raise a fund to help the impoverished family.
[79] The untraced version of *Waiting (An English Fireside, 1854-5*; see p.76, n.15). Neither a Langdale nor Langham (see p.193) are names that appear in the Liverpool Directory. A Mr Langton, share-broker, had offices in Exchange Street East.

30th went & laid out a lot of money for Emma & chicks, have given Emma a dress £4 for having sold her & the child (4 hours).

4th [Oct] Worked at the stolen pleasure picture at the head, from feeling, & at night at William Rossetti's pourtrait till 2 A.M. (4 hours).

7th dined with William Rossetti & after to Brownings where was a woman with a large nose.[80] Hope I may never meet her again. Browning's conversational powers very great, told some good stories, one about the buy gone days of Drury Lane, about the advice that a very experienced stage carpenter of 50 years standing at the theater gave to a young man who wished for an engagement there but had not, it was objected, voice enough. The advice was to get a pot of XXXX & put it on the stage beside him & having the boards all to himself he was first to drink & then to hollow with all his might, then to drink again & so on, which the aspirant litterally did — remaining of course a muff as he had begun, however, I spoil that one. He said that one evening he was at Carlyle's, that sage teacher after abusing Mozart Bethhoven & modern music generally set Mrs C to show Browning what was the right sort of music which was some scotch tune on an old piano with such base as pleased providence or rather, said Browning, as *did not* please providence. An italian sinner who belonged to that highest & in this country scarce to be believed in degree of criminality, which requires that some very exalted dignitary of the church be resorted to before absolution can be obtained for atrocities too heinous for the cleansing powers of the ordinary priest, was likened to a spider, who having fallen into a bottle of ink gets out & crawls & sprawls & blots right over the whole of gods table of laws.

8th painted at William Rossetti till 12 from 8. Gabriel came in, William wishing to [go] early Gabriel proposed that he should wait five minutes & he would go to. When William being got to sleep on the sofa Gabriel commenced telling me how he intended to get married at once to Guggum & then off to Algeria!!![81] & so poor Williams 5 minutes lasted will ½ past 2 a.m. painted at the English Autumn afternoon (8 hours).

9th Out with Emma buing her dress having given her the remainder of her dress money for this year £5.12.1. at 2£ per mensam.

[80] Most likely Ellen Heaton. In her portrait by Thomas Richmond she has an abnormally large nose. She was assiduous in cultivating the Brownings and it is known that she was in London on that date. Furthermore, now or within the next five days she would press upon the Brownings her *Dante's Dream* by Rossetti to keep until their departure for Florence at the end of the month. It seems possible that she had brought the drawing with her that evening, and, though not renowned for tact, she did not refer to it to Brown from whom she had not bought anything a month earlier.

[81] Algeria was recommended as a suitable climate for Miss Siddal's health. Their friend Barbara Leigh-Smith, amateur landscape painter, illegitimate cousin of Florence Nightingale, and advocate of women's rights, was going there in the autumn with her sister Isabella and brother Benjamin. But on this occasion Miss Siddall got no farther than Bath.

10th English Autumn afternoon (8 hours).

11th do. – Lowes, Woolner & the Rossettis here till 12 & the 2 latter till 3.

12th Got up at 12 this morning in consequence & idle all day.

18th Saturday Had Woolner's brother[82] here for the young man's head in stolen pleasures. Yesterday painted at the white Jacket & collar from Susan & the day before at the geraniuns which I was obliged to paint before they all went off – painted at the girls hair from one of the maids – this week (16 hours).

9th November on the 19th of last as I was painting again from Woolner my wrist gradually became so bad[83] that I was obliged to leave off after 3 hours of the worst painting I ever did in my life. All the remainder of the day & night I was in agony or nearly so (3 hours). Monday I went to show it to Marshall who ordered leachs etc said it was rheumatic inflamation on an old sprain. At Finchley I remember while putting the last of England in its frame I made something crack in the back of my hand as I was breaking a piece of wood in two. I never was troubled with it till now. This has kept me from works three weeks nearly, I did nothing till the day before yesterday when I got some of last lilac leaves of this year & painted them under the lay-figures arm & worked on them yesterday (5 hours). To day Sunday I have been to church & out with Emma. I have become fearfully idle, one stoppage after an other having operated in a most prejudicial manner on a constitution already deficient in energy.

Wednesday Mr Plint called, inveigled here by Gabriel Rossetti. He did not fancy landskape nor bite at the Baa-Lambs – & the Christ picture was large & had no women in it. For the same reason the cromwell was unsatisfactory. At length he commissioned me for something for one Hundred guineas, but on seeing the sketch & background of the large picture of "Work" begun at Hampstead He almost agreed to have it gone on with for £420 but said he would write – how I hope He will.[84] This is perhaps the

---

[82] Probably Henry, a young half-brother, aged nineteen.

[83] In photographs of later years Brown is seen wearing a leather glove on his right hand to conceal an arthritic deformity.

[84] T.E. Plint, the Leeds stockbroker, dissenter and patron of the arts commissioned *Work* (Brown's masterpiece), for four hundred guineas. "Brown the brick has a commission to paint that picture", Woolner wrote. "The thorough brick is in good spirits of course – considers himself over the bar at last and on broad water – there is no doubt of how he will manage the ship, being a good captain" (*Letters to Allingham*, ed. H. Allingham & E.B. Williams, 1911, pp.290-1). Rossetti wrote equally enthusiastically. "It will be a most noble affair, and will at last, I should hope, settle the question of his fame, which is making some steps at last" (*Letters*, p.310).

only thing can snatch me from the state of apathy into which I have fallen
– nothing more as yet about a water color for Mr Langham [Langdale].
Rossetti has been here nearly a fourtnight coming daily about 12 & working or not working at his drawing on wood for Moxon of St Cecilia. It is
jolly quaint but very lovely. Also Plint who has already paid Gabriel down
one Hundred of a 400 guinea Commission gave him here on seeing this an
order for a 40 Guin drawing of it.[85] Been to the play twice & altogether very
extravagant.

[85] The price of the projected drawing for Plint of St Cecilia makes it likely that the
commission was to have been a water-colour (see W.M. Rossetti, *Designer and Writer*,
1889, pp.30, 375). There is no evidence that the drawing was ever put in hand. The four
hundred guinea commission can only be guessed at. Perhaps the picture *Found* had been
proposed, though by the following year Rossetti had wheedled its commission from James
Leathart.

1857

16th March Saturday [Monday] Since last entry Plint gave me the commission for the picture of Work & I sent it to be lined by his directions. Then I began upon the naked baby from Arthur, made a drawing of it, then painted it on the enlarged canvas on which I had painted a study of Emma's head one evening in Newman St.[1] I have now sent it to be enlarged a second time, having made an error. After this Emma was taken ill again & had to go to Hastings for 5 weeks, during which I did little more than make a cartoon for a stained glass window of the Transfiguration for Powel of Temple St.[2] for which I charged 16 gnas. Then I finished William Rossetti's Portrait,[3] worked a good bit at the designe for Plints picture which however is not yet done & these four or five weeks I have been at work on the picture itself, drawing in the figures in pencil without nature. Tuesday last I went into Gray's Inn Lane to look for Irish People & after some prowling about found a poor woman & baby in Holborn who next day brought me a young man & [in] six days I painted these 3 into the picture pretty satisfactorily although I can scarce make sure of what I am about as yet. Two days I painted at the head of the man mixing mortar, from the young Irishman, & today I painted in the man leaning against the tree but I see tonight it has been done too quick to be good. Yesterday, Burnett, a young distiller who buys pictures, called to see the Christ & Peter sent by Halliday it seems, who is therefore a brick although somewhat distorted in the baking.[4] I devoutly wish this distiller may distil my picture till nothing remains of it but the pure spirit of the work in the shape of a cheque for £262.10. He promisses to call again with his wife & if he

[1] *Take Your Son, Sir!* (see p.78, n.18). The drawing of the baby is probably the one at the British Museum.
[2] Coloured cartoon (in a painted oval) for stained glass commissioned by James Powell and Son, of Whitefrairs, Temple Street (Untraced).
[3] National Trust, Wightwick Manor, Wolverhampton.
[4] Halliday was slightly deformed (diary, 21 May 1855, p.138). Perhaps John Burnett of Sir Robert Burnett & Co., Distillers and Vinegar makers, of Vauxhall High Street, was the potential buyer.

buyes I make a vow to purchase Nolly a purambulator & myself a glass house with a revolving floor, & two chairs for the parlour, item, a table-cloath for my new table which, by the bye, I have designed among other work.[5] Since my last entry poor Tom Seddon's death has occurd which was rather a startler to us, I must say. It makes one think of spirit land with a vengeance when suddenly informed of the death of an old & dear friend. Poor Tom Seddon, I suppose plenty will be made history of about [him] so it is scarce worth while for one to say much now, particularly as what I now am writing whants the freshness & force of incidents noted down diurnally, while at the same time it is too hasty & careless to be readable history. I went to a meeting of the sub committee about the testimonial at Ruskins,[6] he having noticed my absence from the previous with regret. Ruskin was playful & childish & the tea table overcharged with cakes & sweets as for a juvenile party. After this, about an hour later, cake & wine was again produced of which R. again partook largely, reaching out with his thin paw & swiftly absorbing 3 or 4 large lumps of cake in succession. At home he looks young & rompish at the meeting, at Hunts meeting he looked old & ungainly, but his power & eloquence as a speaker were homeric. But I said at the time that but for his speaking he was in appearance like a cross between a fiend & a tallowchandler. Old Miller was here & dined with me while here.[7] I took him to Lowes Dickinsons Party & to see Woolners statue of Bacon. By the bye, the Tennysson is finished & is a very noble work – & I hope will do Tommy Woolner good.[8] No one deserves it nor indeed wants it more (350 hours). Miss Siddall has been here for 3 days & is I fear dying. She seems now to hate Gabriel in toto. Gabriel had settled to marry at the time I put it down in this book & she says told her he was only waiting for the money of a picture to do so, when, lo the money being paid, Gabriel brought it & told her all he was going to pay with it & do with it, but never a word more about marriage. After that she determined to have no more to

[5] The "glass-house" may have been the popular "Wardian case" (the name of its inventor) for growing small plants. This consisted of a close-fitting case with sides and top of glass. Brown's activity as a designer of furniture anticipated his work for the Morris Firm. In the late 1850s he designed furniture of "solid construction and joiner-made" for the Seddon firm and an oak table for Holman Hunt (see E. Aslin, *19th Century Furniture*, 1962, p.56). Later he designed bedroom furniture for Morris, including a washstand and towel horse all of which were simple and functional and were put into commercial production by the firm. The round-seated "Sussex rush-seated" chair is traditionally attributed to Brown. In 1865 he exhibited a cabinet decorated with a series of panels illustrating the history of an English family from 1810 to 1860.

[6] The meeting on 2 Mar. at Denmark Hill was held to arrange an exhibition of Seddon's work with a view to purchasing his *Jerusalem and the Valley of Jehoshaphat* for the Nation (Tate). Ruskin acted as Treasurer.

[7] The Liverpool patron whom Brown wished to introduce to Rossetti (*Letters*, p.317).

[8] See p.169 n.24.

do with him. However, he followed her to Bath[9] & again some little while ago promissed marriage immediately, when since he has again posponed all thoughts of it till about a fourtnight ago, having found Miss Sid more than usually incensed against him, he came to me & talked seriously about it & settled all he was to do. Again the next morning he called & said the only thing that prevented his buying the licence was want of tin, upon which I said if it was this that prevented it I would lend him some. He agreed to this & a few days after borrowed £10 but spent it all somehow & last night came for one more. This makes with 6 to Miss Sid, £42.10. Of course I am very glad to lend it him but he has quite lost her affection through his extraordinary proceedings. He does not know his own mind for one day.

16th [15th] Sunday Touched again at the man against the tree & all day with Gabriel who is so unhappy about Miss Sid that I could not leave him. In the evening to fetch Emma from Miss Sid at Hampstead, & coming home Hunt came in & talked about a college plan & staid till 12[10] (2 hours).

17th [16th] Monday The Irish man again. Painted 2 hours at him & improved & finished him (2 hours).

Tuesday Wasted great part of the day writing to Miller, then to Hampstead with Emma. Heard Miss Siddall abuse Gabriel & afterwards bought a very dirty old wide awake off the head of a man I met & went home & painted it (1 hour).

Wednesday finished the hat & went off to tell Gabriel what Miss Siddall said of him. Put him in much affliction & brought him back with the intention of waking over to Hampstead to try & induce her to give him an interview, but Emma proposed to go & warn her of his coming.

Thursday This we did but on getting there she would not see him nor me. At length I was admitted but could obtain no favorable speech from her & so Gabriel & I came away again leaving Emma. Gabriel in a sad state. At night to the working mans college with him & then a public meeting & heard professor Maurice spouting & Ruskin jawing. Ruskin was as eloqent as ever & as wildly popular with the men & as absurd & spiteful. He flattered Rossetti in his presence hugely & spoke of Monroe in conjunction with Baron Marit[11] [Marochetti] as the two noble sculptors of England

---

[9] See diary, 8 Oct. 1856, p.191. In December Elizabeth Siddal had gone to Bath for her health.
[10] The scheme in which certain artists were to unite and live under one roof came to nothing. Miss Siddal, who at this period was lodging at Eland House, Hampstead, was hostile to Holman Hunt and refused to live under the same roof.
[11] The sculptor Carlo Marochetti (1805-67), Baron of Italy, was highly regarded and was patronized by Queen Victoria.

whom all the aristocracy patronized & never one word about Woolner, whose bust he had just before gone into extasies about & invited to diner, this at a moment when Woolners pupils of the college were all present, such base spite does not deserve to be recorded but for purposes of elucidation. Rossetti says Ruskin is a sneak & loves him, Rossetti, because he is one too & Monroe because he is one too & Hunt he half likes because he is ½ a sneak, but hates Woolner because he is manly & strait forward, & me because I am do. He adored Millais because Millais was the prince of sneaks but Millais was too much so for he sneaked away his wife & so he is obliged to hate him for too much of his favorite quality. Rossetti was in such a rage about Ruskin & Woolner that he bullied poor Monroe all the way home. I bought a bed on the way to the meeting & Gabriel walked home with me wishing to take every cab he encountered. At home Emma told us she [had] a few lines for Gabriel stating that she would see him today. So Emma & he off in a cab there. I to see Old White, having come down again to that. Met Windus there, he & White having some grand secret between them about me. After he left, Old White showed me the study of heads which I sold at the Winter Exhibition for 10 gnas & which he had bought at Pococks sale for 6£.[12] I forgot to ask if this was what was to please me so. Thence to John P. Seddon's to see his Government offices drawings for the competn.[13] Called on Thomas, then to Hampstead to Miss Siddall's where dined, after which such a scean of recrimination as never — but she seems relenting. Came away leaving Emma. Gabriel went home & I came here & sent off Baby to her.

22nd Up at 10 to work at the Christs Head after time spent in cogitation. Peter's arm & leg till past 6 (5 hours).

---

[12] See diary 4 Feb. 1855, p.120, 2 March p.124. Lewis Pocock's Sale was held at Foster's, 54 Pall Mall on 18 Mar. 1857.
[13] The exhibition of designs for the new Public Offices which opened in May 1857 at Westminster Hall included block plans for Whitehall and individual designs for the Foreign and War Offices. In what became known as the "Battle of the Styles", Sir Gilbert Scott won the competition for the Government buildings.

1858

17th Jan/58 I must now endeavour to fill up this hiatus after some fashion or I shall never be able to proceed satisfactorily. The thought of having to do it, having prevented me all this while from beginning again. After last date I finished the Christs head with much difficulty as usual but it seemed to be successful for it was much liked by Lowes Dickinsons conversatzione where I sent it, & was introduced to professor Maurice[1] who promised to sit for the *Work* picture. About this time I painted in Martineau for the swell in the Work & his horse, also the little girl on her poney. Then till the 13th July (when our poor little Arthur sickened & died in one painful week[2]) I was occupied on 4 things: the little water color view from my studio window of Hampstead[3] (6 weeks). Got up the collection of preRafaël works in Russell Place during the month of June.[4] On this I must have wasted at least 4 weeks. All that came of this was that Ruskins father bought the charcoal of Beauty for 10 Guineas. Painted the body, arm & leg of the man mixing mortar in the work picture, also the dog, loose earth, lantern, & the poney of the girl, & drew in poor little Arthur's head for the baby & began painting it the day he was taken ill & had to rub out what I had done (300 hours). After poor baby's death I was very hard up, the Russell St Exhibition which I paid at first all out of my own pocket (£42) came back to me but slowly (and at this date (17 Jan 58) Millais, Rossetti & Miss Sid have never paid their shares[5]) & obliged to ask Plint for money to bury him.[6] From this time till nearly the End of august Emma

---

[1] The Rev. F.D. Maurice (1805-72), Christian Socialist and founder of the Working Men's College. He stands on the extreme right of the picture beside Carlyle.

[2] The little boy's death on 21 July 1857 had been a heavy blow to his father. Brown made a pencil study of his head wearing a little cap. Inscribed with the child's name and dated: "19 July/57" (Norfolk Museum of Arts, Norfolk, Virginia). A further drawing exists (Private Collection) inscribed "Arthur Gabriel Madox Brown died July 21[18] – 57 From Memory".

[3] Wilmington.

[4] A semi-public exhibition held at 4 Russell Place, Fitzroy Square. Seventy-two works were on view, either executed by the P.R.B. or showing a Pre-Raphaelite influence.

[5] Millais had exhibited four pictures, Rossetti seven and Miss Siddal five.

[6] Arthur was buried in a plot of ground in St Pancras Cemetery, Finchley, bought by Brown with an advance by Plint. Brown himself and most of his immediate family are buried there.

was ill & in bed with a bad miscarriage. But I painted in the young work-man shoveling, the hero of the picture, all but his legs. Also while Emma was in bed I painted at some old studies which I had painted, one head of a humpback in /36, aged fifteen. This head is not altered. Then one day I cooked up a slight sketch once made for Chaucer, also an old study for mary stuart & other rubish. During this time Plint offered me 200£ for Christ & Peter, still at Manchester,[7] which to avoid poverty closing now in on me fast on all sides, I was fain to accept in the shape of guineas. All this while the American Exhibition had been going on. I was to have gone over to hang the pictures, however the scoundrel Gambart put a stop to that & all I had was the trouble of going to select the daubs.[8] At the end of August a letter came from Plint enclosing 38£ without stating for why. However I took it & started off to Manchester as a great relief with Emma & Lucy & staid there a week for we had all of us been getting terribly hipped. But it was the first week in Oct that we visited Manchester & there was near two months interval between this [and] Arthur's death. Some of it was wasted with Emmas illness, some of it I think I painted in some of the wall in Lilac leaves picture. I also forgot to mention that about the month of April I gave two weeks to finishing poor Seddons picture of Penelope.[9] After Manchester as Hunt held out some prospect of Fairbairns coming to buy the Lilac leaves,[10] I set to at it & painted the convolvolus out in the open air, composed & drew in the child, painted in the *Love-lies-Bleeding*, worked at the lovers head & at the girls, in all I suppose 3 weeks. Then I painted at the legs of the hero in the large picture & the figure of the man

[7] Where it had gone to the "Art Treasures" exhibition (June-Oct. 1857). *The Hayfield* was also exhibited.

[8] An exhibition of British paintings to be sent to New York and other American cities had been projected by Captain Ruxton, a retired Army officer. Brown chose the pictures and W.M. Rossetti acted as secretary. The exhibition (1857) met with little success owing to its association with Gambart who had combined with the promoters of the exhibition and had shown water-colours of his own choice.

[9] It was Rossetti's idea that each of Seddon's unfinished works should be completed by one of his friends for showing at the Seddon Memorial Exhibition at the Society of Arts, May 1857. Brown undertook *Penelope* (The Pre-Raphaelite Trust) which had hung at the R.A. in 1852. Unaware that the painting had received attention from Brown Ruskin remarked that "while beforehand he had only regarded Seddon as a landscape painter of great promise, he now saw by the 'Penelope' that he was also a great figure painter" (W. Holman Hunt, *Pre-Raphaelitism and the Pre-Raphaelite Brotherhood*, 1905, vol.ii, p.128). The following year in writing to Lowes Dickinson and referring to J.P. Seddon, *Memoirs and Letters of Thomas Seddon*, 1858, Rossetti commented: "I do think the way that picture *Penelope* is talked about, when the fact is that in its present state it is almost more Brown's than Seddon's, is the coolest thing I ever saw — I believe no one but a thoroughly religious person could have written that passage with such calm aplomb" (*Letters*, p.335). The passage on p.17 of the *Memoirs* refers to Ruskin's energetic praise of the picture and of its "fine breadth and harmony of rich colouring".

[10] *Stages of Cruelty* was not completed until 1890 nor was it purchased by (Sir) Thomas Fairbairn, a patron of Holman Hunt (who bought *The Awakening Conscience*).

with the hod, chiefly in the open air from a navvy I had met in the streets. About this time I worked 3 or 4 days at an old study & at the sketch of Shakespear. Also at the designe for "Work". Since about the 3 weeks in november I have now been making a copy of Christ & Peter in water colors[11] which I finished yesterday, also 4 designes for chairs (500 hours). Tomorrow seriously to work on the Large picture. During this long interval 3 things of importance more require some comments. A visit to Manchester, a visit to the Union club, Oxford,[12] & one to *Carlyle* in company with Woolner.

27th All last week spent in trying to compose Carlyle & Maurice. Called on Rossetti to see about Maurice. Saw Woodward's Crown office.[13] I think the ·most exquisite piece of architecture I have seen in England. Then on with him to Jones'. Saw there, Fanny, their model. Called on Maurice & arranged with him for Monday. Plint has commissioned Jones for an other picture for 350 gns & bought Topsy's (Morris) for 75, his Tristram & Isult.[14]

Saturday Spent a great part in contriving a rail for Maurice to stand against, & to the play with Emma & Lucy.

Sunday Had to work at the rail.

Monday & yesterday had short sittings of Maurice & made an outline cartoon of him. Saw Miss Sterling there, John Sterling's daughter,[15] & she is a jolly girl — would do to paint. To Jones yesterday eve with an outfit Emma had purchased at his request for a poor miserable girl of 17 he had met in the street at 2 am. the coldest night this winter, scarce any clothes & starving, in *spite of prostitution*, after only 5 weeks of London life. Jones gave her money & told her to call next morning which she did & telling her

[11] Tate.
[12] For the visit to Manchester see diary, pp.199-201. The excursion to Oxford was to inspect the murals at the Union Debating Society. Rossetti was the promoter of the scheme to decorate the walls with subjects from Malory's *Morte d'Arthur*.
[13] The Crown Life Insurance Co., built by the architect Benjamin Woodward (1815-61), stood in New Bridge Street, of which Chatham Place formed the southern end.
[14] The painter Edward Burne Jones (1833-98) was living with William Morris in Rossetti's old rooms in Red Lion Square. Plint had commissioned from him a diptych of *The Blessed Damozel* in March 1857 (one water-colour panel at Fogg Museum of Art, Cambridge). "An other" commission may have referred to *The Wise and Foolish Virgins*, executed in 1859 and owned by Plint. Morris's *Tristram and Iseult* has disappeared (if ever executed) though a study exists in a Private Collection. This is the first known reference to Fanny Cornforth, soon to become Rossetti's model, mistress and housekeeper.
[15] John Sterling (1806-44), author and centre of a circle of literary men who founded the Sterling Club in 1838. His wife (whose sister Maurice had married) had died in 1843, a few days after giving birth to a daughter, their sixth child. In his biography of Sterling, Carlyle refers to "little Charlotte" (one of Sterling's daughters). "This bright little creature, on one of my first visits to Bayswater [in 1839] had earnestly applied to me to put her Doll's shoes on for her; which feat was performed" (T. Carlyle, *Life of John Sterling*, 1851, p.245).

story & that she had parents willing to receive her back again in the country. Jones got her to ask Emma to buy her this outfit & has I believe sent her home this morning. He brought Miss McDonald here & I did not ask any questions. This little girl seems to threaten to turn out an other genious.[16] She is coming here to paint tomorrow. Her designes in pen & ink show real intellect. Jones is going to cut Topsy, he says his over bearing temper is becoming quite insuportable as well as his conceite. Hunt who was all hot about Anny M. has somehow quite cooled again in a few days & says now that it is never to be. At Manchester (to give one recording line to it) all that I remember is that an old English picture with Richard II in it was the only really beautiful work of the old masters & Hunt & Millais the only fine among the new. Hunt in fact made the Exhibition.[17] The music was jolly & the waiters tried very hard to cheat (25 hours).

31st Sunday Thursday beastly cold did next to nothing. All Friday in bed with it. Saturday up but not good for much, Letters, colored at one of my lithographs of Windermere to give J. Marshall. At night drew in Maurice into the picture but drawn exactly from himself it looks rediculously stumpy & the head enormous. I must either falsify it or make the navvy's head bigger (7 hours). Today out to see about a photographer for Maurice. To night letters & accounts.

1st Feb. Bothering all the morning about some frames that came home wrong size. Colored at the Litho. of Windermere for Marshall. This eveng letters & colord the letters of the frame for C & Peter. Cough still Bad, could not go this eve. To morrow (3 hours).

---

[16] Is there a shadow of weariness in Brown's reference to Georgiana Macdonald, the seventeen-year-old daughter of a Methodist Minister, who married E.B. Jones in 1860? Is he perhaps thinking of Miss Siddal who also "threatened to turn out another genious"?

[17] Brown is here referring to the Manchester "Art Treasures" exhibition where he admired No. 42 *Wings of a Diptych, with Portrait of Richard II* (Early English), surely the *Wilton Diptych* (National Gallery), now believed to be French. Millais contributed *Autumn Leaves*, while Holman Hunt had five canvases, *The Hireling Shepherd, Valentine Rescuing Sylvia from Proteus, Strayed Sheep, The Awakening Conscience* and *Claudio and Isabella*.

1865

10th Sepr/65 Sunday day of rest, long walk after dinner & in the dusk with Emma & the Children.

11th Monday from 11 till 1.30 & from 2 to 3 at Jacob[1] (drapery of Judah), from 3 till 6 at the nosegay,[2] and Jacob in the evening from 10 till 12 placing drapery for Levi. Nosegay 3 hours (5½ hours).

12th Found the draperies on the lay figure cause delay. Began painting about 12 at Levi till 10 tonight with intervals of rest. Did little good — quite discouraged & can't work (7 hours).

13th To gravesend with Emma to fetch Lucy from Helen Bromley's.

14th Whitewashing ceiling of studio.[3] Painted the convolvolus in the "nosegay" (6 hours).

15th Miss Spartali.[4] Painted at Cathy in the "nosegay". Had to leave off to go after Emma (5 hours).

16th Painted at Cathy & rubbed it out. Put it in again late in the afternoon (8 hours).

---

[1] *The Coat of Many Colours* (*Jacob and Joseph's Coat*; Liverpool, Plate 19) was commissioned in 1864 by George Rae, the Birkenhead banker, and completed in April 1866. It is based on a design for an engraving in *Dalziel's Bible Gallery*. Rae formed an important collection of pictures, mostly by Rossetti (now at the Tate) and had already acquired three works by Brown.

[2] A new patron, F.W. Craven, of Mosley Street, required a pendent to a water-colour made for him by William Henry Hunt who had died before putting it into effect. The companion picture, according to Rossetti, was to have been of "a golden haired female party" (*Letters*, p.559) and Craven hoped that the new drawing might correspond in some degree with Hunt's intention. *The Nosegay* (Ashmolean, Plate 20) was commissioned by Craven in the summer, completed by the end of October and worked on again later.

[3] In Oct. 1862 the Browns had moved to 14 Grove Terrace, Kentish Town.

[4] Marie (Spartali) Stillman, daughter of a Greek merchant who in 1866 was appointed Greek Consul-General in London. She was a pupil of Brown, became an artist of some accomplishment and married W.J. Stillman. Greatly admired for her beauty she occasionally sat to Rossetti for his later pictures.

19. *The Coat of Many Colours*, Walker Art Gallery, Liverpool

Sunday to Rossettis with Marshall. Saw Gough House next the hospital. Emma taken with Cholera in the night.[5]

18th worked at Cathy's head & shoulders. Emma better (6 hours).

19th Tuesday at Cathy's head, hair & dress in the Nosegay (7 hours).

20th W. Cathys head & hair. (To night for 2 hours at making a necklace of [for] Levi). Nosegay (6 hours).

21st Thursday Miss Spartali. Worked at Cathy's head & shoulders. Godwin, the architect,[6] & Marshall to dinner (7 hours).

22nd All day at Cathy. Hair neck & arm (4 hours). Evening placed necklace & worked (2 hours) at Levi (7 hours).

23rd Morning & eve at Levi (5 hours). Afternoon at Cathy's arm in nosegay (4 hours).

24th Sunday Morning & Eve at Levi. Jacob & Joseph (8 hours).

25th Cursed letter from Leeds to answer,[7] requiring much thought, & other letters. At Cathys arm from 3. Nosegay (2½ hours). Evening wrote to Marshall. Sketched Cat for do. (1½ hours). Levi's necklace (2 hours).

26th Tuesday Levi's necklace (2½ hours), evening (1½ hours). Jacob. The cat in the nosegay (4 hours).

27th Worked at Levi's necklace & wrote letters to divers people about the "Work" picture (3 hours).

28th Tried to work at the Cat. Spoilt it. Hunt called (3 hours).

29th White called about "*Work*". Getting dress for the "nosegay". Made a drawing of cat & recommenced it (4 hours).

---

[5] Rossetti had been urging Brown to live nearer the centre of London for the sake of potential picture-buyers and on 9 Oct. he wrote (*Letters*, pp.575-6) suggesting that Howell (see p.208, n.19) would be a likely person to combine with the Browns in a communal dwelling at Gough House, adjacent to the Royal Hospital, Chelsea, which had been until recently a young ladies school. Peter Paul ("Poll") Marshall (1830-1900), the large and exuberant Scotsman who now figures prominently in the diary, was a particular friend of Brown and was married to Gussy, the daughter of John Miller. He was a surveyor, civil engineer and amateur artist and made designs for stained glass for the firm of Morris, Marshall, Faulkner & Co., of which he was a founder member. Cholera had been reported in the Mediterranean since the end of August with fears of its reaching England. Emma's attack seems to have been a mild one.

[6] E.W. Godwin (1833-86), architect and furniture designer, had recently left Bristol and in October opened an office in Baker Street.

[7] Plint who had commissioned *Work* had died in 1861. The painting was completed in 1862 and thereafter Brown was involved in many fruitless negotiations for the re-sale of the picture.

20. *The Nosegay*, Ashmolean Museum, Oxford

30th Sat. Long letter to Leeds about "Work". Painted at cat (4 hours). Placed Lay figure for nosegay (1½ hours).

1 october Sun. Worked at apron & dress in nosegay & walked to Tottenham[8] with Marshall & Rossetti. Beautiful day. Home in Fly with Gabriel. E Finished b- sherry (3 hours).

2nd Mon. Painted at the same. Evening letters. E tried to get cherry Brandy at pastry cook's, I just in time. E very unhappy because failed (7 hours).

3rd Tues. Worked at Apron & dress, then a row, then a walk about the fields with E. Then work again (6 hours).

4th Wed. Miss Spartali. Painted at muslin dress, Nosegay. Letters to Leeds, to Lowes D. & to Green. Walked to Holloway[9] with E. Sulky returning, ungrateful (3 hours).

5th Thursday Worked at Muslin dress (6 hours).

6th friday do. Legros[10] Called & wasted afternoon (4 hours).

7th Saturday Dress in nosegay. Dine with Rossetti[11] (6 hours).

8th Sunday At Rossettis, Home[12] & Stephens & the Marshalls to dinner.

9th Monday till 5 at the dress, cat etc. At night head & shoulders (10 hours).

10th Tuesday Drew head. Background. Evening hand & arm. Campbell[13] called (8 hours).

---

[8] P.P. Marshall's home ("a cheery, reckless household", G. Burne-Jones, *Memorials of Edward Burne-Jones*, 1904, vol.i, p.238) was at Northumberland Row, High Road, Tottenham, a London suburb which was, according to Rossetti, "a very cocknified place" (G. Pedrick, *Life with Rossetti*, 1964, p.150).

[9] This entry recurs again a few days later and again three times in January. It is possible but unlikely that so busy a man as Brown would go for a stroll in country lanes in mid-winter; nor is it likely that he went on shopping errands since he had two daughters and servants who could do this for him. Only in the October entry did Emma accompany him. There was a Working Men's Club in the Holloway Road; perhaps this was the object of the visit. Alternately, but again unlikely, Brown may have been paying a working call on Charles Holloway, painter on glass for the Morris Firm.

[10] Alphonse Legros (1837-1911), French painter and sculptor, taught etching at the South Kensington School of Art. Encouraged by Whistler he had come to England in 1863, had married the following year, and was naturalized in 1864 though never able to master the language. At this time he lived at Victoria Grove Villas, Kensington.

[11] Rossetti had left Chatham Place after the death of his wife in 1862 and later in the year had taken Tudor House, Cheyne Walk, Chelsea, a large house with a garden at the back.

[12] Probably the medium, Daniel Home, who had wakened Rossetti's interest in spiritualism.

[13] Probably James Campbell (*c.* 1828-93), the Liverpool artist who had within the last two years taken up his home in London.

11th Wedy Spartali. Painted at head & hair etc. nosegay (5 hours).

12th Thursd All day at Rose bush & wall (7 hours).

13th Friday All day same. Evening W B Scott[14] (8 hours).

14th Saty all daylight at same. Marshall called, thinks Mr Miller may sell the Work picture for the Leeds people & so get him the commission. Letter from Gabriel & to Gabriel. E.D.[15] eve. Stormy. in consequence (6 hours).

15th Sunday Rest. Rose bush omitted (7 hours).

16th Garden all day at Rose tree. Eveng to Holloway (7 hours).

18th Wed Spartali, Rose bush etc. (9 hours).

19th Thursd At the arranging generally (8 hours).

20th Friday the same (8 hours).

21st Saturday same (9 hours).

22nd Sunday same. Rain all day, never went out (9 hours).

23rd Monday same. Eve to W B Scott with Emma (6 hours).

24th Tuesday All over same. Even 2½ at sketch of do. (8 hours).

25th Wedy Spartali. At Roses etc & finished & sent it off to Mr Craven of Mostley [Mosley] St Manchester who commissd me for it for 125 Guan. (4 hours).

26th Thursday Laid in platform & sundries in Jacob (5 hours).

27th Friday Out after models, worked at Phots of Work (5 hours).

28th Saturday Out about Nolly. After dinner to Tottenham.

29th Sunday With Marshall at Tottenham.

30th Monday home early in the rain to work by 11 painted head of little girl[16] till ½ past 4 & touched it by gas-light (7 hours).

31st Tuesday childs hands and arm & the Jacob (7 hours).

1st November Wedy Childs body. Evening long letter to Craven about an other drawing which he wants[17] (6 hours).

---

[14] Scott had resigned his appointment in Newcastle the previous year and was living at 33 Elgin Road. He was employed at the South Kensington Art School as examiner in Art.
[15] "Emma Drunk".
[16] Jacob's granddaughter, later referred to as "Mary", crouching on the left of the dais.
[17] Presumably the water-colour *Cordelia's Portion* (Port Sunlight) was suggested – and commissioned (see diary, Saturday, Nov. 1865 p.209).

2nd Thursy Childs Legs (6 hours).

3rd Friday Childs legs & foot. Eveng to Legros (6 hours).

4th Saturday Childs foot, & out to get the drapery etc. Evening Placed Lay figure (4 hours).

5th Sunday worked at Childs drapery & Evening wrot lines to a song for Emma (4 hours).

6th Monday at Childs drapery languidly. Evening Emma's songs (4 hours).

7th Tuesday same, Languidly. Out of spirits. Eve finish E's song (4 hours).

8th Wedy same. Miss Spartali. Even. upset looking in to Extravagance (6 hours).

9th Thursday same (4 hours).

10th Friday to London. Cave Thomas's Russian chappel & Gambart's Exhibition.[18] Letter to Craven in Eveg.

11th Saturday Child's drapery & Evening flowers (7 hours).

12th Sunday Levy's scarf (2 hours).

13th monday do. & childs head dress (4 hours).

14th Tuesday Miss Spartali, Jacobs dress (5 hours).

15th Wed Jacobs Dress, ground, Platform etc (7½ hours).

16th Thursday Levi's Foot etc (7 hours).

Friday 17th Out all day, bought horn for Levi. To Mudies; to call on Burgess, out, Livock, C. Thomas, Hine, L Dickinson (at work), Chapman, Swinburn in bed as laet as 3.30 p.m., E Godwin, lost his number; thence to Gabriels & dined there − Fanny & Howel as usual.[19]

---

[18] Gambart's Winter Exhibition took place annually at his gallery in Pall Mall. Thomas was engaged in painting the heads of the twelve Apostles in circular panels for the newly built Russian Embassy chapel in Welbeck Street.

[19] Charles Augustus Howell (1840-90) had become an intimate of Rossetti and assisted him in the disposal of his pictures. Half Portuguese, an adventurer of wit and charm, he had been secretary to Ruskin and was still a favoured friend of Burne-Jones. He married his cousin in 1867 and continued to live in Brixton for some little time. Brown's calls, for the most part abortive, led him across London from the rooms in Buckingham Street occupied by the architect William Burges (1827-81), who was probably at Cardiff for he was restoring the Castle that year, to John Livock, architect and surveyor, at Euston Grove. Cave Thomas was nearby at Torrington Square. H.G. Hine the landscape painter lived in Orchard Street, Algernon Charles Swinburne (1837-1909) was fairly close in Dorset Square; Godwin in Baker Street, and Lowes Dickinson in his Langham Chambers Studio. George Chapman, the impecunious portrait painter, recently back from Spain, had no fixed address.

Saturday Worked at Nosegay which had come back to be framed. Craven called & commissioned me to paint a King Lear & water colour for 525£[20] (3 hours).

Sunday worked at nosegay again with interruptions, evening Webb[21] & Anthony dined with us. E rather D (4 hours).

Monday At the nosegay till 12, then with Emma to Look after Houses. Dined with the Joneses[22] (2 hours).

Tuesday Miss Spartali, & worked at Nosegay, evening to dinner at Scotts. E D there. Marshalls home with us. E talked nonsense to Mrs M. about ill-treatment & separate maintenance (3 hours).

Wednesday only espostulations & waste of time.

Thursday Out after Houses all day & to see Gabriel who was wished to say the size his drawing wd be to have mine the same size, but he refused flat to say. His good word however has got me this commission in some degree.[23]

24th Friday Out after Houses with Emma. Saw one in Euston Sq.

Saturday out again with Emma, took Webb to look at the house, offered to take it for 7 years at £130.

Sunday To church, to call on the Tebbs,[24] & Joneses to dinner with us. Late considering accoants, necessity being of settling with Kentish Town Tradespeople before going.

Monday Painted Levi's Horn & worked Isachar (5 hours).

Tuesday Miss Spartali & out about house. Evening thought about Lear (3 hours).

Wedy Hands & Arms of Judah (8 hours).

Thursday Dog, ground & Coat & drew at Simion (8 hours).

---

[20] Craven appears to have commissioned an oil replica as well as the water-colour *Cordelia's Portion*; the oil was not put in hand until 1867, completed in 1875 (Southampton Art Gallery).
[21] Philip Webb (1831-1915) architect, and a partner in the Morris Firm for which he designed furniture and glass.
[22] In Kensington Square to which they had moved the previous year.
[23] Craven had already three water-colours by Rossetti; in the summer he had commissioned another and wanted Brown's to be the same size. Rossetti knew he was unlikely to begin his drawing for several months and refused to commit himself to specific dimensions. Craven eventually received in 1867 a replica of *The Return of Tibullus to Delia*.
[24] H.V. Tebbs and his wife lived in a cottage at West Hill, Highgate.

Friday [Dec 1st] Simions Head, & to Stephens (5 hours).

Saturday Hous Hunting. Burgess [Burges] & Godwin called.

Sunday House Hunting & letters.

Monday House Hunting & to call on Hunt.[25]

Tuesday Spartali.

6th Wednesday At the Jacob picture (3 hours).

17th Began King Lear drawing for Craven (3 hours).

24th worked at Josephs coat (7 hours).

Xmas day At Josephs coat (4 hours).

26th 27th & 28th at Simion & the tiger skin (16 hours).

Friday 29th, Saturday, Sunday & Newyears day at Simion & also Josephs coat (20 hours).

---

[25] Holman Hunt, engaged to Fanny Waugh whom he married in three weeks time, lived at Tor Villa, Campden Hill. The diary is silent concerning the Browns' move to a larger house, 37 Fitzroy Square. This must have occurred between 6 and 7 Dec. when there are no entries. They lived there for ten years enjoying a hitherto unfamiliar prosperity never experienced in the prevailing years of extreme poverty. The house became distinguished as a centre for men of letters and from the world of art.

1866

Jan 2nd Tuesday Thursday & Friday at Josephs coat, Simion etc (10 hours). Friday night King Lear (3 hours).

Saturday & Sunday at the Josephs coat (10 hours).

8th Monday Same (7 hours).

9th Tuesday same (7 hours).

10th Wednesday Miss Spartali (6 hours).

11th dog . . . & to see Rip van Winkle[1] (5 hours).

12th dog . . . (5 hours).

13th Saturday dog & to Simeon Solomons[2] (5 hours).

14th Sunday out, Scotts etc. Thomas to dinner.

15th Monday out to holloway. Marshalls to dinner.

16th Tuesday Simion. Morris & Scotts to dinner (6 hours).

17th Wednesday (Miss Spartali) Worked at King Lear (5 hours).

18th Thursday Simion. Evening, sandals (8 hours).

19th Sandals. To Holloway. Evening drawing at Juday's feet (7 hours).

20th Feet. To Holloway, evening divers (7 hours).

21st Sunday To dine with Cave Thomas.

22nd Sundries (7 hours).

[1] Dion Boucicault's successful version of the drama ran for nearly two hundred performances at the Adelphi Theatre. An American actor, Joseph Jefferson, played the lead.
[2] The youngest member of a family of artists, Simeon Solomon (1840-1905) of brilliant talent in youth, came under corrupting influences. While his work deteriorated, his homosexual practices made him an outcast from society. In 1866 he was living at 106 Gower Street with his sister Rebecca, also an artist.

23rd Tuesday Judas' foot & dined at Morris's[3] (6 hours).

24th Miss Spartali. Judas foot. Evening Roots of Trees (9 hours).

25th Rae called & saw picture. Evening worked at poppy (3 hours).

26th Friday out with Rae & to dine with Stanhope.[4]

27th Model for Simion. Swinburne wasted my Eveg (6 hours).

28th Sunday Model for Simion. Hughes dined with us (6 hours).

29th Munday Out to see Exhibition.[5]

30th Tuesday Model for Simion (6 hours).

31st Wednesday Miss Spartali. Worked at Simion (5 hours).

1st Feb at Major Gillums to dinner.[6]

2nd Friday Worked at Poppy & sundries (5 hours).

3rd Saturday Model for Simion (6 hours).

4th Sunday model do. (6 hours).

5th out to Zoological after Camel. Eveng general effect (2 hours).

6th All day looking at Green's men stretching Chaucer. (5 hours).

7th Wednesday worked at Divers & Jacob. Spartali. (5 hours).

8th Thursday McLean & Rose called & comissoned entombment.[7]

9th Friday Jacob picture (5 hours).

---

[3] Morris had sold Red House in Kent and had moved to Queen Square towards the end of 1865. The firm's premises were on the ground floor and the family occupied the floors above.

[4] Spencer Stanhope was probably already living in Harley Street which was to be his address for a number of years.

[5] There was a choice of Winter Exhibitions but Brown may have paid a second visit to Gambart's gallery where Whistler's *La Princesse du Pays de la Porcelaine* had been very recently hung. The sitter for the picture was Christine Spartali, sister of Marie.

[6] Major (or Colonel, or Lieutenant-Colonel as given in the Postal Directory) William Gillum, The Moated House, White Hart Lane, Tottenham, had been introduced to Rossetti by Robert Browning. He was associated with the Working Men's College, became a founder member of the Hogarth Club, and was for a short time a pupil of Brown (see N. Pevsner, "Colonel Gillum and the Pre-Raphaelites", *Burlington Magazine*, March 1953, pp.78, 81). The previous year he had bought *Walton-on-the-Naze*, being already the owner of three of Brown's works (including *The Hayfield*, once Morris's).

[7] J. Anderson Rose was a solicitor and a picture-buyer. T. McLean, the art dealer, had premises in the Haymarket. *The Entombment* (Private Collection) may be the water-colour of which Brown made a small oil replica that year.

10th Saturday Jacob (4 hours).

11th Sunday Worked somewhat (5 hours).

12th Monday To Marshalls about self & No1. Out Even.

13th Tuesday Worked & wrote letters (3 hours).

14th Out to Marshall about Emma & to D.T. White.

15th Worked hardly at all at Jacob (3 hours). Evening K Lear (5 hours).

16th Friday Miss Spartali (6 hours).

17th at Background. Eveg Rossetti's, Joneses, Howel to dinner (5 hours).

18th Sunday Out to see Legros, Jones, Stanhope, Prinsep,[8] Hunt, Inchbold Etc.

19th worked at Landscape of Jacob & King Lear (8 hours).

20th at Jacob Background & draperies. Evg to Rossettis (5 hours).

21st out see Arundel Exn.[9] Evening composing King Lear (3 hours).

22nd Miss Spartali. Worked at Jacob. Eveg to Solomon (5 hours).

23rd friday at Jacob & at King Lear (9 hours).

24th Saturday Levi (5 hours).

25th Sunday Model for Levi (7 hours).

26th Monday Levi (5 hours).

27th Tuesday Levi. Eveng King Lear (8 hours).

28th Wednesday Out. Evening King Lear (4 hours).

1st [March] worked Thursday. Spartali. Coat (4 hours).

2nd Friday Coat & king Lear (8 hours).

3rd Saturday levi's leg & dog (6 hours).

4th Sunday Dog & Coat (5 hours).

---

[8] Valentine Prinsep (1838-1904) grew up at Little Holland House, he studied under G.F. Watts and was associated with the Oxford Union mural paintings in 1857. He was now a neighbour of Leighton, living in a house built for him by Webb.
[9] The exhibition at the Arundel Club, where for one day Rossetti was showing *The Beloved* (Tate), before sending it to George Rae. This club in Salisbury Street, the Strand, of which Rossetti was a member, was a meeting-place for actors, dramatists and journalists and enjoyed an unconventional atmosphere.

5th Monday Jacob picture. Dog (7 hours).

6th Tuesday do. dog & Coat (6 hours).

7th Wednesday Coat & Jacobs Dress. King Lear (7 hours).

8th Thursday Spartali. Benjamin (6 hours).

9th Friday out afternoon. Benjamin. Evening, Thomas to dine (4 hours).

10th Saturday Camel. Eve King Lear cartoon (8 hours).

11th Sunday Isachar, Camel, Levi. Eveg K. Lear (8 hours).

12th Monday Scarce worked at Jacob Picture for interruptions. Evening at K. Lear (3 hours).

13th Tuesday Camel. Evening K. Lear (7 hours).

14th Wednesday To dinner at Howell (7 hours).

15th Thursday Spartali. E.D. eveg. R[ow?]

16th Friday Idle in consequence.

Saturday Livock called in the Even.

Sunday 18th Jacob. Evening K. Lear (10 hours).

Monday 19th Jacob (7 hours).

Tuesday 20th do. (7 hours).

Wednesday 21st Jacob. To the Play (6 hours).

Thursday 22nd Spartali (5 hours).

23rd divers in Jacob (6 hours).

24th Same (6 hours).

Sunday 25th To see Hughes (6 hours).

Monday Jacob divers (6 hours).

Tuesday Mary arm in Jacob (7 hours).

Wednesday Mary arm in Jacob (6 hours).

Thursday 29th King Lear. Spartali (3 hours).

Friday 30th Mary arm in Jacob (7 hours). Lear (9 hours).

Saturday Same. Even. Cave Thomas called (7 hours).

Sunday 1st April same. Eve Cogitating ways & means (7 hours).

Monday 2nd out about "Work" picture, Judah blue (6 hours).

Tuesday 3rd Judah blue. Much puzzled about "Work" & ws & ms [ways & means].

Wed 4th out about "work". Judah & Isachar. Eveng King Lear (6 hours).

Thursday 5th out about "Work". Jodah blue. Dine with Morris (3 hours).

Friday 6th Spartali. Simion, Juday etc (7 hours). K Lear (3 hours).

Saturday 7th all over Jacob & cartoon for firm (10 hours).

Sunday 8th divers in Jacob (7 hours).

Monday 9th all day at Jacob (7 hours).

Tuesday 10th all day at Jacob (8 hours).

Wednesday 11th all day at Jacob (10 hours).

Thursday 12th Spartali. Jacob. Eveng to Boys's[10] (6 hours).

Friday 13th child (9 hours).

Saturday 14th child etc & lettering (10 hours).

Sunday 15th child (8 hours).

Monday 16th do. (8 hours).

Tuesday 17th divers (8 hours).

Wednesday 18th Jacob all over (7 hours).

Thursday 19th All day at Jacob. Spartali (8 hours).

Friday 20th worked at "nosegay". Scott to dinner (5 hours).

Saturday 21st Private view of "Jacob" & "Nosegage".[11]

Sunday 22nd Morris dine here & Jones.

Monday 23rd Zoological gardens.

Tuesday 24th

Wednesday 25th Miss Spartali. Botanical.

Thursday King Lear. Out with Emma (6 hours).

[10] Boyce had taken on the Chatham Place rooms once occupied by Rossetti.
[11] At Brown's house. In the autumn of 1866 Gambart showed *The Coat of Many Colours* at his annual exhibition.

Friday to Portrait Exhibition with Emma & Gabriel. [12]

Saturday 28th King Lear (6 hours).

Sunday King Lear (6 hours).

Monday do. (4 hours).

Tuesday [May 1st] do. (4 hours).

Wednesday do. (5 hours).

Thursday Spartali. King Lear (6 hours).

Friday to dine at Rossetti. K.L. (6 hours).

Saturday K.L. cartoon & Gambarts French Gallery [13] (3 hours).

Sunday 6th K.L. eveng accounts (6 hours).

Monday 7th King Le. cartoon (10 hours).

Tuesday 8th King Lear Cartoon (6 hours).

Wedy 9th same (6 hours).

Thursday 10th Spartali. Same (6 hours).

Friday 11th same (5 hours).

Saty 12th do. (7 hours).

Sunday 13th do. (4 hours).

Monday 14th do. (6 hours).

Tuesday 15th . . .

Wed 16th Marshall dined with us.

Thursday 17th Ball.

Friday 18th To dine with Gabriel & slept there.

Sat 19th Spartali.

Sundy 20th King Lear (6 hours).

Monday 21st Spartali. King Lear. Eveg to Scotts (7 hours).

[12] The National Portrait Exhibition was showing over one thousand portraits, arranged chronologically, in what had been the Refreshment Rooms of the International Exhibition at South Kensington in 1862.
[13] Gambart's French Exhibition opened that month.

Tuesday 22nd To Breakfast with Prinsep.

Wedy 23rd King Lear. To dine with Webb (6 hours).

Thursday 24th Spartali. King Lear Model (9 hours).

Friday Out with Emma, worked at a portrait of Lowes D (5 hours). In the evg at a Cartoon of Goliah[14] (2 hours).

Sat 26th Portrait improving for Lowes D. Evg Goliah (11 hours).

27th Sunday Portrait. Eveg walk with Emma & accounts (6 hours).

28th Monday Portrait (5 hours).

29th Tuesday Portrait (7 hours).

30th Wedy

31st Thursday Spartali.

Friday 1st June

Saturday 2nd

Sunday 3rd

Monday 4th King Lear (1 hour).

Tuesday 5th Spartali. King Lear (6 hours).

Wedy 6th King Lear

Thursday 7th King Lear. Spartali.

Friday 8th

Saturday 9th

Sunday 10th

Monday 11th

Tuesday 12th

Wednesday 13th

Thursday 14th Spartali. K. Lear (7 hours).

Friday 15th Portrait for Lowes (7 hours).

Saturday 16th Portrait & K Lear (7 hours).

[14] A cartoon (Untraced) of *David Killing Goliath* for part of a stained glass lancet window.

Sunday K Lear (5 hours).

Monday 18th King Lear cartoon (8 hours).

Tuesday Spartali. King Lear. Leighton called about Drawings (4 hours).

Wednesday 20th King Lear (9 hours).

Thursday 21st King Lear (7 hours).

Friday 22nd King Lear (9 hours).

Saturday 23rd Cartoon Lear, even. Burton, Lowes D, Street, Shields, Holland[15] & D.G.R. to dinner (5 hours).

Sunday 24th to Tottenham with Emma, Chathy & Marshall.

Monday 25th accounts & letters. King Lear, Shields & P.P. to dinner.

Tuesday Spartali. King Lear (6 hours).

Wednesday Lear. To dinner with Holland (7 hours).

Thursday Spartali. (Lear) Thomas to tea (6 hours).

Friday Out after dress King Lear (4 hours).

Saturday 30th

Sunday 1st July

Monday

Tuesday 3rd

Wedy 4th

5th

6th

7th

Sunday 8th

9th

[15] (Sir) Frederic Burton (1816-1900), Irish water-colour painter of historical genre subjects; Director of the National Gallery, 1874-94. G.E. Street (1824-81), architect, had a distinguished reputation as a leading Gothic Revivalist. The Law Courts are perhaps his major achievement. Frederic Shields (1833-1911), of a melancholy disposition, was a painter of religious subjects. James Holland (1800-70), painter in water-colours. On 27 June Brown dined with him at his house in Osnaburgh Street, Euston.

Tuesday 10th

11th

12th

13th

Sat 14th

15th

16th

Tuesday 17th Spartali

18th

19th

20th

21st

Sunday 22nd

23rd

Tuesday 24th Spartali.

25th

26th

27th

Sat 28th

Sunday 29th

Monday 30th

Tuesday 31st

Wednesd 1st [Aug]

2nd

Friday 3rd

Sat 4th

Sunday 5th

Monday 6th

Tuesday 7th Spartali

Wednesday 15th Spartali.

Wednesday 22nd Spartali.

Wedy 29th Spartali

Wedy 5th Sepr

6th

Friday 7th

Saturday 8th

Sunday 9th

Monday 10th

Tuesday 11th

Wedy 12th

Thursday 13th

Friday 14th

Saturday 15th

Sunday 16th

Monday 17th

Tuesday 18th

Wednesday 19th

Thursday 20th

Friday 21st

Saturday 22nd

Sunday 23rd

Monday 24th

Tuesday 25th

Wedy 26th

Thursday 27th Spartali.

Oct 4th Spartali.

11th Spartali.

18th Spartali

25th –

1st Nov Spartali.

8th Spartali.

10th do.

15th do.

22nd

29th

6th Dec Spartali wheen

13th Spartali

27th Spartali wheen

1867

Jan 67 Spartali.

Feb 14 –

21st Spartali. Worked at Coat of many colours

28th Spartali.

March 7th Spartali.

16th Spartali.

21st

27 Sp.

April 6th Spartali.

13 Sp.

27th Spartali.

May 2nd do.

9th do.

16th do.

23rd do.

27th do.

June 3rd

14th
17th

July 1st Spartali.
29th Spartali.

August 5th —
12th —

Nov 4th
11th
do. 20th
do. 27th

Dec 4th
do. 20th
27th

1868

Jan 68 1st
3rd
24th Spartali.
31st

12th
26th

4th

APPENDIX I

Letter from D.G. Rossetti to Ford Madox Brown (see p.36), (D.G. Rossetti: His Family Letters with a Memoir ed. W.M. Rossetti, vol.i, 1895, pp. 116-17).

50 Charlotte Street, Portland Place.
March, 1848

Sir,

I am a student in the Antique School of the Royal Academy. Since the first time I ever went to an exhibition (which was several years ago, and when I saw a picture of yours from Byron's *Giaour*) I have always listened with avidity if your name happened to be mentioned, and rushed first of all to your number in the Catalogue. The *Parisina*, the *Study in the Manner of the Early Masters, Our Lady of Saturday-night*, and the other glorious works you have exhibited, have successively raised my admiration, and kept me standing on the same spot for fabulous lengths of time. The outline from your *Abstract Representation of Justice* which appeared in one of the Illustrated Papers constitutes, together with an engraving after that great painter Von Holst, the sole pictorial adornment of my room. And, as for the *Mary Queen of Scots*, if ever I do anything in the art, it will certainly be attributable in a great degree to the constant study of that work.

It is not therefore to be wondered at if, wishing to obtain some knowledge of colour (which I have as yet scarcely attempted), the hope suggests itself that you may possibly admit pupils to profit by your invaluable assistance. If, such being the case, you would do me the honour to inform me what your terms would be for six months' instruction, I feel convinced that I should then have some chance in the Art.

I remain, Sir, very truly yours,
Gabriel C. Rossetti.

APPENDIX II

Text of verso and recto adjoining missing pages (see p.163).

as we were putting up holly in the parlour (our drawing Rooms) for/ folding doors looked so beautiful that I thought I had as/ yet undecided, but it will be a family on Christmas eve putting/ but this idea is as yet in *embryo*. She will be *ill* somehow seated/ to her children. Katty will be lugging nolly along to see the/ years old − & she holds him under the arms & drags him about by/ & paint. Yesterday I worked at thinking it over & settled much/ nothing & the frame I have although not paid for. I stick/ already painted save the figure. Last eveng I did little but send/ to church with Lucy & the sermon being unutterably dull/ work a pretty way of doing it some will say. After church I/ plaid as a tartan the same that was painted in the last of England/ to spread out & I rather ashamed of it being of a faded light/ an other this winter, money goes so fast & fearfully. The/ my dressing & lumber room. I find by a rough calculation/ 29 yesterday I began at Lowes Dickinsons painting in a black silk dress/ insisted on making it £40 instead of £39.9. & paint for the/ am to designe & show him, after this home found a letter from/ save for bare outlay so of course this is knocked on the head/ to Maria feeling forced to decline their kind offer, Lowes/ 8th Feby To Dickinsons again before 10 at work at the black silk/ I worked at drawing in the parlour in the "Holly" Picture also at the/ Wednesday 31st to Dickinsons & there on going in at a man in [illegible]/ [?chin] for all intricate outlines from nature not figurs/ sound knowledge of the human figure does anatomy/ persuaded me & Lucy is go there for £35 per ann./ kind persuasion to this favour. Sunday all/ at night Cromwell. Wednesday spent straining a / Hunt & William Rossetti called & we had a grand/ of the Accadm. Hunt thinks a curse hangs over all/ approve of the doings of the R.A.s we will have nothing/ of his travels & a stout hearted traveler he has been/ left at ½ past one. Thursday to Dickinson as above / idea of it. Cromwell one hand in pocket looks at/ on his active period) his horse is to be old & *pale* as/ foreground crosses the grass touching the horses./ seen through the horses legs. A straw yard to the/

over the meadow behind through the gateway into/ Huntingdon town in the distance the Ouse &/ worked late & enthusiastically at this in a state/ to designing in earnest. Yesterday morning saw/ are marvellously fine some of the others so so./ the eveng from 9 till past 12 at the Cromwell design. 9 hours/ began it, eveng went to Princess's at half Price with Emma 6 hours/ 10£ on account home, had the butcher boy, painted him in Woolners sketch 8 hours/ morning from 10 to 5 at Lowes. Painted Bonnet etc very tired after Dinner – slept 6 hours.

INDEX

Acland, Dr Henry 186n
Addison, Laura 30
Allingham, William 106, 173n, 176; *Day and Night Songs*, and *Poems* 105
Anderson, Charles 140, 148
Annersley, Lord *see* Tenterden
Ansted, D.T. 27, 31
Anthony, Mark 12, 14, 15, 16, 17, 21, 27, 28, 30, 31, 42, 45, 49, 56, 137, 148, 166, 167, 209; buys from Brown 74, 80; at St Albans 86; pictures at Pantheon 132, and at Miller's 189; *Landscape and Figures, Village Green* 26n; *Stratford-on-Avon, Evening* 116
Art Journal 70n, 131n,
Art Union, The 8, 32, 45, 46, 59, 61 103
Art Union Monthly see Art Journal
Arundel Club 213; Society 171n
Ashley, Miss, Mrs 27, 30, 31, 35, 48, 49, 55, 59; travels 95
Athenaeum, The 40n, 61n, 72n, 131n, 154n
Atkinson, Miss 156

Bacon, Francis 135
Baily, E.H. 61, 70, 122; *The Graces* 61n
Baldung, Hans *Portrait of a Man* 108n
Bamford family 9, 14, 17, 20, 21, 28, 29, 33, 34, 40, 44, 45, 49, 52, 56, 104, 112; and *Lady Nugent* 103
Barker (model) 69
Barlow, T.O. 163
Barnet Union 86, 111n
Barraud, Henry and William 27, 39, 63; *Lord's Cricket Ground, We Praise Thee, O God* 27n
Barry, Sir Charles 1n
Beggar's Opera, The 62
Bellini, Giovanni *Virgin and Child* 186
Bishop, W.J. 66
Black Prince, The 2, 12, 13, 14, 41, 74, 163

Boddy, 40, 45
Bonington, R.P. *The Indian Maid* 125
Boyce, George Price 138, 173, 181, 215
Boyce, Joanna *Elgiva* 138
British Institution 29, 62, 113, 114, 121, 144
Brodie, J.L. 30
Bromley, Clara 24n, 48, 145,
Bromley, Elizabeth 110, 111
Bromley, Helen 4n, 6, 10, 12, 15, 21, 23, 28, 110n, 139; her daughter ill 103, dies 139
Bromley, John 16, 20, 25, 31, 40, 42, 45, 63
Bromley, John James 40
Bromley, Sir Richard Madox 11, 24n, 34
Broussais, Dr 58
Brown, Arthur Gabriel Madox 188, 194, 198, 199
Brown, Bessy, (aunt) 5, 6, 7, 8, 10, 12, 14, 23, 24, 27, 30, 31, 32, 33, 39, 42, 103
Brown, Catherine (Katty, Cathy) 84, 87, 95, 102, 103, 142; birth, baptism, marriage 72n; cuts eyelid 112; as model 76, 127, 128, 178n, 202, 204; out with father 92, 96, 134, 140, 180, 187; frightened by Rossetti 107; character 126-7; at Ramsgate 176
Brown, Elizabeth (1st wife) 2-3, 4n, 6n, 10, 11n, 18, 28, 154
Brown, Emma (2nd wife) *passim*; as model 14n, 66, 74, 76, 78, 80, 88, 93, 106, 117, 126, 128, 129, 134, 140, 151; to Ramsgate 67, 176; marriage 72; to Dover 78; unwell 80, 90, 92, 102, 111, 115, 126, 132, 155, 159, 187, 194, 204; to Rossettis 84, 125, 145, 164, 166; pregnant 87, 107, 110, 188, and confined 117, 188; shops 90, 104, 123, 125, 131, 135, 137, 142, 143, 146, 175; irritable 92; extravagant 115, 129, 139, 208; intoxicated 129, 162n, 207, 209,

Brown, Emma *cont.*
214; quarrels 141, 178, 182, 206;
miscarriage 199
Brown, Ford Madox cartoon competition
1n; pleasures of painting 2, 91, 113,
and disappointments 2, 142; at Rome 2,
4, 6, 28; and lay figures 4, 5, 8, 9,
10, 12, 13, 21, 23, 32, 33, 34, 56, 76,
94, 95, 96, 106, 107, 113, 182, 206,
208; Ravensbourne Wharf and Tan
Yard 5n, 11, 31, 32, 115, 116, 117, 118;
and use of pigments 6, 7, 9, 35, 39, 48,
49, 50, 52, 53, 64, 70, 76, 183; and
daguerreotypes 14, 66, and calotypes
157, 162, and photographs 187, 207;
versifies 23, 101, 102; to Dickinson's
Academy 24, 25, 26, 27, 30, 41, 42, 43,
44; and framing 35, 91, 92, 104, 109,
122, 123, 124, 125, 131, 134, 146-7,
151, 177, 201; teaches 36, 118n, 136,
137, 143, 212; and School of Design 45,
114, 117; his studio 6, 7, 69, 194; and
North London Drawing School 70n, 71,
78, 164; at Stockwell 74, 76, 78,
Hampstead 78, 95, Hendon 80, Grove
Villas 80, 94, 104; sacks maid 86-7;
difficulty in writing 93-4; views on
poetry 105; as model 105n, 106, 126,
151, 167, 178n, 183; dislike of Ruskin
105n, 113n, 126, 130, 131, 144, 170,
196, and dreams of 142; irritated by
Rossetti 107-8, 110, 115, 130, 137, 149,
154, 178; troubles with Emma 129, 132,
139, 141, 142, 145, 175, 178, 182, 203,
206, 207, 209, 214; goes house-hunting
152, 154, 155, 209, 210; lives at Fortess
Terrace 155, at Grove Terrace 202n, at
Fitzroy Square 210n; his chimney alight
160; works for Dickinsons 162-3, 165,
166, 167, 169, 172, 173, 174, 177;
Liverpool prize 187; designs furniture
195, 200; is buried 198n; American
Exhibition 199. Suffers from: ague 16,
40, 175; apoplectic numbness 141, 143;
boils 110, 146; bowels 122, 143, 151;
colds 9, 30, 46, 105, 112, 120, 133,
186, 201; discouragement 96-7, 119;
dizziness 37, 172; face ache 184; fever
76, 126, 154; flea bites 90; headache 95,
115; indigestion 9, 20, 158; inertia 121;
laziness 7, 9, 13, 18, 21, 52, 82, 83, 84,
91, 92, 102, 103, 117; melancholia 78,
82, 84; mulligrubs 153; rheumatic
inflamation 192; the sulks 5, 6, 123,
137; toothache 5-6, 11, 49, 59, 182;
vomiting 189; want of money 4, 78, 91,
94, 96, 99, 107, 110, 111, 112, 114,

Brown, Ford Madox *cont.*
115, 121, 122, 182. Visits: Blackheath
5n, 17, 21, 27, 31, 42; Crystal Palace
140, 171; Decoy Farm 94; Eel Pie Island
8n; Foot's Cray 5n, 17, 21, 22, 27, 40,
45, 53, 54, 55, 68, 76, 186; Gravesend
4n, 6, 10, 18, 21, 25, 30, 40, 41, 42, 44,
45, 48, 49, 53, 61, 63, 64, 65, 68, 95,
103, 107, 109, 125, 139, 140, 159, 202;
Greenwich 5, 10, 11, 25, 40, 49, 64,
103; Hampton Court 8, 64; Holloway
206, 207, 211; Isle of Wight 74; Lakes
46, 82; Liverpool 46, 188-90; Margate
67; Mill Hill 92, 134, 142; Paris 44;
Ramsgate 67; Richmond 8, 42, 68;
St Albans 84-6, 115; St Ives 176-7;
Southend 4, 82; Tottenham 206,
207, 218; Zoological Gardens 66, 212,
215. Works: *Adam and Eve* 1n; *Beauty
Before She Became Acquainted with
the Beast* 68, 83, 84, 87, 88, 90-1, 92,
109, 110, 120-1, 152, 198; *The Body of
King Harold . . . the Battle of Hastings*
1n; *The Brent at Hendon* Pl.15, 88, 90,
91, 92, 93, 94, 104, 108, 109, 125, 131,
141, 186; *Carrying Corn* Pl.16, 90ff,
122, 123, 124, 131, 141; *Chaucer at the
Court of Edward III* Pl.2, 2ff, 40n,
63ff, 84, 121, 122, 123, 124, 125, 212,
and studies 7, 41n, 199, and landscape
65, 72, and Paris exhibition 113, 116,
119, 121, 157, 162; *Christ Washing
Peter's Feet* Pl.10, 76, 82, 83, 84, 105n,
111, 112, 180, 181, 182, 183, 184, 185,
186n, 192, 194, 197, 198, 199, water-
colour 200; *The Coat of Many Colours*
Pl.19, 202, 204ff; *Cordelia's Portion*
207ff; *Cromwell on his Farm* 153, 163,
164, 165, 170, 171, 172, 175, 176, 192;
David Killing Goliath 217; *Emma Brown*
Pl.9; *An English Autumn Afternoon*
Pl.12, 78, 80, 82, 84, 91, 113, 121,
122, 144, 186-7, 191, 192; *An English
Fireside* 76, 110, 113, 114-5, 116, 118,
120, 124, 125, 126, 127, 185, 190; *The
Entombment* 212; *The Execution of
Mary Queen of Scots* 159, 199; *Major
Freulich's Horse* 161-2; *Hampstead
From My Window* Pl.3, 198; *The
Hayfield* Pl.17, 146, 151, 152, 156, 157,
158, 159, 160, 161, 162, 178, 185, 212n,
The Last of England Pl.13, 80, 91ff,
157, 168, 185, 186n, sold to White 153;
Lear and Cordelia Pl.7, 50, 52, 53, 54,
55, 56, 57, 61n, 67, 80, 82, 84, 131,
158, 159, etching of 72, 82, untraced
version 156, 157, 158, 159, 161, 162;

Brown, Ford Madox *cont.*
  The Lord Jesus 69, 70, 71, 71; *The
  Medway* 72; *The Nosegay* Pl.20, 202,
  204, 206, 207, 209, 215; *Our Ladye of
  Good Children* 80, 87, 90, 94, 101, 102,
  103, 104, 122, 131; *The Parting of
  Cordelia* . . . 72, 80, 82, 123, 131, 186;
  Paul's Cray Church 76; *The Pretty Baa
  Lambs* 74, 76, 78, 80, 82, 152, 192;
  The Prisoner of Chillon 165, 166, 167,
  168, 169, 171, 182, photographs of 178;
  The Seeds and Fruits of English Poetry
  2, 8n, 63, 72, 76, 141; *Shakespeare* 69,
  70, 71, 72, 200; *The Spirit of Justice* 1n,
  125, 152; *Stages of Cruelty* Pl.18, 178,
  180, 182, 183, 184, 188, 191, 192, 199;
  Take Your Son, Sir! 78, 195; *The Transfiguration* 194; *Two Studies of Girl's
  Head* Pl.14, 82, 90, 91, 106, 109, 110,
  120, 124, 127, 197; *Waiting* 76, 78, 80,
  82; *Walton-on-the-Naze* 212n;
  Windermere Pl.6, 46, 48, 49, 50, 62,
  63, 67, 80, 82, 83, 84, 87, 123, 125,
. 134, 145; *Work* Pl.11, 78, 106, 113,
  114, 115, 118, 119, 134, 135, 153, 159,
  192, 194, 196, 198, 199, 200, 201, 204,
  206, 207, 215; *Wycliffe Reading his
  Translation of the Bible* . . . Pl.4, 17ff,
  apparel for 26, 27, 33, 34, 74, 76, 80,
  82, 103, 123, 125, engraving of 44, at
  Liverpool 46; *The Young Mother* Pl.5,
  48, 49, 50, 52, 53, 54, 55, 56, 57, 61n,
  67, and sketch 80
Brown, Dr John 118n
Brown, Lucy *passim*; portraits of 18, 25;
  at Herne Bay 44; and Christmas 53; her
  birthday 66; to Margate 67; holidays 80,
  95, 159; at Church 95-6; at piano 96;
  and school 97, 110, 132, 145; as model
  126, 142, 178n, 183
Brown, Oliver Madox 129, 134, 142, 145,
  149, 154, 207; birth 117, registered 124;
  portrait of 118, 119, 136; clothes for
  123, 124; appearance 117, 121, 126; as
  model 126, 127, 140, 151; vaccinated
  134; baptized 156; weaned 161
Browning, Elizabeth Barrett 43n
Browning, Robert, 181, 185, 186n, 187,
  191, 212n
Bruce, H.A. 166
Builder, The 48, 49, 50
Bulford, Emmeline *see* Seddon, Mrs
  Thomas
Burcham, R.P. 138, 140
Burchett, Richard 115
Burges, William 208, 210
Burnett, John 194

Burns, Robert 2, 5, 6, 11, 12, 14, 41, 42,
  44, 45
Burton, Sir Frederic 218
Bury (model) 34
Buss, R.W. 20
Byne, Miss (model) 74
Byron, Lord 2, 5, 6, 7, 10, 11, 12, 13, 14,
  15, 16, 41, 43, 44, 46, 48, 49

Campbell, James *Eavesdroppers – the
  Asking* 173
Campbell, Thomas 29
Cardigan, 7th Earl of 142n
Carlyle, Jane 191
Carlyle, Thomas 119, 183, 187, 191, 198,
  200; *Critical and Miscellaneous Essays*
  158-9, 160, 161; *Latter Day Pamphlets*
  134n; *Oliver Cromwell's Letters and
  Speeches* 176-7
Carruthers, James 111, 118
Casey, Daniel 4n, 6, 32, 33, 44; and Mrs
  153; *Catching a Mermaid* 158n
Caxton, William 2n
Cayley, Charles 140, 143, 153, 164
Chamberlayne, Miss (model) 9, 10, 24
Chapman, George 208
Chaucer, Geoffrey 1, 2, 9, 10, 11, 13, 20,
  21, 23, 24, 25, 26, 27, 33, 36, 37, 38, 39
Cholera 87, 90, 93, 96, 97, 99, 204
Claude 115
Clayton, John 162
Claxton, Marshall 13; Florence *The
  Choice of Paris: An Idyll* 13n
Coates, Mrs 78
Cobden, Richard 109
Cockerell, C.R. 61n
Cole, Sir Henry 82n, 114, 115, 116, 117,
  164,
Colin, Monsieur 66
Collins, Charles Alston 128, 132
Constable, John 189
Cook (gilder) 38
Cooper, John 10
Cornforth, Fanny 200, 208
Corrie, James *see* Carruthers
Coulton (model) 25, 39, 57
Cox, David 190
Crabbe, George 130, 134
Craven, F.W. 202n, 207, 208, 209, 210
Crayon, The 157
Creswick, Thomas 82n
Crimean War 31n, 88n, 97, 118n, 120,
  133, 150, 153, 175n; Brown
  philosophizes on, 97-9, 100-1
Cromwell, Oliver 120, 176
Cross, John 30, 49, 103n, 148, 159, 189;
  Lucy Preston's Petition A.D. 1690 174

Cushman, Charlotte *The Stranger* 10

Daily News 186
Dallas, E.S. 173
Dalziel, Edward 165, 166, 171, 172, 182; *Dalziel's Bible Gallery* 202
Danby, Francis *A Calm After Heavy Gale* 29
Dante 57, 140, 143, 149
Davis, William 189, 190; *Wallasley Mill, Cheshire* 174-5
Deakin, Dr Richard 6, 17
De Bathe, Colonel 164, 165, 166, 167, 168, 169
Deighton *see* Dighton
Delacroix 157
Delessard, A.J. 189
Deverell, Walter 45n, 64, 83n, 120n, 187
Deverell, Wykeham 120n
Dibdin, T.C. 13
Dickinson Brothers, Academy 15, 24, 25, 26, 27, 30, 41, 42, 43, 44; Firm 66, 69, 116, 162; Gallery 72, 119, 121, 122, 123, 125, 169
Dickinson, Lowes Cato 15, 50, 53, 121, 134, 135, 136, 145, 146, 153, 160, 164, 166, 169, 170, 181, 184, 195, 198, 206; buys *Chaucer* 74, and *An English Autumn Afternoon* 82; his studio, 116, 162, 171, 208; signs portrait 162n; portrait of 217
Dickinson, Robert 15, 50, 103, 121, 123, 157, 169, 175, 184; proposes scheme to Brown 162
Dighton, W.E. 74
Dobell, S.T. 105n
Dürer, Albrecht 106, 108
Dyce, William 98, 108; *Christabel* 138

Ealing, Phil (model) 33
Edward III 2, 8, 9, 10, 86
Elliott, Robinson 32, 36, 52, 56, 59, 74; *Negro Emancipation: An Allegory* 10
Elliott, Rev. William 186
Emerson, Ralph W. *English Traits* 188
English Academy 2
Ensgrubber, Miss 28, 29-30
Etty, William *The Shipwrecked Mariner* 87, 125
Examiner, The 141
Eyck, van, Brothers 109

Fair Maid of Kent, The 14
Fairbairn, Sir Thomas 199
Fenton, Roger 31, 42, 52, 53, 61, 70n, 71; *You Must Wake and Call Me Early* 62
Fielding, A.V. Copley 29

Foggo, James and George 12
Foley, J.H. 24
Fowke, Captain Francis 120
Free Exhibition 13, 15, 16, 17, 20, 21, 31, 32, 33, 39, 41, 44, 59, 60; Private View 40, 61
French Revolution 31, 32
Frost, W.E. 29
Fry (model) 42

Gambart, Ernest 199; exhibitions 138n, 208, 212n, 215n, 216
Garrett (model) 21
Gaunt, John of 2, 9, 20, 24, 26, 28, 30, 31, 38, 40; his dress 34n, 35, 36, 37, 39
Germ, The 6n, 72, 105n, 108n, 154
Gilbert, Sir John 166
Gillow & Co. 156
Gillum, Major 212
Giotto 171
Glasgow, Royal Institute of Fine Arts 80
Glass, J. 108, 148, 150
Gloucester, Humphrey, Duke of 85-6
Glyn, Isabella 60n, 156
Godwin, E.W. 204, 208, 210
Godwin, William *Life of Geoffrey Chaucer* 17
Goldsmith, Oliver 9
Goodall, Frederick 35
Government Schools of Design 98n; Belfast 116, Cork 116n, Limerick 116n, London 45, Newcastle 108n
Gower, John 2, 20, 23, 25, 26, 32, 33, 36, 37, 38, 39
Greenaway, Kate 120
Gregson, Miss (Mrs Lee) 74
Grundy, J.L. 76

Hall, S.C. 70
Halliday, Michael 138, 166n, 167, 184, 194
Hancock, John 42; *Christ's Entry into Jerusalem* 59
Hannay, James 143; *Satire and Satirist* 126
Hawart *see* Howard
Haydon, Benjamin 1n, 83, 96, 115, 125
Heaton, Ellen 130, 157, 187, 191
Herbert (model) 71
Herbert, J.R. *Lear Recovering his Reason...* 138
Herbert, Louisa Ruth 164n, 165
Hess, H.M. von 6n
Hewlett, D. 13n, 16, 21, 31, 32, 34, 37, 39
Highschool, Professor 14
Hill, Mrs (Catherine) 91, 95, 118, 124, 129, 150; and Mr 83n

Hill, Emma *see* Brown
Hilton, William *The Crucifixion* 190
Hine, H.G. 208
Hogarth, Joseph 70
Hogarth, William 178n
Holland, James 218
Holst, Theodore von 132n
Home, Daniel 206
Hook, J.C. *Bonny Boat, The Brambles in the Way, The Fisherman's "Goodnight", A Passing Cloud, Welcome* 174
Hough, William 180
Household Words 133n
Howard, Frank 30
Howell, Charles Augustus 204n, 208, 213, 214
Howitt, Anna Mary 156; Mary 118, 156; William 133, 156
Howlet *see* Hewlett
Hueffer, Ford Madox (Ford) 72n
Hueffer, Franz 72n
Hughes (model) 24
Hughes, Arthur 138, 143, 212, 214; *April Love* 153
Hunt, William 83n, 137
Hunt, W. Holman 4n, 45, 61, 62n, 138, 167, 174, 195n, 204, 210, 213; as model 83n; and Cobden 109; in Near East 113n, 117, 128, and returns 161; and Annie Miller 154n, 181, 184, 201; at Pimlico 166; character 172, 197; unwell 183; at Liverpool 188, 189; plans communal living 196; engaged 210n. Works: *The Awakening Conscience* 181n, 199n, 201; *Claudio and Isabella* 201; *The Finding of the Saviour in the Temple* 167; *The Hireling Shepherd* 201; *The Lantern Maker's Courtship* 167, 184; illustrations to Tennyson's *Poems* 128n; *The Scapegoat* 174, 181; *Strayed Sheep* 201; *Valentine Rescuing Sylvia . . .* 201
Hurlstone, F.Y. 12, 82n

Illustrated London News 83, 115
Inchbold, John 168, 213; *The Moorland: Tennyson* 138
Ingram, Herbert 150
Ingres, 157, 190
Inskipp, James *Reaping* 29
Isecole *see* Highschool

Jefferson, Joseph 211
Jerusalem, Bishop in 181
Jones, Anna 139n, 140

Jones, Edward and Georgiana Burne 201, 209, 213, 215; *The Blessed Damozel, The Wise and Foolish Virgins* 200
Jullien, Monsieur 157, 158

Kean, Mr and Mrs Charles 164n, 175n
Keats, John 46
Knight, Charles, publisher of *Chaucer* 9, 18; *Pictorial History of England* 12, 58n, 65n, 165
Krone (model) 37, 57, 60

Ladies Beware 9n
Lambert (model) 71
Lance, George 29
Landseer, Sir Edwin 159n, 163n
Lauder, R.S. 31
Lawrence (boy) 9, 10, 11
Layard, Sir A.H. 123
Legros, Alphonse 206, 208, 213
Leifchild, brothers 143
Leigh-Smith, Barbara 191n
Leighton, Frederic Lord 213n, 218; *Cimabue's Madonna Carried in Procession . . .* 136; *The Triumph of Music* 174
Leslie, C.R. 30
Lewes, G.H. *Life of Goethe* 165
Lewis, John *An Account of Dr Wiclif* 17
Lightfoot, Robert 21
Linnell, John 189
Lippi, Filippo *St Bernard's Vision of the Virgin* 108
Liverpool Academy of Arts 46, 76, 174n, 180, 185, 188; St Georges Church 190n; St George's Hall 61
Livock, John 208, 214
London: Bertolini 181; Bishopsgate Station 10; Bricklayer's Arms 32; British Museum 1, 17, 18, 42, 43, 84, 88; Camden Town 4n, 70n, 97; Campbell's Scotch Stores 132; Charlotte St 36n; Cheapside 4n, 9n, 10, 25n; Cheyne Walk 206n; Chinese Gallery 13, 39, 40; Clerkenwell School 120; Cleveland St 45n, 61n; Clipstone St 4n, 9n, 36n, 40, 74n; Cremorne 181; Cumberland Market 156; Egyptian Hall 160; Five Bells 102; Furnival's Inn 121; Gray's Inn Road 28; Great Coram St 5n; 8, Great Portland St 4n, 70n; Gough House 204; Gower St 61n, 62n; Haymarket 70n, 156n; Haverstock Hill 13, 20; Highgate Cemetery 4, 8, 13, 18, 23, 28, 29, 40, 41, 118n, 167; Hyde Park 20, 153; Kentish Town 95n, 117,

124; Lechertier Barbe 4, 32; Lombard St 5n; Maddox St 15n, 24, 25, 26, 30, 41, 42, 43, 44, 82, 122; Marlborough House 120, 121; Mary St 112n; Mivarts Hotel 143; Mogg's 4, 5n; Mudie's 188, 208; Newman St 61n, 62n, 72, 76; Oxford St 7, 20, 26; Pantheon 132; Percy St 12n, 152; Portland Gallery 13n, 31; Primrose Hill 7, 20, 71; Queen's Head 124n, 149, 155; Red Lion Square 118n; Reeves 10; Regent's Canal 37; Robert St 30; Royal Institute of British Architects 62; Royal Panopticon 178, 180n; Russell Place 198; St Pancras Cemetery 198n, Church 116, Rd 5n, Workhouse 5; Sass's Academy 36n; Shoolbred 31; Society of Arts 42n; Somerset House 45; Somers Town 4; Spaniards Inn 102; Stafford House 148; Strand 4, 27, 33; Suffolk St 12n; Swiss Cottage Tavern 122, 124, 154; Tavistock St 11n; Tom's Coffee House 88; Tottenham Court Rd 8; Tudor Lodge 4, 34; University College Hospital 5n, 29n, 167; Upper Albany St 84n, 138; Westbourne Grove 116; Westminster, Abbey 10, 174n, Hall 6n, 43n, Palace of 1n. Theatres: Adelphi 211n; Astley's 149, 150; Drury Lane 154, 191; Marylebone 40; Princess's 9, 10, 62n, 164, 175; Sadler's Wells 30, 60, 156; Strand 164, 165

London Lady, The 60n

Longfellow, Henry W. 105

Love, Law and Physic 9n

Luard, J.D. 168, 169

Lucia di Lammermoor 52, 62n

Lucy, Charles *passim*; teaches 4n, 15, 70n; criticizes 25; and French Revolution 31; assists Brown 38; to the Lakes 45, 82; to Rossetti 148; to Paris 157; *Mrs Claypole . . . at Hampton court . . . A.D. 1659* 59, 60; *Cromwell Resolving to Refuse the Crown* 153; *The Landing of the Primitive Puritans . . .* 17

Lucy, Mrs Charles 6, 7, 10, 12, 13, 157; and fuchsia 18; and Lucy Brown 44

Macaulay, T.B. Lord *History of England* 175

MacCracken, Francis 74, 80, 82

Macdonald, Georgiana *see* Jones, Mrs E.B.

McDowall, Patrick 159

McIan, R.R. *Highland Girls Winnowing Corn* 60

Mackintosh, Sir James 1

McLean, T. 212

Maclise, Daniel 1; *As You Like It* 138; *Sleeping Beauty* 60; *The Spirit of Chivalry, The Spirit of Justice* 1n

Macready, W.C. 40

Madox, James Fuller 5n, 16, 17, 22n, 27, 31, 32, 39, 45, 52, 54, 61, 122, 186; and Mrs 27, 53, 122, 186

Madox, Tristram Maries 22

Maitland (model) 23, 24, 31, 34, 36, 37, 41, 53, 54, 55, 60, 64, 65, 67, 74, 163

Manchester, Art Treasures exhibition 199, 200, 201; and Royal Institute exhibition 46, 80, 145

Mantegna *Triumph of Caesar* 8; *The Virgin and Child . . .* 186

Marochetti, Baron 196

Marshall, John 5, 12, 17, 24, 28, 29, 30, 31, 32, 37, 40, 42, 49, 52, 59, 60, 135; and the Chartists 38; professional attendance by 46, 192; work by Brown for 63, 76, 80, 201; as model 65, 74; appearance 108; and family 167; and corpse 167

Marshall, Peter Paul 204, 206, 207, 209, 211, 213, 216, 218; and Mrs (Gussy) 204n, 209, 211, 213

Martin, J.F. 13, 16, 17, 21, 35

Martineau, Robert 143, 166n, 198; *The Taming of the Shrew* 138

Massaccio 108

Maurice, F.D. 15n, 196, 198, 200, 201

Memling, H. *The Last Judgment* 109

Mencken, Ada, and Mazeppa 150n

Mendoza (model) 42, 43, 44

Mercers' Company 25

Millais, Effie 130, 144, 169, 170-1, 197

Millais, John Everett 62, 138, 141, 143, 163, 198; advises Brown 76; Brown's reference to 113n; visits Seddon 127, 128; character 132, 172, 197; eats out 132-3; and R.A. row 135, 136-7; abuses Holman Hunt 168-9, Brown 169, Rossetti 169; discourses on Ruskin 170-1. Works: *Autumn Leaves* 168, 173n, 201; *Blind Girl* 169n, 174; *The Bridesmaid* 125; *Byron's Dream* 182; *The Huguenot* 125; *The Kingfisher's Haunt* 87-8; *Lorenzo and Isabella* 61, 125; *The Order of Release* 132n; *Peace Concluded* 169; illustrations to Tennyson's *Poems* 128n, 166, 169; *The Rescue* 69, 132, 135; *Wandering Thoughts* 125

Miller, Annie 136n, 154n, 181, 183, 184, 201

Miller, John 169, 188, 189, 190, 195, 196, 204n, 207

Milton, John 1n, 5n, 6, 8, 11, 41, 43
Mogford, John 109
Montaigne 101
Monti, Raffaelo 140
Morris, Marshall, Faulkner & Co. 185n, 195n, 204n, 206, 209n, 212n
Morris, William 178n 185, 195n, 211, 212, 215; character 201; *Tristram and Iseult* 200
Moser, Mrs Robert 24, 40
Moxon, Edward 46n, 128, 169, 172, 187
Mulready, William 42, 159, 189
Munro, Alexander 138, 143, 148, 153, 168, 196, 197
Murcott, Mrs 16, 32, 34

National Gallery 32n, 40, 46, 65, 110; acquisitions 65, 108, 186
National Institution 13n, 31n
Never Despair 164n
New Water-Colour Society 40
Nicholl, W.G. 61
Nicholson, Sir Charles 178
North London School of Drawing 70, 71, 78, 118n, 164
Northumberland, 4th Duke of 29

Old Water-Colour Society 40
Oliver, William 32
Olympic Theatre 158
Omnibus Service 124
Oxford, Museum 186n; Union Debating Society 200, 213n

Palmerston, Viscount 123, 159
Papworth, E.P. 70, 122
Paris 28, 31; revolution in 44, 154; Universal Exhibition at 82, 84, 114, 119, 155, 156, 157, 159
Parris, E.T. 24, 26
Patmore, Coventry 168, 176; *The Angel in the House* 105, 119; and Mrs 95
Paul, B.H. 97n
Peel, Sir Robert 33n
Pelham, James 189
Pemberton, Charles 189
People's Journal 44, 103, 133n
Perrers, Alice 8, 11
Perugino *Virgin and Child with SS Raphael... Michael* 186
Phelps, Samuel 60n
Phillips (Auctioneers) 60, 82, 187
Pickersgill, H.W. 189
Plint, T.E. 192, 193, 194, 198, 199, 200, 204n
Pocock, Lewis 196
Poets of the Nineteenth Century 165n, 182

Polidori, Charlotte 88
Polydore, Henry 119
Pope, Alexander 5n, 8, 10n, 23, 42
Potter, J.P. 29, 68
Powell & Sons 194
Powers, Hiram *The Greek Slave* 43
Pratt, Samuel 50, 52
Pre-Raphaelite Brotherhood 36n, 45n, 46n, 61n, 74, 98n, 117, 125, 128n, 138n, 150, 154n, 173n, 185; and Ruskin 105n; exhibition 198
Prinsep, Valentine 213, 217
Pugin, A.W.N. 18

Rae, George 202n, 212, 213n
Raphael 8
Redgrave, Richard 82n
Reeves, Sims 52
Rembrandt *An Elderly Man as St Paul* 108
Reynolds' Miscellany 103
Richmond, Thomas 191n
Rip van Winkle 211
Rob Roy 154
Robertson, J.E. 190
Robinson, George (Auctioneers) 76
Robson, Frederick 158
Romance of the Rhine, A 9n
Rose, J. Anderson 212
Rossetti, Christina 97, 118, 122, 140, 155, 183; as model 83n; pupil of Brown 118n
Rossetti, D.G. 56, 102n, 127, 142, 171, 198, 206, 213; teaches 15n, 105n, 118; Brown visits 36n, 62, 104, 119, 124, 143; pupil of Brown 40, and Holman Hunt 45n; as model 57, 59, 74, 83; acquires studio 62n, 88, and shares Brown's 78; his nature and habits 78, 104, 110, 137, 138, 154, 173, 174, 187; Brown's observations on work by 90, 101, 106, 148, 163, 168, 193; studies of "Guggums" 101, 148, and of Ruth Herbert 165; abuses Effie Ruskin 130, Cave Thomas 137, Emma and Katty 149, Munro and Ruskin 197; and Miss Siddal 106, 126, 133, 157, 173, 174, 175, 191, 195-6, 197; praises Ruskin 130, 133, 169; visits Brown 134, 149, 153, 164, 170, 177, 182, 186, 190, 192, 218; and the theatre 149, 150, 154, 164; and Annie Miller 154n, 181, 183, 187; appearance 160. Works *Arthur's Tomb* 130n, 156; *La Belle Dame Sans Merci* 130n, 170; *The Beloved* 213; *The Blessed Damozel* 108; *Carlisle Wall* 163; *Chapel Before the Lists* 163; *Dante's Dream* 126n, 130n, 168, 191n; *Dante's*

Rossetti, D.G. *cont.*
Vision of Matilda Gathering Flowers
130n; *Dante's Vision of Ruth and Leah*
130n, 149, 156; *Ecce Ancilla Domini!*
23, 71; *Ford Madox Brown* Pl.8; *Found*
90, 101, 105n, 106, 107n, 108, 109,
193n; *Fra Pace* 163, 166; *The Girlhood
of Mary Virgin* 48, 52, 61n, 62n, 113n;
King Arthur and the Weeping Queens
138n; *The Nativity* 130n; *Paolo and
Francesca da Rimini* 130n, 157, 170;
The Passover in the Holy Family 88;
illustrations to Tennyson's *Poems* 128n,
172; *The Return of Tibullus to Delia*
209n; *Ruth and Boaz* 130n; *St Cecilia*
193; *The Seed of David* 131, 166;
Stratton Water 105
Rossetti, Gabriele 62n, 140n, 159
Rossetti, Mrs Gabriele, Brown calls on 84,
103, 104, 119n, 133; and Lucy Brown
132, 164; and Miss Siddal 133
Rossetti, Maria 137, 139, 145, 159, 162
Rossetti, W.M. 28n, 62, 97, 115, 124, 136,
140, 143, 148, 162, 168; as model 74,
83; visits Brown 107, 131, 139, 167;
advice sought 119, 121; and Millais 131,
132, 169; and Howitts 133; character
138; as critic 155; portrait of 164, 181,
182, 191, 194; engaged 181
Royal Academy 40, 78, 124; Professor of
Anatomy at 5n, 66; sending in day at
37, 131; rejects work by Brown 63n, and
exhibits 76n; and Millais 128, 169;
Brown visits 44, 174-5
Ruskin, Effie *see* Millais
Ruskin, John 98n, 105, 108, 143n, 173;
teaches 15n, 105n, 196; buys from
Rossetti 90n, 156, 157, 166, and Miss
Siddal 133; writes to *The Times* 105n;
admires *The Angel in the House* 119,
Leighton's *Cimabue* 136; praises and
abuses *An English Autumn Afternoon*
144; calls on Rossetti 144, 154; abused
by Millais 170-1; and Arundel Society
171n; *Academy Notes* 173; appearance
195; as sneak 197
Ruskin, John James, 68, 198
Russell, Lord John 100-1, 162n, 172, 173,
174, 175
Ruth (servant) 88, 90, 107, 111
Ryan, Miss (model) 76

Saulter, W. 24
Scharf, Sir George 32, 35
School For Scandal, The 165n
Scott, W.B. 83n, 117, 142, 143, 163, 180,
187, 207, 209, 211, 215, 216; Brown

Scott, W.B. *cont.*
admires 108, 144; *Poems by a Painter*
108n, 119
Seddon, Charles 118, 137; and *An English
Autumn Afternoon* 82, 113, 114, 186,
187
Seddon, J.P. 103, 141; buys *Lear and
Cordelia* 82, 157; competition designs
197
Seddon, Emily *see* Tebbs, Mrs H.V.
Seddon, Firm 23n, 28n, 61, 156, 195n
Seddon, Thomas 23, 28, 39, 50, 56, 65,
122, 127, 134, 148, 153, 161, 166, 167,
183; to Covent Garden 52; works in
Brown's studio 66, 165, 171; and
Drawing School 70n; given *The Medway*
72; witness at Brown's marriage 72n; as
model 83n, 178; in Near East 113n, and
returns 117; letter from Brown 113n,
144n; and marriage 117, 139, 141,
142-3; wears Arab dress 118; and
exhibition 125, 130, 199; Brown visits
128, 131, 136, 138, 139, 140, 145, 151,
153, 159, 164; sells pictures 132; to
Holman Hunt 184; death and
testimonial 195; *Jerusalem and the
Valley of Johoshaphat* 195n; *Penelope*
199; *Pyramids of Gizeh* 136, 170, 171
Seddon, Mrs Thomas 117, 141, 142-3,
145; as model 178, 180, 181, 182, 183
Seddon, Thomas, senior 28n, portrait of
67, 68; fondness for Emma 113;
financial advice sought 115, 119; lends
money 122, 123, 170n; and Mrs 67, 74,
107, 113, 123, 170
Shakespeare, William 1n, 2, 5n, 8, 11, 16,
41, 42, 43, 44, 103; and birthplace 7;
portrait of 69, 70, 71, 72; *Anthony and
Cleopatra* 20, 83; *Henry VIII* 164;
King John 60; *King Lear* 40; *The
Merchant of Venice* 165n; *Twelfth
Night* 30; *The Winter's Tale* 175n
Shaw, Henry *Specimens of Ancient
Furniture* 28
She Stoops To Conquer 9n, 10
Shelley, Percy Bysshe 8
Shenton, H.C. 103
Shields, Frederic 218
Siddal, Elizabeth, appearance 101, 137,
148; Brown admires 101, 126; Rossetti
visits 106, 196, 197; exhumation 118;
Ruskin's praise of 126; and marriage
126, 175, 191, 195, 196; visits Ruskin
131, who buys her work 133; visits Mrs
Rossetti 133, and Brown 134, 149, 173,
174, 175, 177, 195; and Emma 144n,
149, 173, 174, 175-6, 182-3, 196, 197;

Siddal, Elizabeth *cont.*   travels 156, 157,
176, 177, 191n;
    complains of Rossetti 183, 195; health
    191n, 195; *Sir Patrick Spens* 187
Slade, Sir John and family 136, 137, 138,
    139, 140
Smart, John (grocer) 106, 118
Smith (model) 20, 34, 37
Smith, Albert 160
Smith, Alexander *Poems*, and *Sonnets* 105
Smith, Bell 59
Smith, W. Collingwood 16, 31, 65; and
    father 31
Society of British Artists 12, 14, 27, 40
Society of Freemasons of the Church 7, 29
Solly *see* Sully
Solomon, Simeon 211, 213; and Rebecca
    211n
Sonnambula, La 154n
Southey, Robert *Book of the Church* 17
Spartali, Marie (pupil) 157n, 202, 204,
    206ff
Spectator, The 127, 130, 135, 181n
Spenser, Edmund 1n, 2, 5n, 14, 42, 43
Stanhope, J.R. Spencer 212, 213
Stephens, F.G. 5n, 83n, 154, 166n, 206;
    Mort d'Arthur 167
Sterling, John and wife and daughter 200
Stevens *see* Stephens
Stillman, W.J. 157n, 202n
Still Waters Run Deep 158n
Stone, Miss (model) 56, 59, 66
Street, G.E. 185, 218
Suffolk Street Exhibition *see* Society of
    British Artists
Sully, W. 45, 46
Swinburne, Algernon Charles 150n, 208,
    212

Tebbs, Henry Virtue, Mr and Mrs 118,
    209
Tennyson, Alfred, Lord 105; and Emily
    128; Woolner's bust of 169, and
    medallion of 169n, 187; *Morte d'Arthur*
    128; *Poems* 128, 130, 166, 187
Tenterden, Lord 155
Thackeray, W.M. *The Newcomes* 103,
    150
Thomas, Ralph 132
Thomas, William Cave *passim*; Brown
    admires 10, 29; and metaphysical art
    15; designs for Mercers' Company 25,
    and London University College 28;
    argues with Brown 41; works in Brown's
    studio 45; and Art Union 46, 59; and
    the *Builder* 48, 49; teaches 70n; travels
    to Russia 88n; and cholera 99-100;

Thomas, William Cave *cont.*
    appearance 138; works for Dickinsons
    166, 177, and for Russian Chapel 208;
    reconciliation 170; *The Heir Cast Out
    of the Vineyard* 174; *Rivalry* 137; *The
    Russian Dealer* . . . 88
Thomas, W.C., senior 29, 30, 146, and
    Mrs 143
Time Tries All 164n
Times, The 33n, 105n, 119, 120, 128,
    173, 175n
Titus, Emperor 5
Tonge, Robert 189
Trevelyan, Sir Walter and Lady 187n
Truefitt, George 62, 70n
Turner, J.M.W. 125, 144, 163n, 177,
    189; *The Shipwreck* 115, 116

Vernon, Robert, and National Gallery 65
Vitruvius 25

Wappers, Baron 4n
Ward, E.M. *The Last Parting of Marie
    Antoinette* . . . 175
Ware, Samuel 155
Warren, Fred 118, 164
Warren, J. Neville 70n
Waterford, Marchioness of 143
Watts, G.F. 213n
Webb, Philip 209, 213n, 217
Weir, William (editor) 186
Weire, Mr *see* Ware
Wentworth, W.C. 108, 110
Westminster, Duchess of 148
Whistler, J.A.McN. 206; *La Princesse du
    Pays* . . . 212n
White (model) 25, 34
White, David T. 91, 103, 110, 121, 122,
    142, 157, 178, 204, 213; buys Brown's
    work 74n, 80, 82, 87, 94, 104, 141,
    143, 153, 157, 162, 163, 197;
    characteristics of 82n, 125, 131, 162,
    185; and Rossetti 163, 166
Wild, Julia 24, 36, 37, 65, 74
Wilkie, Sir David *The Parish Beadle* 108
Williams 113, 115, 116
Williams, Rev. Theodore 103
Windus, B.G. 123, 124, 125, 131, 157,
    168, 178, 197
Windus, W.L. 189, 190; *Burd Helen* 173,
    175
Wollstonecraft, Mary 180
Woodville, R.C. 150
Woodward, Benjamin 200
Woolner, Thomas 94, 104, 112, 131, 135,
    137, 168, 176, 180, 189, 200; emigrates
    80n, 174n, and returns 103; to the

Woolner, Thomas *cont.*
Rossettis 104, 148; visits Brown 106, 107, 115, 149, 192; discourses 119, 134, 136, 137, 138, 159, 185; and *Work* 159; and White 162; recommends Brown 178, 185; and Ruskin 197; and Henry Woolner 192; statue of Bacon 185-6, 195, medallion of Browning, and of Carlyle 187; bust of Tennyson 169, 195, and medallion 169n, 187; statue of

Wentworth 108, 110; Wordsworth monument 174
Working Men's College, The 15n, 105n, 118, 196, 212n
Wornum, R.N. 131
Wycliffe, John 2, 20, 21, 23, 24, 25, 26, 35, 36, 37, 38, 39

Yates, Mrs 21, 27, 38, 41, 42, 43; and Mr 21, 27